TURKEY

Publisher: Aileen Lau
Editorial Manager: Bina Maniar
Editors: Bina Maniar
                     Aileen Lau
                     Emma Tan
DTP Design & Layout: Sares Kanapathy
Illustrations: Koh Hong Teng
Cover Artwork: Susan Harmer
Maps: Rebacca Fong

Published in the United States by
PRENTICE HALL GENERAL REFERENCE
15 Columbus Circle
New York, New York, 10023

ISBN 0-671-87909-X

Titles in the series:
Alaska - American Southwest - Australia - Bali - California - Canada - Caribbean - China - England - Florida - France - Germany - Greece - Hawaii - India - Indonesia - Italy - Ireland - Japan - Kenya - Malaysia - Mexico - Nepal - New England - New York - Pacific Northwest USA - Singapore - Spain - Thailand - Turkey - Vietnam

USA MAINLAND SPECIAL SALES
Bulk purchases (10+copies) of the Travel Bugs series are available at special discounts for corporate use. The publishers can produce custom publications for corporate clients to be used as premiums or for sales promotion. Copies can be produced with custom cover imprints. For more information write to Special Sales, Prentice Hall Travel, Paramount Communications Building, 15th floor, 15 Columbus Circle, New York, NY 10023.

Printed in Singapore

TURKEY

Text by Sevan Nisanyan

With contributions from:
Emma Tan
Bina Maniar

Editors
Bina Maniar
Emma Tan
Aileen Lau

Prentice Hall Travel

New York   London   Toronto   Sydney   Tokyo   Singapore

C O N T E N T S

C O N T E N T S

C O N T E N T S

C O N T E N T S

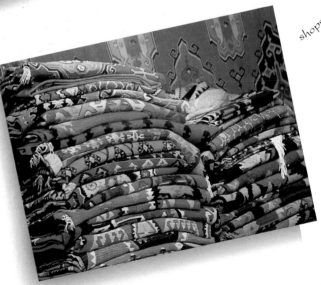

Turkish rugs, kebab

shops,

camels on the street and fresh fish … scenes of Turkish life!

Age and youth, beauty and character –

the Turkish spirit.

Portraits of pleasures, pleasurable portraits of

Turks at work and play.

Türkiye' ye Hos Geldiniz – "Welcome to Turkey" the legendary cradle of mankind called Asia Minor by the ancients. This land bordered by the Eastern Mediterranean, the Black Sea to the north, the Aegean to the west and the Arabian Deserts to the south has played a key role in history: it has been the dividing line between the Orient and the Occident; it sat at the root of classical civilization and was at the core of the Byzantine Empire with its capital at Constantinople; it was where Christianity first took root, and Noah's ark is said to have anchored at Ararat; it is the site of the world's oldest "city" – Çatal Höyük (7,500 BC), the birthplace of Omar Khayyam and Celaleddin Rumi, the poet, mystica and founder of the "Whirling Dervishes", as if that was not enough Turkey was also the focus of the colourful annals of Ottoman history; the place where Xerxes the leg-

Introduction

1

A giggle, a laugh, a hug and a chat with some modern Turkish belles.

The spectacular minarets and domes of the Suleymainye
Mosque captured at night.

endary Persian king crossed westwards on his way to a victory at Thermopylae and a resounding defeat at Salamis, and finally the site where Alexander the Great, history's greatest conqueror and expander of kingdoms made a great about-turn reversing his Macedonians troupes eastwards across Anatolia towards India thereby becoming the heartland of classical Hellenistic culture...

More Than Deserts

Turkey often conjures up stereotypical images of oriental splendour, sultans, harems, belly dancers, plush carpets, Turkish massage, kebab cuisine...

But the reality of modern times is of a country with a multi-racial identity traversing the uneasy ground between an eastern identity and western economic aspirations with hopes for EC membership, she is also the only NATO ally in the Middle East, her landscape (which is bigger than France and England put together) is dotted with mosques and Orthodox churches, archeological remnants of the old Roman empire are scattered alongside ancient Hittite sites and a strong Islam fundamentalism pervades this surprisingly secular state.

Spirit of the Turks

At one time the frontiers of the empire stretched from the Persian Gulf to the

Three pretty girls all in a row – Turkish folk dancers in Istanbul.

Atlantic and from the Indian Ocean to Vienna.

Over The Passing Centuries

However, over the passing centuries this once grand empire slowly disintegrated as did the original fighting spirit of the Turks.

Both the country and the people were resurrected by Mustafa Kemal (Atatürk) rising from the ashes of post-WWI through the Turkish war of independence or liberation which successfully purged Turkey of western imperialistic designs while at the same time removing the ruling House of Osman.

Today, the Turkish population (according to 1990 figures the population is estimated at 56 million) whose majority are Turks is remarkably heterogenous with large numbers of Muslim Slavs, Kurds, Greeks, Armenians, Albanians, Laz, Assyrians, Jews and Caucasians creating a vast diversity of people whose reputation for friendliness, warmth, generosity and hospitality to strangers is well deserved and sincere especially when historical annals reveal that most outsiders came as conquerors!

Yet, today there are still vast disparities in the standards of living between the western educated urban elite and the more backward eastern interior whose living standards in some cases have remained unchanged over the centuries.

Bask in the sun at Cleopatra's Beach, Sedir Islands on the Turkish coast.

The ruins of Ephesus – hints of a great civilization.

Something For Everyone

Follow us on our journey through mysterious, enigmatic Turkey as we travel from Istanbul to Bursa and then onto Edirne before reaching the Aegean region which boasts the town of Izmir. Then onto Antakya and its environs before moving eastwards to Mount Nemrut, north to Elâzığ and Lake Van. From Van we will switch westwards and southwards to Diyarbakir, completing the loop at Urfa.

Next comes Central Anatolia with its capital at Ankara, Cappadocia and Konya meandering via Sivas and Erzurum to Mount Ararat and Ani to Artvin before we reaching the Black Sea.

Do A Caesar

With her high mountain ranges, vast plateaus, fertile river valleys and splendid coastlines bordering azure seas, Turkey offers something for everyone – archeology cum history students, pilgrims, sunseekers and the erstwhile tourist looking for new and unchartered territories enabling him or her to utter Caesar's immortal words at Zela, east of Ankara *"Veni. Vidi. Vici"*. or "I came. I saw. I conquered".

History

Few countries have shed their cultural skin so often and so radically through the ages as Asia Minor, the landmass that was called Anatolia – the "Orient" of antiquity, which is today better known as Turkey.

At The Crossroads

Situated at the proverbial "crossroads" of East and West, Asia Minor was destined to be at the meeting point of many of the key events in world history. In the last 5,000 years of its known past it was invaded by innumerable nations from east and west, who brought an alternation of both devastation and civilization in their wake. Its historical accounts recall more than half a dozen periods of splendor that were unfortunately set apart by dark gaps of devastation and depopulation. Most Turkish

The material figure of the statue of Artemis greets visitors to most Turkish museums.

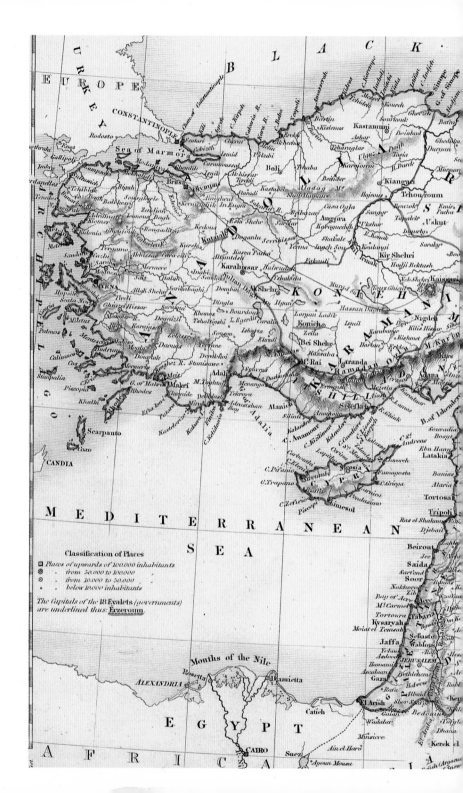

Classification of Places

- ▢ Places of upwards of 100.000 inhabitants
- ⬡ " from 50.000 to 100.000
- ⊙ " from 10.000 to 50.000
- • " below 10.000 inhabitants

The Capitals of the 18 Eyalets (governments)
are underlined thus: <u>Erzeroum</u>.

TURKEY IN ASIA

Scale of English Statute Miles
20 40   80   120   160

Gallipoli – The monument built to New Zealand forces.

towns carry the marks of some or all of these epochs in their midst. An important example is in the center of Istanbul, where the Hagia Sophia and the Blue Mosque face each other across a park, looking fairly similar to the uninformed eye but in fact separated by time (1,100 years), culture (Byzantine vs Ottoman), language (Greek vs Turkish) and religion (Christian vs Muslim).

In Antalya, one courtyard contains the relics of a Hellenistic wall, a Roman temple, a Byzantine church, a Selçuk mosque and a late-Ottoman *tekke*, just one example of the layers of history that make up Turkey's sites. Fortresses throughout the country telescope into their walls the different stone-laying techniques of the Hittites, Lycians, Ro-

mans, Byzantines, medieval pirates, European Crusaders, early Turkish barons and Ottoman engineers. No wonder Turkey is such an archeological paradise.

Striking Continuity

In some cases the historical continuity is striking. Take religion: At Ephesus, the Lydian and Carian inhabitants in archaic times worshipped a mother-goddess whom they knew as Kubaba/Cybele. Under the Greeks, the same city became a center of the cult of Artemis, a virgin who was also the goddess of childbearing; and in AD 2 after the Christians threw out the worship of idols the

Wander through the ruins of the Temple of Hadrian, Ephesus.

veneration of the Virgin Mary spread from Ephesus into general Christian practice.

A mountain called Samandaa "Saman's Mountain") near Antakya n southern Turkey was famous far and vide throughout the Christian world of Byzantine times as the pilgrimage site of St Simeon the Stylite, who initiated he unusual custom of living alone on op of a pillar for the greater glory of God; it is now visited every year by vast crowds of Turkey's Alevis – an ancient emi-Muslim sect whose lore bears a remarkable similarity to the stories of he 4th century saint.

Take architecture: The mysterious ock-carved beehive tombs which the Phrygians built in west-central Anatolia in 700 BC were faithfully reproduced more than a millenium later in the Christian monks settlements of the Cappadocia.

Take traditions: The bazaars of old Turkish towns perpetuate the habits of Byzantine guilds, which in turn, no doubt, owed much to the traditions of the Assyrian merchant colonies which had introduced organized commerce to Anatolia in 2 BC. And, if you are tempted to regret the hustle of souvenir-sellers in modern tourist resorts, you can take comfort in the fact that in Ephesus, 2,000 years ago, St Paul was nearly lynched for interfering with the work of a mob of artisans who sold icons of Artemis to the pilgrims, a trade "which brought no small gain to the crafts-

Historical Chronology

BC

7000	First settled agricultural communities in Anatolia
5600	Earliest fortified towns
3000-2200	Early Bronze Age ("Proto-Hatti") civilization
1700-1200	The Hittite Empire
1200-700	"Dark Age"
800-670	Phrygian Kingdom in west-central Anatolia
850-590	Urartu Kingdom in the East
700 BC-AD 395	Greco-Roman antiquity
700-494	Archaic Ionia: Greek cities on the Aegean coast
546-334	Persian rule 334/333 Alexander conquers Asia Minor
281-30	Hellenistic kingdoms: Seleucids, Pergamum, Pontus, Commagene, Armenia, Cappadocia.
133	Romans take over kingdom of Pergamum (Western Anatolia)
66/63	Romans subjugate all Asia Minor
30 BC-AD 180	Prosperity under early Roman emperors

AD

331	Constantinople becomes the capital of the Roman Empire
391	Christianity made state religion
395-1453	The Byzantine (Eastern Roman) Empire
538-565	Justinian I
620-750	Persian and Arab invasions destroy Anatolian cities
1071	Battle of Malazgirt: Turks conquer East and Central Anatolia
1096/98	First Crusade
1204-61	The Fourth Crusade captures Constantinople
1090-1306	Selçuk Kingdom of Konya
1270s-1516	Turkish emirates in Anatolia
1299-1922	The Ottoman Empire
1451-81	Mehmed II "The Conqueror"
1453	Conquest of Istanbul
1512-20	Selim I "The Grim"
1520-66	Süleyman I "The Magnificent"
1683	Second siege of Vienna
1826/1839	Start of Europeanizing reforms
1914-18	The empire disintegrates in World War I (WWI)
1919-22	War of Independence
1923	Proclamation of the Turkish Republic
1923-38	President Atatürk
1938-50	President İnönü
1950-60	Prime Minister Menderes
1965-71, 75-78, 80	Prime Minister Demirel
1980-83	Military regime of Kenan Evren
1983-89	Prime Minister Özal

men". Elsewhere it is the discontinuity of history that makes its traces the more fascinating. In many parts of Europe, medieval towns have grown impercep- tibly into modern times, often with thei buildings, institutions and even family

Elements of Christianity spring up all over Turkey. Akdamar Church in Lake Van, Eastern Turkey.

rees intact. Turkey's history is one of violent breaks. Time and again the ruling classes of older states were wiped out, their documents destroyed, their homes taken over by their serfs or their conquerors for whom the buildings of an earlier age were either a thing of indifference or of uncomprehending superstition. Instead of changing organically with the times, their monuments were left to slowly decay, standing in alien surroundings like a haunted sign from the past.

Ancient Temple & Medieval Walls

Bits of ancient temples and medieval walls now stand in the back alleys and marketplaces of all Turkish towns, unnoticed, undocumented, without parking lots for tourists and ticket offices for sightseers. Few countries have as much history as Turkey that they can afford to take it for granted; most Turkish towns are at least 2,000 to 5,000 years old.

Also few countries, have so many abandoned, forgotten and ruined cities dotting their landscape – over 50 well-known ones in the west and south alone and countless others, (many of them hardly discovered), scattered throughout the rest of the country. Architecturally some are more and others are less interesting. What makes them all unforgettable is that they have stopped growing, left embalmed in a distant

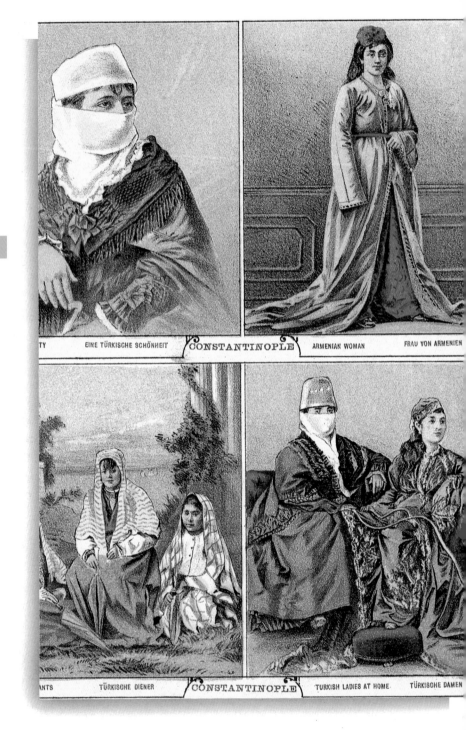

EINE TÜRKISCHE SCHÖNHEIT • CONSTANTINOPLE • ARMENIAN WOMAN • FRAU VON ARMENIEN

TÜRKISCHE DIENER • CONSTANTINOPLE • TURKISH LADIES AT HOME • TÜRKISCHE DAMEN

The Turkish beauty captured over a hundred years ago.

point of time. They are history without the banalizing touch of the present; a past that has not been domesticated by continuous use.

The Turks are relative newcomers to this ancient country, they first arrived in the 11th century, descended to the southern coast in the 13th and did not complete their conquest of the western part of the country until the 15th century. For a millenium and a half before them Anatolia had been one of the core lands of Greco-Roman civilization, in both its pagan and Christian phases.

Anatolia's language and culture had been predominantly (though by no means exclusively) Greek. Homer, Thales and Heraclitus were Anatolians; so were St Paul and St Nicholas the bearer of gifts. The first great masterpieces of ancient Greek architecture were erected in western Anatolia.

Greek philosophy had its origins at Miletus, now a nondescript village near Kuşadasi, while Herodotus, the Father of Historiography, hailed from Halicarnassus, better known today as the popular tourist resort of Bodrum. Christianity first emerged as a religion of general appeal in Antioch and owed its first great theological debates to the Cappadocian fathers, who came from central Turkey and made their church in Constantinople. All seven of the ecumenical councils of the early church were convened in various towns in what is now Turkey. However Hellenism itself, came to Anatolia by conquest and never fully succeeded in penetrating the

Crags and peaks of Goreme Valley.

eastern half, where the native cultures proved to be much more susceptible to Persian and Middle Eastern influences than to the call of Greece and Rome.

The Greek language and culture arrived in Anatolia when a string of colonies settled along the Aegean seaboard around 1,000 BC and later spread thoughout the country through the conquests of Alexander the Great c. 334 – 333 BC. Its grip was consolidated under the political umbrella of the Roman Empire, but it was not before the advent of Christianity as a mass religion that a majority of the peasants and common people of Anatolia converted to using Greek speech and an approximation of the Greek way of life.

In doing this, they shed a bewilder-

A Cradle of Christianity

Shortly after the crucifixion of Christ, his apostles moved the base of their operations to Antioch (Antakya), whose mixed Greek and Jewish population had shown itself to be more amenable to the gospel than conservative Jerusalem. It was here that the new sect called themselves "Christians", and the word "church" first came into use.

St Paul, a native of Tarsus in Cilicia, came to be the chief organizer, proselytizer and thinker of the new sect in Antioch. Unlike the original 12 apostles, simple men from Galilee, Paul was a Roman citizen and an educated man schooled in the Greek philosophical tradition. His four evangelizing journeys were turning points in transforming Christianity from a local creed into an universal religion.

On his first journey (c. AD 36), Paul traveled with Barnabas to Cyprus, Perge (near Antalya), Pisidian Antioch (Yalvaç in central Turkey) and Iconium (Konya). A momentous turn of events came about in Pisidian Antioch. Here as elsewhere, the apostles first preached at the Jewish synagogue. However, when word of their preaching got out, they were invited by an excited crowd to address the whole city. This caused consternation among the Jews, who tried to stop the meeting from taking place. Then Paul "waxed bold, and said, It was necessary that the word of God should first have been spoken to you: but seeing ye ... judge yourselves unworthy of everlasting life, lo, we turn now to the Gentiles." On his return to Jerusalem he was criticized for this rash decision, and there was much "dissension and disputation" within the church *(Acts of the Apostles 13-15)*.

A more amusing incident took place in Lystra,

A religious multihued mosaic in Aya Sofia, Jstanbul.

an unidentified place near Iconium. Here Paul and Barnabus performed a miracle by healing a crippled man, whereupon the local folk took them to be Zeus and Hermes in disguise and began to offer worship. The high priest of Zeus led the people by making a sacrifice of oxen and garlands and could scarcely be persuaded otherwise.

The second journey (AD 49-51) took Paul

ing variety of ethnic identities and languages which had characterized Asia Minor since pre-classical times.

"Anatolian" Nations

Some of these "Anatolian" nations, like the Pisidians and the Isaurians of the Taurus highlands or the myriad peoples of the Black Sea coast, had been relatively primitive tribal groups. Others, like the Phrygians from whom the Greeks borrowed many elements of their religion and art, the Lydians who were the first to invent coined money and the

through the Assyrians and Persians.

through Cilicia, Lycaonia, Galatia, Phrygia, Mysia, Thrace, Macedonia, Greece, and to Ephesus, where he founded the core one of the most important communities of the early church. He returned to Ephesus on his third journey (AD 52-57), staying there for two years. His proselytizing activities drew the wrath of the local artisans who made silver icons of Artemis, a trade "which brought no small gain to the craftsmen" *(Acts 19.25-41)*. A riot broke out when Paul tried to reason with an angry crowd in the theater, where he was silenced by a mob crying out "Great is the Ephesian Artemis". Reason prevailed when the city magistrate addressed the assembly, pointing out that the greatness of Artemis could not be harmed because some people spoke out against her and that if anyone had a complaint he could seek redress in the courts. Paul departed shortly afterwards, spending some time in Greece, Assos and Patara on his way back. On his fourth journey, he was taken as a prisoner to Italy with St Peter and was martyred near Rome.

Some years later, the apostle John took up residence in Ephesus, bringing with him (according to tradition) the Virgin, whom Jesus had commended to his care shortly before his death. Mary is said to have completed her days in a modest house not far from this city. St John wrote the *Revelation* (Apocalypse), one of the most powerful books of the *New Testament,* in Ephesus, addressing it to the "seven churches of Asia" – seven dioceses of the Roman province of this name. The dioceses were Ephesus, the capital, Smyrna (Izmir), Pergamum (Bergama), Thyatira (Akhisar), Sardes, Philadelphia (Alaşehir) and Laodicaea (Denizli).

Lycians who had their own alphabet and sophisticated urban institutions, boasted a mature culture of their own.

The Cappadocians of inner Anatolia, the Armenians of the east and the many city-states of the southeast belonged firmly to the cultural traditions of the ancient Near East, as imparted

A Separate Identity

The Urartians of the Lake Van area spoke a language akin to an Indian dialect. The Galatians (or Celts) of the Ankara region came from western Europe and brought with them the Druid religion. A sense of a separate identity, if not a separate language, survived (in the case of many of these nations) well into the Byzantine era.

The origins of these nations are largely obscure. The most powerful of them, the Phrygians, had arrived from the west with the so-called "Invasion of the Peoples of the Sea", which devastated the eastern Mediterranean world around 1220 BC. Others may have immigrated then, or were displaced from earlier areas of settlement and tossed about in that chaotic period.

Whatever their particular roots, each preserved something of the shadow of an ancient and powerful civilization, which with the onset of classical antiquity had long vanished from historical memory, but whose achievements lived on in Hittite tradition and legend, in religious belief and architectural forms.

The Hittites

The Hittites, who have the distinction of being the earliest Indo-European nation known to have had a written lan-

The ancient city of Ephesus.

guage, dominated Asia Minor from their base in the central plateau for most of 2 BC. At the height of their power, Hittite kings held transit routes to the Aegean ports, traded with Caucasia and fought with Egypt for the control of Syria. At home, their rule was limited by a code of laws and a powerful council of nobles; their constitution was feudal, with vassal princes presiding over a population that spoke over 20 different languages; their scribes maintained a fantastic royal archive dealing with every imaginable detail of bureaucratic procedure, religious ritual and business transaction, at the capital city of Hattusha. Their bazaars were the meeting place of Assyrian merchants, who introduced the art of writing and the techniques of bookkeep-

ing and tax evasion and native artisans who produced some of the finest examples of metalwork in the Near East.

Natives of the Land

The Hittites, in turn, were no more the *Urvolk* (natives) of the land than their various successors. Their arrival on the scene has been placed at between 2200 and 1900 BC. The designation of their rulers as "Kings of Hatti" referred not to the ruling nation but to the previous inhabitants of the land which they had subjugated. These, the People of Hatti (or Proto-Hatti as some scholars call them), had already built many of the walled cities which were to form the

Ancient stairs and a semblance of a forum in Termesses, Turkey.

nodal points of the Hittite state.

This the first civilization of the Bronze Age in Asia Minor contributed he basic patterns of Anatolian lifestyle hat remain more or less unchanged right up to the twentieth century including: village architecture, agricultural methods, carpet motifs, folk myths and rites.

Heyday of the Hittites

The language of the Hatti, partly preserved in Hittite texts, remains undeciphered. Their heyday (c. 3000 to 2200 BC) corresponds to that of the sister civilization of Troy II, whose artistic achievement is spectacularly exem-

plified in the famous Treasure of Schliemann.

Before the Bronze Age

The two millenia preceding the onset of the Bronze Age are relatively obscure; but before this, the remnants of yet another substantial culture have emerged. The settlements from this period were spread over a wide area, but are especially concentrated in southern Turkey.

Çatalhöyük

The most important one, at Çatalhöyük,

A Turkish bashaw receiving a petition of the most humble kind.

near Konya, flourished from c. 6500 to 5500 BC. Its intricate wall paintings and statues are among the oldest works of art created by a settled civilization.

The town of Çatalhöyük, rather like the pueblos of southwestern USA, formed a single architectural block of mud-brick walls, where dwellings were entered through roof openings. Whereas at Hacblar, a settlement near modern Burdur (an important centre c. 5600 BC), houses were separate, often two-storeyed high and opened on clearly defined streets. Their industries included painted pottery and kilim-weaving.

Products were traded over considerabl distances. Some of the figurines found at Çatalhöyük and Hacilar bear a strik ing resemblance to the cult idols wor shipped in Anatolia during the Hellen istic era, more than 5,000 years later!

Even older settlements, dating from c. 7000 BC, have been discovered around Mersin, Tarsus, Adana and Diyarbakır they are among the oldest in the world alongside those of Syria and Mesopota mia. Over 60 settlements existed in the plain of Antakya alone, which thus qualifies as one of the oldest continu ously inhabited places on earth. When

a new capital for the empire (Constantinople) in the ancient city of Byzantium.

The Split of the Roman Empire

Seventy years later, Theodosius split the administration of the empire into two, with an eastern half governed from Constantinople and a western half taking orders from a co-emperor in Ravenna. The west collapsed under the onslaught of the Germanic tribes by the fifth century but the eastern half survived for another 1,000 years.

The east changed its state language from Latin to Greek and adopted the style and institutions of oriental monarchies. Later, in the Middle Ages, Europeans began to mockingly term it the "Byzantine" empire. But its official designation – the Roman Empire – never changed and it never gave up its claim to universal rule. Today the Greeks of Istanbul, carry the proud title of *Romaioi*, (Romans).

St Peter and St Paul met at Antioch to set the ground rules of their novel religion, that city already had a history of 70 centuries behind it – about four times longer than the oldest northern European town today!

The Eastern Empire

The Roman empire adopted Christianity as the state religion in several steps from AD 325 to 391. Constantine's imperial edict convening a great congress of Christian bishops in Nicaea, in AD 325, was also the occasion for another momentous move – the decision to build

Byzantium's Peak

Byzantium reached the peak of its power under Justinian (AD 538-565), the rest of its history is largely a succession of disasters. The Muslim Arab conquests of the seventh century swept over Egypt, Syria and the southeastern half of Anatolia. For the next two centuries, iconoclastic controversies, kept the remaining territories in a state of permanent civil war.

A Slight Revival

A slight revival in the eleventh century was followed in 1071 by the Turkish conquest of two-thirds of Anatolia. The shock of this loss was hardly over when another menace appeared on the western front – the crusades of 1097, 1147 and 1189 which cut a swathe of devastation across Anatolia and undermined whatever was left of Byzantine strength.

The Fourth Crusade captured Constantinople in 1204, putting a temporary end to the empire. The Byzantine empire which was later revived in 1261 was reduced to occupying only a small part of the Balkan peninsula and the coastal strip of western Turkey. Politically and economically, it was a dependency of the Italian republics of Venice and Genoa.

Byzantine's Revival

However, in the artistic and intellectual fields, Byzantium began to display a degree of vitality that was wholly out o measure with its previous sterile centu ries. Some of the most interesting Byz antine artworks in Turkey (and the Bal kans) date from the final days o this empire.

After the 1380s, Byzan tium was no more than a city state con sisting of Con stantinople and its en virons. I was elimi nated from the map by the Ottoman Turks in 1453.

The Turkish Conquest

The Turks, a semi-nomadic nation from central Asia, broke through Byzantine defences at the battle of Malazgir (Manzikert) in 1071, and occupied most of Anatolia by the following decade From the 11th to the 14th century the Selçuk kingdom, based in Konya in central Anatolia, brought the various Turkish warrior clans under one rule. While the 12th century was spent fighting the Byzantines, the Crusaders and the unruly Turkish princes, the 13th century brought an overall revival of Mediterranean trade from which the Selçuks benefited hugely.

The scores of fortified *caravanseraie*

Engraved
for Middleton's
Complete System
of Geography.

MAHOMET
the Turkish Emperor murdering the beautiful
IRENE.

Garbed in western-like dress Mahomet the Turkish emperor
murders the beautiful Irene.

Jtars Castle, East Anatolia.

(public inns serving merchant caravans) strewn along the ancient trade routes of Anatolia stand as a living testimony to the enduring Selçuk preoccupation with commerce.

At its zenith under Sultan Alaeddin Keykubat (1220-1237), the kingdom came to be distinguished more for the graceful culture of its court than the warlike traditions of the Türkmen tribes on whom it depended for its power. Persian was used in preference to Turkish as the language of state and the influence of Byzantium was transmitted by the cities which remained largely Greek in character.

The leading intellectual figure of the era was Mevlana Celaleddin Rumi, the founder of the Mevlevi order of "whirling dervishes" who combined Muslim theology with Persian poetry and Byzantine music to develop a unique brand of mystical humanism.

The End of the Selçuks

However the era of Selçuk brilliance was short-lived. It came to an abrupt end when the Mongol hordes of the sons of Genghiz Khan burst into Anatolia dealing two devastating blows to Selçuk power in 1243 and 1256 from which the kingdom never recovered, though it maintained a shadow existence for another half a century. The country was now plunged into two centuries of chaos in which scores of Turkish warrior

A fresco of the Last Supper in the Christian Cave chapel, Goreme Valley, Cappadocia.

princes staked their claims to various bits of the former Selçuk domain. These dynastic chiefs had a code of military valor far removed from the effete manners of the court of Konya and their brand of Islam was of a far more zealous sort than the tolerant syncretism of Mevlana.

The Conversion of Anatoli

Within a short time, the conversion of Anatolia was completed. Administration, trade and the arts fell into Turkish hands.

A majority of the natives were assimilated to Islam, those who did not convert survived in the poor and backward pockets of the Christian population.

The Turkish Emirates

In many ways the Age of the Emirates represents a more radical turning point for the history of Anatolia than the kingdom of Konya. Many of the existing towns of western and central Turkey owe their birth, or their rebirth with a Turkish identity, to having served as the capital of one petty principality or another in the critical decades of the late 13th century. These towns include: Balbkesir, Kütahya, Bilecik, Manisa, Aydbn, Selçuk, Milas, Elmali, Antalya, Burdur, Beycehir, Ermenek, Karaman,

An ancient past – Pergamon.

Adana, Elbistan, Sinop and many others. Neither the Selçuks nor, the Ottomans were notable city-builders outside their respective capitals. in fact, it is the obscure dynasties from this period that gave the historic towns of the Turkish provinces what they possess in terms of civic monuments, mosques, princely tombs, public baths and bazaars.

The Karaman Dynasty

The most influential among these Emirates was the Karaman Dynasty, which had its capital in the city of Laranda (now Karaman) and controlled a large part of the old Selçuk patrimony, including the city of Konya. The Aydin and Menteşe lords of the southwest and the Ramazan dynasty of Adana maintained a considerable cultural vitality. Meanwhile, a breakaway Byzantine principality styling itself the Empire of Trebizond ruled the coasts of the Black Sea (until 1461). A crusader-state governed by European knights survived in Antioch (until 1268) and a dynasty of Armenian warlords controlled the impregnable castles of Cilicia (until 1375).

An Epic Struggle

Half a dozen Emirates continued in an epic struggle featuring chivalry, religious zeal and the appetite for plunder along the Byzantine border. One of these,

The library of Celsus in Ephesus.

the Ottomans (Osmanli) from the Bursa region eventually prevailed above all others. In 1453, they captured Constantinople, the last sad relic of the Roman empire in the Orient.

In 1475, they successfully brought the Karaman Dynasty to its knees, thereby eliminating their oldest and most dangerous Turkish rival in Anatolia and the country was once again united under a single imperial administration.

The Ottoman Leviathan

The growth and collapse of the Ottoman state is one of the most phenomenal stories of empire-building in the annals of history. From a small border march from the hills of Bilecik in 1299, the family of Osman came to rule over half of western Turkey, Thrace, Macedonia and Bulgaria by 1390; Greece, Albania and Serbia fell following the capture of Istanbul in the 1450s; Crimea became a tributary state in 1480; the Romanian princes followed c. 1500 thereby completing the conquest of eastern Turkey by 1514. In 1517, the destruction of the Memluks of Egypt added Syria, Egypt, Palestine and part of Arabia to the empire. Hungary came under Turkish rule from 1526-41. Western Georgia was subjugated around the same time, just as Turkish privateers brought the *beys* (governors) of Tunis and Algeria under Istanbul's control. Baghdad and Basra were captured in 1539 and Yemen and

Aden became Turkish possessions later.

Era Of Expansionism

Expansion came to an end with the naval defeat at Lepanto in 1571. In 1683 over a century later, Turkish armies marched to the gates of Vienna. Defeat at Vienna led to the collapse of the frontier along a broad front, and the loss of Hungary. In the next 200 years, Austria and Russia warred against the Ottomans no less than 12 times, either singly or in conjunction with other European powers. The Europeans vacillated at Turkey's expense. The secession of Serbia in 1808 and Greece in 1830 added speed to the disintegration.

The End Of The Osmans

By the time the last members of the House of Osman left the scene at the end of WWI, no less than 20 countries had been carved out, wholly or in part, from the carcass of the Ottoman empire – Hungary, Yugoslavia, Romania, Bulgaria, Albania, Greece, Cyprus, Syria, Iraq, Lebanon, Israel, Jordan, Kuwait, Saudi Arabia, Yemen, Egypt, Libya, Tunis, Algeria, Turkey and parts of The Ukraine, Moldova and Georgia.

Modern Times

The 19th century saw the collapse of the Ottoman empire on the battlefield, but, it was a time of improvement in domestic affairs. Trade was revived as Turkey became a supplier of products (tobacco, cotton, olive oil, citrus fruit, opium) to Europe. A cash economy penetrated the provinces, followed by European institutions, fashions and ideas. A new middle class arrived on the scene armed with banks, modern schools, hospitals, clock towers and courthouses. The new residential quarters that arose reflected a lifestyle more concerned with comfort than self-defense. The gracious "old quarters" one now sees in Turkish towns all date back from this period. With the exception of a few half-ruined manorial houses, there are practically no examples of residential architecture in Turkey that are actually older than the 1820s.

Economic Beneficiaries

However, the fruits of economic revival, were not evenly distributed; the Christian minorities of the empire got the better part of the deal. Thus, the Aegean tobacco trade was in the hands of the Greeks, while the Greek, Jewish and Levantine (expatriate European) banks of Izmir held the purse-strings. The French introduced a lucrative cotton industry into Adana, which was controlled by a class of French-educated Armenians and Christian Arabs.

Hundreds of new churches were built throughout the land after the toleration edicts of 1839 and 1854 (practically no mosque of any significance dates from the same era). Greek schools in Milas, Aydın, Tire, Antalya and elsewhere taught Plato and Rousseau, the laws of thermodynamics and the rules of modern bookkeeping. The Turkish *medreses* concentrated on teaching its pupils to reciting the **Quran** from memory.

Political Results

The Greeks of Turkey began to agitate for reunion with the newly created state of Greece, with Constantinople as the capital. The Armenians with the aid of Russia and England demanded an independent state in eastern Anatolia. Things came to the boiling point at the beginning of the 20th century, revolts and massacres following each other in an escalating vicious circle. Many cities in the east were burned down in ethnic rioting. Most of the remaining Armenians perished during WWI, when they were suspected of collaborating with the Russian enemy.

National Sentiment

Turkey emerged from the war having lost all of its Balkan and Arab possessions. What was left was placed under British, French and Italian occupation pending a final settlement at Versailles. The Greeks, who had been promised Izmir, were allowed to occupy that city in 1919, before being allowed to expand their occupation to include most of western Turkey as far as Kütahya and Afyon. This event precipitated a backlash of Turkish national sentiment. A revolutionary government was formed in Ankara under the leadership of Mustafa Kemal and a War of Independence was fought against various occupying forces, which ended with the spectacular defeat of the Greek army in August 1922.

Abolished Sultanante

The sultanate was abolished in November 1922 and the Turkish Republic was established on October 29 1923, with Mustafa Kemal as its first president. By agreement with Greece, all remaining Greeks in Asia Minor were evacuated in 1923-24 in exchange for Turkish immigrants from Greece. The Turkification of Anatolia inaugurated 850 years earlier, was now complete.

One Party Regime & "Europeanisation"

In the first 27 years of the Republic, the one-party regime of Atatürk and his successor, Ismet Inönü, began to create a modern, "European" nation out of a devastated, depopulated, and destitute country. From 1950 Turkey took off economically, with her more democratic government and her young, hard-working, and increasingly mobile population creating a new identity for itself.

The portraits of the Father of Modern Turkey frown sternly from every shop and office, on every banknote and postage stamp. His statues stand in every schoolyard and public square in the country – there even exists a line of trade specializing in mass-produced Atatürk busts! Banners proclaim his principles: "How happy is he who calls himself a Turk!" "Peace at home, peace abroad!" "Science is the truest beacon of life!" At football stadiums: "I prefer an athlete who is also a gentleman!" In hospitals: "Trust me to Turkish doctors!" In aeroplanes: "The future belongs to the skies!" Disrespect for his name is a legally punishable offence and his reforms (including the famous Hat Law of 1928 which orders all male Turkish citizens to wear hats instead of the *fez*) are embalmed in the constitution.

Symbol of a nation – a star and crescent moon on a red background.

Government

31

Atatürk – Father of Turkey

Mustafa Kemal (1881-1938) who was later called Atatürk, was a brilliant strategist, a spellbinding orator

and a risk-taker of grandiose proportions. The War of Independence (1919-22) and the resurrection of Turkey from the debris of the Ottoman empire were to a very real extent the products of his own solitary vision and will. The Republic that he founded in 1923 owed much to a world whose rising stars were Lenin and Mussolini. His methods were not extreme by the standards of the time: only a few hundred of the regime's opponents died in the purges of the early years and only a few political prisoners marred the peace of the 1930s and 1940s. He created a single party, the Republican People's Party, or CHP which embodied the state until 1950 and pledged "one nation, one party, one leader" as their creed. The party nationalized the economy, glorified the state and rewrote historical annals to prove that the Turkish nation was the source of all light and civilization since the beginning of time.

Atatürk's reforms were of a radical-progressive cast. Among other things, they introduced the Latin alphabet and a western legal framework, enfranchized women and suppressed Islam as an organized force in public life. The new calendar counted years from the birth of Christ and the citizens of Istanbul and Ankara were encouraged to adjust their dress to European fashions. The unfulfilled dream of successive generations of the Turkish elite since the 1830s – to be accepted as a *bona fide* member of the European family of nations – was almost reached.

However opponents of the CHP won a landslide victory during the first free elections, held in 1950 and they have remained in power (with only sporadic short interruptions) ever since. They opted for a policy of caution and consensus, never making a direct attack on the basic principles of the Republic and keeping the name of her founder above criticism. Today, of the more than 20 European and semi-European countries that have finally succumbed to democracy, only Turkey has never formally repudiated its totalitarian past.

However, with only brief interruptions Turkey has also been a parliamentary democracy since 1950. Only a handful of Asian countries possess a comparable record. Of the Muslim nations of the Near East, only Turkey has been governed by a freely elected government.

Political Partying

Turkish political parties are powerful, with great cohesion and strong grassroots support. They have become important channels of patronage and social advancement, more so in the countryside than in the cities. Even if Turkish politicians may seem weak at defending the abstract principles of democracy, they are very adept at bringing roads, jobs and contracts to the remotest parts of the country. Partly because of this, none of the military governments which tried to readjust Turkey's political course in recent decades was able to last

A nation's hero and father – Mustafa Kemal.

more than a couple of years

The basic battlelines of Turkish politics were drawn in 1945-50. On one side stand the CHP and its successors. Their traditions are "radical" in the old French sense of that term: secular-anticlerical in ideology, pro-intellectual in sentiment, nationalist in economy and neutralist in world affairs. They adopted a semi-socialist line in the 1970s under the leadership of Bülent Ecevit (Prime Minister in 1974 and from 1977-79). The party was banned by the military junta of 1980, and two new formations now dispute its legacy: The SHP (Social Democratic People's Party) is led by a son of Ismet Inönü, the second President (1938-50) of the Republic and the rival DSP (Democratic Socialist Party) of Ecevit.

The winners in every fair election held since 1950 have been the conservatives, under their three successive incarnations: the Democratic Party of Adnan Menderes (Prime Minister from 1950-60); the Justice Party (AP) of Süleyman Demirel (Prime Minister during the following periods: 1965-71, 1975-77, 1979-80, 1991-) now renamed the True Path Party (DYP) since 1980; and the Motherland Party (ANAP) of Turgut Özal (Prime Minister from 1983-89 and President 1989-1993). Conservatives are characterized by a tolerant attitude towards Muslim opinion, a pragmatic approach to business and farming interests, and a pro-American line in foreign policy. Their stronghold is in the well-to-do small towns and farming villages of western Turkey, where Menderes and Demirel enjoy the status of secular saints. Demirel, who has been the dominant figure of Turkish politics for three decades, was overthrown twice by military coups and banned from politics by the junta of 1980; nevertheless he managed to reorganize his party and returned to power in 1991. Özal started his political career as a protegé of Demirel, but parted ways with him by accepting a job with the military government of 1980 and rising to power at the time when his mentor was banned from entering politics or having any involvement in the political arena. A personal feud now separates the two men and their parties, although few real differences exist between their policies.

The "Third Force"

No discussion of Turkish politics can be complete without the armed forces – the "Third Force" which has traditionally held the balance in Turkey's political system. The army, with 800,000 men under arms, forms the largest organized force in the country. Three generations of political leaders have tried to bring this behemoth under civilian control, without notable success; three generations of generals have in response dumped civilian governments (in 1960, 1971 and 1980) in order to steer the country back to what they perceived to be the abandoned path of Atatürkist

orthodoxy – equally without long-term success. It is a mistake to suppose that the Turkish armed forces have unbounded power to dictate their will: the fact that they were compelled to oust a civilian elected government three times in a row shows the limits of their power; however, it also shows, that Turkish democracy remains incomplete in one key respect, the subjection of all branches of government to elected organs.

Restless Kurds

Some eight million Kurds live in eastern and southeastern Turkey; as many as four million more are scattered in the cities to the west. They speak various dialects of an Indo-European language that is related to Persian and the majority are *Sunni* Muslims. Their refusal to lose their ethnic identity in the Turkish melting pot has been the single biggest obstacle in the road towards national integration charted by the Turkish Republic.

Since 1980, a guerrilla movement professing the aims of Kurdish nationalism has caused Turkish governments much headache. Until a generation ago most Kurds lived in a tribal form of society. The early Republic made an effort to break Kurdish feudalism for which it was met with fierce resistance and a succession of revolts which shook the country between 1925 and 1938. Thereafter, Ankara preferred to put the problem out of its mind.

The Kurds were declared non-existent. Old Ottoman law had recognized their tribes as administrative units: the new western-style civil code did not recognize any such body, except as a private association or a criminal society.

Before 1983, the Kurdish language was not banned, it just ceased to exist. Many educated Kurds, eager to throw off the stigma of tribalism, were too ready to admit that the language spoken by their fathers was not a language at all but an idiom of formless grunts and homey phrases. Dictionaries were published to prove that all Kurdish words were derived from ancient Turkish roots, while prominent scholars "proved" that the Kurds were in fact Mountain Turks.

A part of this astonishing rejection was psychological: the Kurds represented the primitive underside of a society which desired to see itself as modern, bourgeoisie and European. Part of it was simple ignorance: until recently it was possible to find perfectly well-educated and well-meaning people in western Turkey who were unaware that a completely different nation lived in the far part of their country. No one traveled to the east, and those who traveled there were too embarrassed to admit what they saw.

In 1991, after a decade of fruitless struggle against guerrilla attacks from the east and diplomatic pressure from the west, the Turkish government finally agreed to come to terms with the matter. The existence of the Kurds was recognized and a promise was extracted to meet some of their linguistic and cultural demands. However, the chances of Turkey granting independence to its Kurdish provinces, remained as remote as a Basque, Corsican or Welsh secession. Unfortunately, not only do Turkish sentiment and pride militate against an easy disengagement, but so do the mammoth waterworks which resulted when Turkey recently harnessed the Euphrates and Tigris Rivers, deep inside Kurdish territory. These waterworks supply a large part of Turkey's energy needs and also give her an enormous strategic advantage over her Middle Eastern neighbors – an advantage which Ankara has shown every sign of planning to exploit to the full extent in the future.

I n 1950, Turkey was a backward agricultural country with practically no paved roads, less than 8,000 telephones, a literacy rate of 20 percent and an annual external trade volume of $250 million.

Its towns, except for the main centers, had hardly changed in appearance and habits over the centuries; in some respect they had regressed from the peak of perfection reached in the 16th century.

Eating under a clear blue sky – cotton pickers munching in the midst of work.

From Tenfold to Ten Million

In the four decades since 1950, Istanbul grew nearly tenfold to ten million and many lesser cities expanded at an even faster rate. A stupendous housing boom changed towns beyond recognition, and a vastly expanded road network introduced the remotest parts of the land to the joys of

Economy

After the cotton is picked and packed into bales, they are
weighed before further processing.

motor traffic. Industry grew exponentially to a point where Turkish firms now play a leading role in supplying credits and industrial know-how to the republics of the ex-Soviet Union. In agriculture Turkey is one of the very few countries in the world that is self-sufficient in food.

In western Turkey agricultural methods succeeded in revolutionizing village life after several thousand years of immobility.

The country's literacy figures approached 80 percent for the whole country and exceeded 90 percent in the west and over 90 percent of all households own their own personal television and one in five possess a car.

A turning point in this economic revolution was the program of economic liberalization that was introduced in 1980, and which has been unremittingly pursued since.

The name Turgut Özal was closely associated with the reform, first as the chief economic advisor of Demirel, then as the economics minister of the military regime and later as civilian Prime Minister and as President. His policies freed investment and trade, reduced import barriers, encouraged exports abolished currency controls, rationalized the banking system and introduced proper financial markets.

These reforms ushered in a decade of explosive economic growth without creating the dire income imbalances predicted by critics.

Harvesting tea on the Black Sea.

Of Poverty and Slums

However success, must be examined in perspective. Poverty is still widespread, particularly in the economically depressed east. But, one will not find the slums of Bombay, Lima, New York or Liverpool in Turkey.

More intangible but equally significant is the absence of the depressing, forlorn quality of the back streets of Sophia, Moscow or Havana. For 30 years it had been customary to deplore the *gecekondus*, (illegal "slum" houses) that ring the bigger cities: what is less noticeable now is that these have become one of the most profitable investments of a booming economy, bringing instant middle-class status to vast numbers of first-generation immigrants from the countryside. On average it takes less than a decade to turn a brick-and-tin illegal house into a seven storeyed apartment complete with satellite dish antennas poking out of every pore. The minimum wage is under $120, but an extraordinary entrepreneurial culture has ensured that 82 percent of the working population is either self-employed or working in enterprises employing fewer than 50 workers, where the minimum wage has little application. One only needs to observe shopping crowds in Istanbul (or Bursa, Konya, Aydin, Adana), or see the astonishing conglomerations of middle-class holiday housing that have disfigured the shores of

The inviting blue waters off the Turkish Coast have created a boatyard industry as in Bozburun, Turkish Coast.

the Aegean and Marmara Seas in the last decade, to realize that Turkey has made that critical – and perhaps sad – transition to a modern, materialistic, mass consumer society. Or, to be exact, only a part of it has. The east remains an economic nightmare. Much of the rural interior, abandoned by the younger generation for city jobs and the good life, is in the process of a slow death. It only yields good photographs of gnarled ancient folk and nostalgic ways as well as some wheat, but little else of use.

Neo-Ottomanism?

A ghost has been stalking the capitals of the Balkans and the Near East: the ghost of Neo-Ottomanism. Greece had long fidgeted about the security of its eastern Aegean Islands and the status of its Turkish minority in Thrace.

In the 1980's, Bulgarian nationalists joined it with a sudden panic over the rights of Bulgaria's own Turkish minority. Syria and pre-war Iraq wondered aloud about Turkey's newly acquired control over the waters of the Tigris and Euphrates. Iran is wary of Turkish policy toward Caucasia, Central Asia and the Kurds. Russia has been eager to court Turkey's economic favor, while visibly worrying about its increasing entanglement in Caucasia and Central Asia and Armenia and Georgia are

Of world renown – Turkish carpets.

continually vacillating between seeking Turkish aid and panicking over Turkish intentions. For half a century after the collapse of the empire, Turkey's foreign relations were characterized by caution and apathy. Having lost 20 consecutive wars and enough land to create 19 new countries, the country

Sea, sky, sans surf on Yalikavak Bay near Bodrum on the Turkish Coast.

took time out to lick its wounds. Relations with the Balkan countries which had been governed by the Turks for 550 years, were reduced to nothing and the ban on Arabic instruction in universities slashed all cultural bonds with the Middle East. The republic looked westwards for allies and was humiliated by wealthier nations.

Second-Class Citizen Of NATO

Turkey was made a second-class member in NATO and allowed special trading status with the EC, but when she applied for full membership in 1987 she was refused and a visa rule was imposed on Turkish subjects.

The first step out of inertia came with the invasion of northern Cyprus in 1974. Having lost countless lands where ethnic Turks, while always a minority, formed a significant part of the population, Turkey decided to hold the line at the insignificant island of Cyprus which had a 20 percent share of Turkish population threatened with incorporation into Greece. To its great surprise and relief, it worked: the world grumbled a little, then forgot about Cyprus.

In the Balkans, a series of mini-states had been created before WWI through the policies of Austria-Hungary and Russia, and maintained after 1945 through the dynamics of the Cold War. The collapse of the Soviet Union

No agricultural shortages here – corn husking in Ma, Mugla.

eft a vacuum and Turkish firms and government agencies rushed into the Eastern European nations before other Europeans could step in. The disintegration of the Soviet Union afforded Turkey with the opportunity to rediscover Azerbaijan, whose people speak a nearly identical version of Turkish and share many aspects of Turkish culture, and also unearthed a virtual slew of Turkic cousins (Turkmens, Uzbeks, Kazakhs, Kyrgyz, Tatars) who looked up to Turkey as a model of a modern, secular, capitalistic Muslim state. Armenia and Georgia wedged between the two branches of the Turkic world, also fell into the field of Turkey's diplomatic interest. In the Middle East, many of the region's intractable conflicts had always contained hidden elements of the unresolved legacies of Ottoman rule.

Gulf War

When the Gulf War broke out in 1991, for the first time Turkey adopted an active role in a regional conflict in which it had a historical and strategic interest. Not that Turkey seeks to regain lost Ottoman territories. But, it should not be surprising if an economically successful and diplomatically more self-confident Turkey begins to effectively use its influence in a part of the world which has only known unity under the Byzantine and the Ottoman empires ruled from the shores of the Bosphorus Sea.

Let us start with what is not there. First of all, there are no deserts in Turkey: there are some pretty dry areas around the Great Salt Lake in the central basin and near the Syrian border in the southeast, but otherwise nearly the whole surface of the country is cultivable, and has been cultivated more or less continuously for the last 5,000 years.

The second not-there follows naturally: the total camel population of Turkey stands at only 2,500. Long ago camels used to be a popular mode of land transportation; now Ford trucks have taken over, and in only a handful of tiny southern pockets where motor roads are a relatively recent arrival (the Bodrum peninsula, around Kafl-Kekova, the villages of Silifke) does one see an occasional dromedary humping up a bale. In addition to them, a number of beasts are bred for camel-fights, a popular form of entertainment in the Aegean and Mediterranean regions.

Finally, nowhere in Turkey do

Craggy cliffs of the Goverme Valley.

Geography & Climate

45

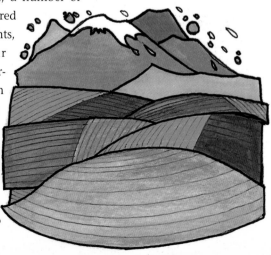

Snow in the desert? Pamukkale, Ephesus.

palm trees grow naturally. You see a few lonely date-palms in the gardens of the affluent in Istanbul, and some municipal plantings along the boulevards of southern towns, but that is all. Palms thrive on frost-free winters, and that rules out 97 percent of Turkey's landmass where winter temperatures regularly dip below freezing point. And even the balmy southern coast gets freak winter ice and snow once every few years.

Five Geographical Zones

Apart, from these, the variety of climates and landscapes that Turkey does offer is pretty phenomenal, making it hard to single out any one snapshot as "typical" of the country as a whole. Yes it is a Mediterranean country, with pretty much the same sort of natural landscape as Italy, Greece or Southern France. It is also the land of the vast, bleak volcanic wastes of Inner Asia, and at the same time one of green alpine pastures ringed with snow-capped mountains. The beaches of Antalya stay full of tan-seekers through early December; at the same time, a two-hour drive away, the Taurus passes will already be snowed under and the thermometer in Erzurum, in the frosty northeast, may have dipped to – 30°C. The 400 kilometers drive between Istanbul and Ankara crosses no less than five geographic zones, ranging from temperate farmland to pine forest and arid steppe. And the drive

cross ony one of the mountain passes
f the northeast, where the treeless vol-
anic plateau of the interior suddenly
plunges into the mist-shrouded forests
of the Black Sea Coast, is one of the most
unforgettable travelling experiences
anywhere.

Contrasting Environments

urkey is a large country: at 780,000
quare kilometers, it measures more than
rance and Great Britain put together. It
s also an extremely mountainous coun-
ry, with a complex physical structure
accounting for a sharp variety of natu-
al environments.

Two chains of mountains bracket
he Anatolian peninsula to the north
and south. The northern mountains run
along the Black Sea Coast, starting a
hort distance east of Istanbul and gain-
ng altitude towards the east; at their
eastern extremity near the Georgian
order, the Kaçkar range forms a solid
wall rising directly from the sea to a
eight just under 4,000 meters. In the
outh, the coast is cut off from the inte-
ior by the Taurus mountains, a young
alpine chain with many peaks standing
over 3,000 meters, which start at the
majestic knot of the Lycian peninsula in
he southwest, reach their highest point
at the 3,700 meters peaks of the Aladağ
range, curving inland behind the
Cilician plain, then branching eastwards
along a broad arch to join the wild
Kurdish highlands of the southeast. Be-

Snow-caps and streams of Mount Agri.

tween these two ranges lies the Anatolian
high plateau, occupying an average
height of 800 meters above sea level in
the central part, and rising to an average height of 1,200 to 1,600 meters
further east.

Five (some say seven) regions of
very different natural landscape, climate, flora and even distinct history
and culture, result from this geography.

The Northeast

The Northeast – the region of the
Marmara Sea – is an extension of the
Balkan peninsula: a fertile land of rolling hills, fruit orchards, and compact,
prosperous villages of red-tile roofs pok-

No need to journey to the moon, experience the 'lunar' landscape of the Goreme Valley.

ing through verdant greenery. It rains throughout the year here, although not often, and snow is common in winter. The natural vegetation mixes moderate-zone leaf forests with patches of Mediterranean maquis (especially on south-facing hillsides), though the land is so densely cultivated that wild nature has few opportunities to exhibit itself naturally. The Mediterranean element gets stronger as one goes south along the Aegean coast, but the same basic landscape continues to dominate as far as Izmir or thereabouts.

The Mediterranean climate breaks forth in full glory south of the Izmir peninsula, producing a dazzling tapestry of sunshine, sea salt and aromatic grass along a 1,000-mile coastline. The

region is sharply mountainous as far a the Syrian border. The typical landscape is craggy white-grey limestone, covered with thorny bush and a wild variety o odorous herbs – thyme, rosemary, sage mint, tarragon and laurel bush. Many hillsides are planted with forests of 500 year old olive trees. It practically never rains on the coast between May and September, though the torrential down pours of winter and early spring still make parts of the region (notably the western face of the Lycian peninsula and the plain of Antalya), on the aver age, some of the wettest parts of the country. Such flat land as exists be tween the crevices of the mountains is as a result, fertile with a subtropica luxuriance; here grow the largest part o

Bridge over the river, Northeast Turkey.

Turkey's greenhouse vegetables – tomatoes, cucumbers, peppers, eggplant – and cotton, and nearly all of its citrus fruit, figs and bananas.

The Interior

The Interior of Anatolia is a lonely, rolling plateau with a grandeur of landscape all its own. Its main product is wheat, endless fields of which cover the land, alternating with bald patches where wind and water erode the volcanic soil into fantastic landscapes. Villages of the Anatolian interior seem to grow directly from the earth with their huddled clusters of low, flat houses, built of mud-brick and adobe using tech-

niques perfected 5,000 years ago. Many villages form a sort of low mound, formed over many millenia as successive generations of villagers build their houses over the debris of their ancestors. Brown, yellow and ochre are the dominant colors pervading throughout most of the year – except in spring, when nature breaks forth for a few brief weeks in a most extraordinary display of greenery and wild flowers.

Eastern Turkey

Eastern Turkey forms an extension of the Iranian-Afghan landmass, a vast and awesome land of extinct volcanoes and high lava plains. Several of its mountains, notably the 5,165 meters high Ağri Daği – Mount Ararat of the Bible – stand higher than the highest point in Europe, with solitary volcanic silhouettes which impart them with a terrible majesty which chain-mountains could never match.

Lake Van, one of the largest highland lakes of the world, stands at 1,650 meters above sea level; the city of Erzurum is located at 1,900 meters, while the broad plateau of Kars rises to 2,100 - 2,200 meters. These areas suffer from winters of proverbial harshness, which often bring temperatures below minus 40°C, making many villages inaccessible by snow for months at a time. The land is more fertile than Central Turkey, but the long winter rules out most forms of agriculture. As a result the dominant economic activity is cattle and sheep rearing, and a considerable part of the native population pursues a nomadic way of life in continual search of fresh pastures.

The Black Sea Coast

The Black Sea Coast is quite unlike the rest of the country. Its unbroken chain of mountains blocks out any southern influence, while the predominant north-westerly winds bring heavy rainfall – 230 cm per year at the eastern end of the coast – which averages approximately 200 days of rain per annum. As a result the land is covered with a jungle-like mantle of forest and fern, with wild

streams and waterfalls bursting out of every clearing in the woods. The south-eastern "elbow" of the sea, squeezed between the Kaçkar range in the south and the Caucasus mountains in the northeast, enjoys the climate of a natural greenhouse: it is the only corner of Turkey that is completely immune to

A view of the coastline in Marmaris.

frost, and therefore grows a variety of products – oranges, bananas, and above all tea – that one would hardly expect to find this far north. Patterns of habitation, too, have also adapted to nature: instead of cluster-villages which are the norm throughout Turkey, the individualistic, fiercely independent inhabitants of the Black Sea Coast live in isolated farms scattered throughout the forested valleys, cultivating fields which are often more vertical than horizontal.

T

he Turkish people appear to many through the eyes of myth and legend. Beautiful princesses and genies haunt our imagination from tales such as a **Thousand and One Nights**, to which we often think that all things exotic belong.

The Turks especially the women, are indeed renowned with a mystique of eastern seductiveness and the apppeal of the mixture of both east and west. The men on the other hand are often depicted as mischievous wide-boys on the go for another wife – another rather gross misconception. Turkey has the appeal of a nation lured by the piety of Islam, but with a vivacious charm of its own.

The shy smile of a young Turkish maid bids you welcome to her land.

53

Search For An Identity

At home, even today the Turks are searching for an identity which they can call their own. This is however not merely

(although partly) due to the mixture of east and west. It is never quite clear whether Turks are Easterners or Balkans, of the Orient or of the Occident, while participants in the Mediterranean spirit.

Of Tough & Persevering Stock

Confusion over national identity has developed throughout history during which their lines have been greatly influenced by powerful and authoritative rulers.

History has proved that the people of Turkey are of a tough and persevering stock. Their forefathers came to Turkey as herdsmen who while seeking an oasis in a barren and harsh land fought for and raided towns.

Out of this tough history were born the likes of Genghiz Khan an awesome hero of the land. During this time when the Turks were seeking to establish themselves in the land, the practice of exogamy took place, whereby tribes intermarried establishing blood ties which can be seen in the mixed blood of the people of today.

Through The Centuries

Through the centuries Turkey grew up into a great and mighty nation, led by the omnipotent Süleyman the Magnificent whose empire was one of the great-

est the world has ever seen. The T
needed such awesome rulers to ins
them in the years ahead: after yea
subservience to northern Europe,
nation suffered a severe defeat in W
which left 50 percent of the popula
either dead or displaced.

It was out of this terrible defeat
national and individual identity v

A Muslim man caught unawares in the midst of prayer in Istanbul.

formed, shaped by the infamous "Father of the Nation", Atatürk. Atatürk deliberately dealt with the issue of identity from the premise of "Happy is he who calls himself a Turk". This great leader forged the identity of "Turkish European" instead of "Islamic Turkish", which had enormous implications and consequences for all Turks. "European", meant the replacement of the *fez* by the hat, the Arabic alphabet was abolished and there was a purge campaign against Persian words. This new system left the Turkish people in cultural isolation from

With twists of scarves and layers of cloth, the Turkish woman is protected
from the vagaries of climate and prying eyes.

hundreds of years of their ancient culture.

Secondly as Turks were now first and foremost "European", not Islamic, Islam was to be tolerated as a religion but banned as a lifestyle, *de facto* making Turkey a secular state.

In 1926 a law was made banning religious marriage, which was replaced with a civil institution. In 1935 another law made Muslims take up a family name in addition to other names, for administrative i.e non-religious purposes.

Position of Islam

The new position of Islam in opposition to the new laws of the state, had much influence on the people, especially the women, who encountered the seeds of liberation in Atatürk's speeches in favor of the education and equality of women. In essence Atatürk managed to produce a nation out of a melting pot of races and cultures in which Islam had been the dominant form. Far be it however to say that Atatürk had created a uniform identity.

The Turkish language today still reflects its cultural roots, sounding very different from the tongue of any northern European. The Turkish language belongs to the Ural-Altaic family of languages spoken in various parts of the middle east. The early tribes had also adopted other religions besides Islam which are still existent today.

A child sits secure on its mother's back as she husks corn in Ula, Mugla.

Today the population of 56 million is comprised not entirely of Turks, but also a number of "significant" minorities. The Kurds of South east Turkey are perhaps the most significant; an ethnic group with their own language and tribal affinities, whose plight for survival has been graphically portrayed recently in Iraq, where their brutal treatment has incurred considerable Turkish empathy and practical help.

Other minorities include Greeks, Armenians, Laz, Assyrians and Jews – there has been a Turkish Jewish community since the 1500s when considerable immigration took place.

As apart from political and ethnic influences on the Turkish identity, one must always stress the enormous im-pact of religion, which has posed a major issue in dialectical tension with politics concerning the status of women.

Women's Issues

Turkey is still very much a gender-segregated society, and despite many of the so called "feminist" reforms, it must be said that it is a consevative nation. The veil is still worn by many women, though in the cities western style is more in vogue.

Women tend to go around in groups during the daytime and are seldom seen after dark and especially not in bazaars or restaurants as women are often seen to be certified prostitutes if they work

Turkish football and its youthful afficionados caught in a pre-game upbeat mood.

anywhere where alcohol is served.

Since WW1 when women first went to work in the munitions factories, the status of women in Turkey has indeed changed. In 1925 polygamy was abolished, women were given equal status in divorce and a minimum age for marriage was fixed. Women now had considerable control over their marital staus. Again, equality of inheritance and equality of testimony was granted before a court of law, such that women could at last hold individual power. Finally in 1930-34 female suffrage was introduced.

Although these drastic reforms seemed to spell a revolution for women, progress in reality was not as fast. Turkey still to a considerable extent remains a patriarchal eastern society and women are continually fighting for their rights.

As late as 1987 Mrs Semra Özal, the wife of the Prime Minister, called for the end of the practice of taking a second wife and the practice of religious marriage (where the girl was often underaged and forced into it) – which had been banned in 1926! It is at an elite and rural level that "feminist" reforms are not always welcomed, even by women themselves; in parts of the south and east many women wear veils as an Islamic Fundamentalist statement against the legacies of Atatürk's reforms and the secular state.

There are still many contradictions regarding the staus of women as in

many countries; despite the legalization of brothels, the vitue of chastity is
widely extolled. Various feminist organi-
zations and feminist magazines speak
out for many of those who suffer, including beaten wives who are often
afraid to speak out, being silenced by
tradition.. In the face of apparent progress the issue of feminism is still very
much evolving and requiring public recognition in Turkey today.

ordained perhaps from their imperial
history. For instance it is customary to
say all the polite words you can think of
when you ask for something or when
someone has done something for you.
Sign language also varies from other
parts of the world; for instance moving
your head from side-to-side in Turkey
does not mean "no", but "I don't understand".

The Influence Of Tourism

A final influence
on the people of
Turkey has been
the vast en-
croachment of
tourism onto
her shores. Turkey
has become a highly poular holiday
destination for thousands of tourists –
especially westerners – who enjoy her
gorgeous seas. Despite semi-nudism and
the mob mentality of many tourists, the
Turks remain generously respectful of
foreigners who they see as cultured, educated and wealthy, thus deserving or
not you will usually find them friendly
and polite.

Do not point your finger at anyone
or show them the side of
your foot. Do not engage
in heavy petting in
public as this is con-
sidered offensive.

The Turkish Character

Turks are a
friendly people
but are deservedly proud of their nation.
Their passion is perhaps most publicly
and vehemently displayed in a love of
soccer – a victory is cause for jubilant
celebration, but defeat often ends up in
a fight between supporters, the losing
sides fans sometimes even attack their
own team.

A Turkish Debate

Turkish men do love to debate. They will
be amenable to your participation but
do not become too personal. Intellectu-

Standards of Etiquette

Turks do have standards of etiquette,

A Turkish man complete with beard and knitted cap.

alism is respected and the men love to gather over tea, to discuss issues of the day. Intellectuals see it as their personal duty to guide the nation to democracy in this developing state.

Finally the Turk is addicted to nightlife, for the men at least. People stay up to 1-2am even on weeknights in a country where enjoyment is important as well as devotion.

A jovial, friendly and fun-loving people, getting to know locals will be a big factor in making your trip an enjoyable one.

Every traveler in Turkey has his favorite story of that first night in the hotel, when an ungodly din blasting through his pre-dawn sleep sent him flying for the fire-escape. One gets used to it in a few days; one also learns to avoid hotel rooms facing a mosque! Thus, the first palpable signal to remind you that you are in a Muslim country: five times a day beginning at dawn a *müezzin,* or rather his disembodied voice through a tuneless loudspeaker, will proclaim the greatness of Allah from every minaret in the land, urging the faithful to perform their devotions. The vast majority of Turks simply ignore it – unless the holy month of *Ramazan* (fasting month) comes around to stir their residual piety, or advancing age makes their soul more receptive to the call of God. Only at Friday noon will sizeable numbers – especially the merchants and artisans of the traditional bazaars – congregate at the mosque to hear the ser-

The Aya Sofia in Istanbul stands in domed and minareted silhouette in the sunset.

mon and perform *namaz* (collective rites).

Proclaim the Name of God

Nearly all Turks are technically Muslim, though not all obey the word of God with equal scruple. The surest way to measure someone's Islamic soundness is the degree of *tesettür* (covering) practised by the women in the family. Practically all rural women cover their heads with some sort of simple or elaborate headdress, but this is more a matter of local tradition than an overt expression of piety. Serious religious orthodoxy as shown in head-to-toe feminine *çarşaf* (covering) is usually found among the wives of bazaar merchants in the small towns. On the other hand, zealots from the born-again Islam school (a mainly urban phenomenon), flaunt their faith by sporting an off-color long coat and a loose-ended *türban* (headscarf). The males from the latter two groups are likely to have followed all of the Prophet's injunction to brush their teeth by the bark of the *misvak* tree and will under no condition consent to shake hands or come into physical contact with a female stranger.

Other rules of Islam are more universally observed. During the month of *Ramazan* (fasting month), which occurs 11 days earlier each year following the lunar calendar (February-March in 1993), a majority of Turks observe *theoruç* (fasting), during which time they avoid food, drink, smoking and sex from dawn to sundown; only after hearing the canon–shot officially announcing sunset can they feast amidst the sentimental pleasures of a family get-together. In the western parts of the country nobody will bother a sinner publicly flouting the fast, but in the more conservative central and eastern parts of Anatolia this is considered offensive behavior, eliciting a nasty snicker at best and serious violence at worst.

A more exotic occasion is presented by *Kurban Bayrami,* or the Feast of Sacrifice (May 31 – June 3 in 1993), when all devout Muslims are expected to slaughter a ram, a bull or even a he-camel depending on their financial ability and distribute the meat among their neighbors and the poor. The queazy and weak-of-heart are advised to stay off the streets at this time. However, most middle-class Turks honor this feast by flocking to sea resorts for their annual vacation.

The months preceding the Feast of Sacrifice are considered the most propitious for another ritual involving the knife – the *sünnet* (circumcision) of boys. One often finds six-to-twelve-year old heroes parading the streets all aglitter in kitsch-prince's outfits accompanied by gloating grandmothers and envious sisters, holding a brand-new bicycle with one hand and the offensive foreskin in the other.

The Holy Book explicitly bans the consumption of wine, but this has not prevented Turkey from being a pro-

The Muslim movement at Erzurum University. An informal gathering.

ducer of excellent table wines or a good many Turks from being avid drinkers of *raki*, (alcoholic liquor distilled from grapes). However, the Quranic injunction against pork, is universally respected: do not ever try to tell even a free-thinking Turk that pigs can be cute animals, let alone tasty chops!

What Allah Said...

The **Quran** (Holy Book) was revealed to the Prophet Muhammad in Mecca, Arabia, from AD 624 onwards. Over the next one and a–half centuries the Prophet and his successors spread the message over a vast territory from central Asia and the borders of India to

Spain and the Sahara. These lands, many of which continue to adhere to Islam today, can rightfully boast of having numerous common social institutions and a stronger sense of joint community than those which follow most other world religions.

The fundamental idea of the religion of Muhammad was its uncompromising stress on the unity of God. Allah stands pure, apart and above, untainted by human characteristics, unnamable, inconceivable, and perfectly alone in His majesty. He is rarely spoken of and is never depicted in human form. His power is never shared nor delegated: Muhammad is a simple messenger, as are the scores of Jewish and Christian prophets which Islam recognizes as pre-

The holy Quran being read at a religious shrine in Istanbul.

ceding him. The worship of saints is rejected, except for the respect one holds for venerable men. Icons are also prohibited; so Muslim religious art largely consists of abstract non-figurative design, reaching its highest form in the art of calligraphy.

Another important characteristic of Islam is the absence of a formal priesthood. An *imam* (the nearest thing to a Muslim priest), is any person whom the community considers qualified to lead collective prayers and to deliver the Friday sermon. In countries practicing the *unni* form of Islam (including Turkey), the state has traditionally appointed *imams* and paid their salaries from the public purse. In countries professing the *shiite* faith (like Iran), prayer leaders are elected and supported by the community, forming in effect a financially independent and self-perpetuating clergy.

Muslims

The Turkish state has been secular since 1924. Laws of property, marriage, inheritance, commerce, banking and criminal procedure are adopted from the west; they are un-Islamic in the sense that Islam entails an elaborate *seriat* (legal code) of its own.

Islam was persecuted in Turkey in 1923-50. Mosques were closed down, demolished or turned into government depots; religious education was made practically unavailable, with the unintended result that a whole generation of *mullahs* (religious teachers) grew up semi-illiterate and correspondingly narrow in their worldview; the study of Arabic was discontinued in the universities; The Islamic orders and brotherhoods were banned, and the meeting of their sectaries was made a criminal offence; *vakif* (religious foundations) – one of the most widespread forms of property under Islamic law, were taken over by the state and the priesthood became a department of the civil service, with *imams* that were appointed by Ankara and closely monitored by the Ministry of the Interior.

After 1950, the rules were relaxed and Islamic re-awakening has been part of Turkey's agenda since the 1970s. One result is visible throughout the land: after half a century in which practically no mosque was built, new mosques are now propagating the landscape. The number of mosques built since 1980 now exceeds the total number constructed in the previous nine centuries of the country's Islamic history. A similar growth in the number of *imam-hatip okulu* (religious seminaries), has benefitted universities with extra graduates. Covered women who were once a rare sight in the cities of western Turkey; now form part of the urban landscape of Istanbul and Ankara – although they still remain scarce on the sunny Aegean-Mediterranean coast. The holy month of *Ramazan*, which 30 years ago went nearly unnoticed in Turkey's cities, has become a nationwide month of piety, with round-the-clock media coverage and half the nation's restaurants closing down for the month.

But one could easily exaggerate the extent of Islam. Islam is a fact of Turkey's political life – no more than Catholicism in Italy, and a lot less than Baptism in America's Bible Belt; it will continue to play a sometimes greater, sometimes lesser role as part of the democratic process. Chances of an open conflict with the constitutional order are slim: fundamentalist parties were first allowed to compete in the elections of 1973; they won 12 percent of the vote

A wealth of devotion as Muslim men in Erzurum bow their heads in benediction.

and have never done better than 9 percent since, with nearly half their support coming from Kurdish tribal areas to the east. Many politically active Muslims prefer to work through the established conservative parties, notably through the pragmatic, business-minded ranks of the Motherland Party (ANAP) or the True Path Party (DYP). Although their influence is likely to grow as an increasingly complex society breaks the taboos of the Atatürkist state, their radicalism will undoubtedly diminish as affluence turns people's con-

exactly constitutes Islam. A majority of about three-fourths follow the mainstream *(Sunni)* version of the religion, which used to be the state creed until 1924 and is still supported (more or less overtly), by the official establishment.

The *Alevis*

That leaves out 20 percent or more of Turks who are *Alevis* – adherents of Ali, a son-in-law of Muhammad who they believe was deprived of his rightful succession and martyred by his rivals in the seventh century.

Often classed as a branch of *Shiite* Islam, *Alevism* as practiced in Turkey and Syria, (the only other country where it is widespread) actually has little in common with the religion of Iran. The origins of the sect go back to the peasant rebellions of the 13th and 16th centuries when her adherents were persecuted under the Ottoman regime, thereby developing an ethos of suffering and martyrdom. Many elements of their creed are secret; they appear to involve, among other things, a belief in the transmigration of souls. Their rituals include the celebration of the spring equinox, in which red-painted eggs announce the end of a month-long fast. Communal houses of worship – like mosques or churches – are shunned, instead there exist small shrines called *ziyaret* ("pilgrimage"), which are often set in unusual and awesome natural sites which devotees visit in order to perform private

cerns toward less transcendental avenues.

Children of Other Gods

Approximately 99.6 percent of the population of Turkey belongs to the Muslim faith. However, not all agree, on what

Four young maids off
for a stroll.

rites or to pray for the fulfillment of wishes. There is no formal priesthood; instead, each community has a *dede* (venerable sage) .

Alevi communities exist in all parts of Turkey. In fact, Turkish *Alevis* form a majority of the rural population of the east-central Anatolian plateau (provinces of Amasya, Tokat, Sivas, Erzincan, Malatya and K Maraş). The province of Tunceli is inhabited by Kurdish-speaking *Alevis*, while the city and district of Antakya is the home of their Arabic-speaking co-religionists.

which played a crucial part in the early history of this religion. **Armenians** belong to a national church (the Gregorian) which split from Greek Orthodoxy during the doctrinal disputes of the fifth century. So do the **Syriac Christians** (Jacobites), who live around the southeastern city of Mardin.

The **Melchites** who inhabit the region of Antakya, are Arabic-speaking Christians who observe the Greek Orthodox rite. The **Chaldean** and **Maronite** churches, with congregations similarly to those in the Southeast, are uniate sects who recognize the supremacy of the Roman Pope. Finally a small number of **Orthodox Greeks** remain in Istanbul

Christianity

Some 150,000 native Christians continue to live in Turkey, the land

Feet folded under him, eyes cast down, prayer beads in hand – a Muslim man meditates.

A place of pilgrimage in Ephenis for the nation's Catholics.

and the Aegean Islands of Imroz and Bozcaada.

Judaism

Most of Turkey's 25,000 **Jews** trace their roots to the Sephardic communities which were invited to settle in the Ottoman Empire when they were driven out of Spain in 1492; a majority of them still speak Ladino, a derivative of medieval Spanish. Nearly all Turkish Jews reside in Istanbul and Izmir, where they enjoy a distinguished position in the business community. An Arabic-speaking Jewish congregation survives in Antakya, one of the oldest centers of the Jewish diaspora.

The Yezidis

The **Yezidis** are devotees of an ancient non-Muslim sect which combines elements of Islam, Zoroastrianism and the occult.

The sect spread in the 13th century among the Kurdish population of upper Mesopotamia. Although it was cruelly persecuted in later ages there are still many adherents in remote areas of Iraq and southeastern Turkey. Its tenets are secret, but seem to involve a reverence for Melek-i Tavus, the Peacock-Angel, who is sometimes identified with Lucifer, the fallen archangel. Muslims regard Yezidis as abominable Satan-worshippers.

T

he land of Turkey is that of one of the world's most ancient civilizations. Dating back before biblical times it is a land of cultural gems teaching us about ancient peoples, rulers, religions and lifestyles. Turkey was once a land ruling over a great empire, a glory evident in the many sites and relics that history has bequeathed. It was in Ephesus that Saint Paul preached the Gospel of Christianity to the Genlites, it was in Constantinople–modern day of Istanbul – that Süleyman the Magnificent established his great Muslim Empire and Constantinople shone as one of the greatest cities of learning and authority in the east. The wonder of Turkey is that evidence of these peoples is still found in abundance, and through archaelogical findings, history is still being discovered. Traditions – mostly Islamic – have been

Torso – less bodies and ancient pillars abound in Nemrut Dag.

73

The intricate detailing of imperial residences of the Harem housed in Topkapi Palace.

handed down through generations and are still being lived out, among these ancient peoples of diverse descent preserved especially in their festivals. The people of Turkey have endured much suffering, particularly during the devastating world wars and probably the two greatest influences in their continuation have been Islam and Atatürk, the state and religion are today completely separated, but they have been the bulwarks of the nations survival and the restoration of the Turkish culture.

The great Ottoman Empire which succeeded the Byzantine Christian period established a Renaissance of the arts in Turkey, which is prevalent wherever you go in the country today. Süleyman the Magnificent established

a precedent for an artistic tradition by giving himself the title "Patron of the Arts".

For Süleyman the arts were to be the tools of Islam's Allah, to whom the peoples of his vast empire belonged. Süleyman was a considerable artist himself, as a gifted goldsmith and an outstanding poet. He encouraged the development of calligraphy, ceramics, textiles and painting. He commanded the building of countless mosques and other beautiful buildings. Süleyman prided himself on a philosophy with an intellectualism which is still evident in many of the bohemian bars of Istanbul, Izmir and many other towns today. During Süleyman's reign, there were great literary developments especially in poetry with the Sultan's vested interest Süleyman himself published his *Divan* (collected poems) and patronized the poetry of Fuzuli, Hayali and Baki who was the Sultan's poet laureate.

Süleyman was probably highly flattered for many of the poems were about himself and sung his praises unstintingly. With the Ottoman empire Islam was securely fastened as the lands religion and has remained dominant ever since then. The desire for progressiveness in culture sometimes clashing with reactionary elements within the church.

Turkish Carpets

When Marco Polo journeyed through

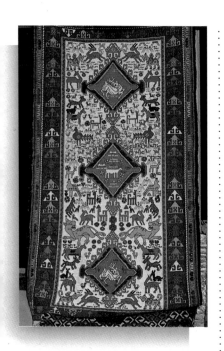

Silken threads, intricate patterning and nimble fingers create a Turkish carpet.

Anatolia, in the 13th century, he remarked on the beauty of the carpets and woven silk which he saw. Turkish carpet was already hugely famous and was being exported to Europe, usually presented to honoured guests as prestigious gifts. Since carpets were the pride of their maker they were usually woven with the sign of the maker's tribe.

The signs were often of a bird or a beast, another distinctive one was that of a woman with her hands on her hips. Such signs gave the carpets an authenticity such that many carpet-makers today include such signs on their products, remembering their nomadic and hardworking ancestors, they also make carpets more unique.

In recent years, bright colours have been used to make the carpets, the strength of the colours believed to be a mark of beauty. Today an organization called DOBAG Pojesi is trying to encourage the use of vegetable dyes, which was the traditional way of making these carpets though the dyes impress weakened colours.

Note when buying a carpet that the Grand Bazaar in Istanbul is not the best place to make a purchase as the salesmen are generally too keen for you to be ensured of a reliable purchase. If the dye runs when something is spilled on the carpet, it is not a high quality one. *Kilims* (pile-less rugs) are probably the most popular purchase and the ideal souvenir.

Kuala in West Turkey is the center for carpet making and Hereke for silk and wool carpets. In order to see the pride of Turkish carpet and *kilim* making, visit the **Museum of Turkish and Islamic Art** and the **Konya Museum**, both in Istanbul.

Silk & Other Handicrafts

The silk industry is also an ancient Turkish prerogative. Since the time of the Ottomans silk brocades and velvet weaving have been of the highest quality.

Bursa is the focal point for the silk industry today and an interesting event is the annual **Silk Cocoon Festival**, where cocoons are sold after being carefully nurtured for a few weeks. This is a most meticulous process but the prod-

A photographer's cheer brings on a serial smile at the loom.

ucts are gorgeous. There are a wide array of other handicrafts practiced in Turkey today which though rather mundane, are ancient and simple traditions which have been taken for granted for hundreds of years. Knitting for instance is an ancient Turkish craft and the knit-

ting of shawls and scarves that one sees the Turkish people wearing so often, are parts of a cultural tradition. Knitting is especially established in Siras and in Ankara where Mohair goats provide the material for the most beautiful soft and comfortable jumpers. A tradition of

Glitz and intricacy are the hallmarks of Turkish embroidery.

pron making has descended from Thrace, aprons being called *kesans*. Feltmaking is also a Furluch institution in this land of fabrics and is still used to make felt caps to warm the shepherds as they lead their flocks in the cool months. Such handicrafts are extremely useful in this tough and once nomadic country.

Other handicrafts include leatherwork and broom-making. The main leather workshops are now in Izmir and Istanbul, though they were originally based near the source of tanning in Western Anatolia. Copperworks was traditionally a popular commercial item and an essential for newly weds, demand has greatly fallen with the modernization of society and it is really

supremely in the tourist oriented bazaars that such items – especially tea sets– will be found. The **Turkish Handicrafts and Costume Museum** in Ankara, has a good selection of the above mentioned items and traditional costumes.

Ceramics

Perhaps the other great Turkish art is ceramics and in this land of the *fez*, ceramics have always had great religious overtones. Most of the greatest displays of tiling are on mosques intricate detail being born out in text from the **Quran**.

The **Mosaic Museum** in Istanbul

Handmade leather shoes crafted in Bodrum along the Turkish coast.

Mosque in Edirne also has beautiful tiling of a *Mihrap* style, the tiles are hexagonal and turquoise blue and white chinoiserie-style tiles interspersed. Tiling was patronized by the Ottoman courts who had several Court controlled kilns – for example that of Nicaea in the 16th century. Since Islam does not allow the presence of any form of icon or image of God, ceramics often with inscriptions from the **Quran**, beautify the interior and also serve to cool worshippers who have entered from the hot sun.

Painting

Because of the ban on iconography and because of the preoccupation with religion in Turkey, there is little in the way

Fine cottage industries enjoy pride of place in Turkey.

bears witness to these beautiful treasures, but they can be seen in full splendor on buildings themselves. In Istanbul the Iznik tiles on the interior walls of the Blue Mosque are a most beautiful example of the art of tiling.

There are over twenty thousand of these tiles and they exhibit a variety of designs from plain to flower and tree patterns and geometric designs. Tiling is an Islamic heritage and the tiling that you will see in Turkey follows Islamic motifs:- circles, stars, geometric designs, often in turquoise, green, white and blue.

In Edirne the Green Mosque has a marble exterior of detailed design. The tiles are mode of polychrome and are of blue and green colour. The Muradiye

Porcelain painting is executed by each craftsperson to create personalized pieces.

f Islamic painting. However, a rich legacy has descended to us from the Byzantine era, whose paintings are to be found in the greatest museums of the world. These paintings were mainly in the form of icons of the apostles and Jesus Christ. In Istanbul, the Haga Sophia contains some internationally famous example of Byzantine Mosaics such as the Deëis Mosaic of Christ.

In the late Byzantine empire restrictions of economy meant that mural painting replaced mosaics, an example being the series of murals of the resurrection of Christ dated 1310-20 in the Cariye Camii – formerly the Church of the Saviours, in Chora, Istanbul.

Such Islamic painting as there was featured landscape scenes, an example being that of Summer Landscapes, from the *Album of the Conqueror* (Sultan Mohammad II) which can be seen in the Topkapi Palace Museum, Istanbul.

In more recent centuries foreign painters have depicted Turkey rather savagely as a place of violence and passion. Along this line are J. Ingres' *The Odalisque*. Nineteenth century frescos can be seen everywhere in the town of Sinassos, from government building to ordinary houses. An important fresco is at the Hotel Sinassos which contains an 1893 painting of the Russian-Japanese war.

The Main Art Museums in Turkey are:- the **Gallery of Fine Arts** in Antalya, the **State Art Gallery** in Ankara and the **Panagia Convent** in Trabzon which houses some of the finest examples of Byzantine painting in the world.

Literature

Again in terms of foreign ignorance, literary foreigners such as Byron depicted Turkey with a passion, as of a life of sex and harems and the intrigues of Sultans. In reality literary origins were more pious. The illumination of texts found its way from the writing of scientific material to that of the calligraphy of religious texts.

Calligraphy became a developed art form – probably influenced by the Chinese –- which reached almost abstract proportions. A good example of such calligraphy can be found in a range from the **Album of the Conqueror** (Sultan Mohammad II) in the Topkapi Palace Museum, which includes a 15th century imaginative calligraphy of the word Allah.

Literature was highly patronized by Süleyman the Magnificent, who advanced the genre of poetry as an art form. Philosophers such as Al Farahi also encouraged the development of intellectual debate in Turkey, his form of philosophy blending Aristotelian, Platonic and Sufi thought.

During the Byzantine era. The area of modern Turkey was also the venue for important the logical discussions: the Covention of Nicaea in AD325, defined the Christian Churches creed of Faith, which is still a major doctrinal basis for the religion today. Modern day Turkish writers include Edouard Roditi , a American based Turkish writer known for his elegant prose, and Ayse Özakin who wrote a controversial book Th **Prize Giving** which questioned the in stitution of marriage.

Architecture

Architecture was one of the greates manifestations of the power of an em pire, such that the Roman, Byzantin and Ottoman empires, all manifeste their rule over Turkish civilization with a host of architectural forms. A fin example of Roman architectural can b seen at the altar of Zeus at Pergamon One of the most important architec tural structures in Turkey is however th Hagia Sophia in Istanbul, representin as it does, a juxtaposition of architec tural styles. The building was inaugu rated during the "Golden Age" o Justinian (527-565) at the time of Ro man rule.

However characteristic minaret were added after the Turkish conquere in 1453, when it became a mosque Thus the axis forms a Christian basilica but the additions impart a notably Turk ish flavour. Classical Hellenistic styl art can be seen at Ephesus, where th Great temple – one of the 7 wonders o the world – is built in classical style Further evidence of Roman culture ca be seen in the theatre of Ephesus, and in the Roman theatre at Demre, which i

Gold relief in the Harem sectnoney Topkapi Palace.

still in an excellent condition.

Bursa is the finest example of Ottoman architecture, with the characteristic eyran style of architecture. The Ottoman style of mosques was modelled on the form of a main dome joined by four half domes, the perfection of this design can be seen at the Mosque of Sultan Ahmed I in Istanbul, (1609-16) Muradiye mosque northwest of Ankara, is another of the finest of Ottoman mosques. Divriği in northeastern Turkey has fine examples of pre-Ottoman architecture. Other styles of architecture to be found throughout the country are the examples of Lycian Funeral architecture at Myra and timber and stucco architecture in the Black Sea region. The most eclectric range of style is however to be seen in Istanbul. Sinan was one of Turkey's greatest architects.

Theatre & Cinema

From the days of the Roman Empire, theatre was a popular form of entertainment in what is now the land of Turkey. In the 16th century *Karagoz* (shadow theater) was brought over from Egypt by Selim I. For modern productions of plays there are both state controlled and private theaters, the private ones are to be found out of the main areas.

Cinema is also developing as an art form in Turkey, since the 1950's when it capitalized on the genre of melodrama, expanding into a home-grown art form.

The fabulous Blue Mosque stands in symmetrical splendour in Jstanbul.

Yblmaz Güney is the most famous film director. After making a social political film about Turkish life in the 1970s he was imprisoned on the charge of murdering a judge. His most famous film *Yol* (the Road) was written from his prison cell. The film follows the lives of 5 prisoners who are released for 1 week or parole.

The ***Istanbul Sinema Derneği*** (Istanbul Cinema Association) is a major intellectual haven where thinking people gather to discuss the state of this and other art forms.

Music

Presidential Symphony Orchestra Concerts can be heard in the Ankara state concert hall and less grand performances around the provinces. Turkey's most famous composer is Ulri Erkin, who adapted Turkish folk music to choirs. The main traditional folk music instruments are the *tambur* – a long necked lute with double strings – the *ud* (lute) and the *kanun* (lateral zither). Turkish folk music called *asik*, can be heard in Erzurum and Kars. A new kind of music is currently evolving in Turkey which has been given the name of arabesque.

Other Museums & Festivals

Important museums to see in Turkey, are: The **Atäturk Cultural Centre**, in Istanbul; The **Rodrum Museum of Underwater Archaeology**, contains findings form the Cape Gelidonya Wreck (1960) and the Seylam Deresi wreck among others; The **Pergamin Archaelogical Museum** – with artefacts from this important ancient cultural center, The şanakkale Archaelogical Museum features exhibits from Troy. The **Izmir Archaelogical Museum** isthe scene for international Arts festivals – a vital part of the local cultural scene.

The ancient pipe and a young fan in Jstanbul.

Istanbul

For all the "third-world" ills of overcrowding, dirt, smog, chaotic growth and traffic that have unrelentingly gripped it in modern times, Istanbul remains a beautiful city. To appreciate it fully one must get there by boat (as countless travellers from the past have done), watching the silhouette of a thousand minarets grow slowly over the horizon, then come to rest in the world's most splendid harbour surrounded by the seven hills of the Old City and the steeper heights of Pera and Asia, with the *fjord*-like bends of the Bosphorus vanishing in background. Few great cities of the world embrace the sea so intimately, blue, choppy and fresh smelling – not the grey leaden liquid of other seaside cities – at the very center of the city.

Now—days you are more likely to arrive in Istanbul by plane or car, entering by the Western

Ortakoy on the waterfront in Istanbul.

Zek•

Belgrad Ormani

Petnahor

Belgrad Ormani

Valide Bendi

Mahmu Bendi

Büyük Bendi

Bahçeköy

Pirinççiköy

Habibler

Kemerburgaz

EUROPE

Şeyhan

K

Alibey Baraji

Cebeciköy

Kâğithane Deresi

Ayazağa

HASDAL

Kadi Yapili D.

Çavuşabasi Deres

Alibey Deresi

Kâğithane

METRIS

Küçükköy

Alibeyköy

MAHMUTBEY BATI

MAHMUTBEY

Metrisköy Atişalan

020

ZINCIRLIKUYL
Cerve Yolu

CAGLAYAN

Uzunca

DOGU

Mahmutbey

ESENLER

SISLI

OSMANBEY

OKMEYDANI

Rami

EYÜP

HALICIOĞLU

BES

Esenler

Çirp Deresi

HASKÖY

DOLMABAHÇE

Kirazli

TAKSIM

Güneşli

Bağcilar

BEYOĞLU

GALATA

FENER

Medisi Mebusan

B

ORTA AKS

Güngören

Litros

VATAN CAD.

Vidos Deresi

TOPKAPI

Fezzi Pasa Cad.

FATIH

Kocasinan

ÖSNANIYE

Millet Cad.

SIRKECI

BEYAZIT

Safraköy

Siyavuspaşa

MERTER

ALTIMERMER

KUMKAPI

SULTANAHMET

SELI

Kuleliçifliği

INKIRLI

E5

SAMATYA

HAYD

Sirinevler

100

YEDIKULE

ISTANBUL

ÇOBANÇEŞME

ATAKÖY

Yeniköy

Zeytinburnu

Yeşilköy Havalimani

Ataköy

Bakirköy

Yeşilköyburnu

Yeşilköy

SEA OF MARMARA

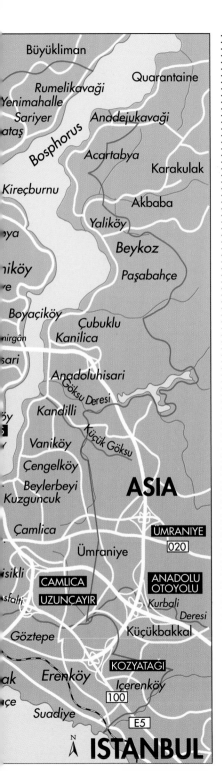

Highway. Ignore the ramshackle new districts, the smoke-belching vehicles, the dusty roads and dismal crowds that accompany your first ten miles or so into the city.

Head straight for the center, and do not open your eyes until you get to the harbour. Get off only when you reach the **Galata Bridge**: this is where you see Istanbul in all its glory, the 2,600-year old mistress of two world-empires, still alive and magnificent beneath all the menacing shabbiness that has so far failed to submerge it.

A View from the Bridge

It is still simply *the Bridge* for the natives of Istanbul, although no longer unique since the 1950s (two other bridges have been built across the Golden Horn and two spectacular suspension bridges span the Bosphorus), nor even old.

In 1992, a bold new bridge the product of modern technology and German steel, replaced the ancient floating bridge of Galata which had been the revered symbol of Istanbul for many generations.

The hoary old pontoon has now been towed away to the deep end of the harbour, its downstairs fish restaurants, smokers' dens, fishing-rod renters and resident bums all seemingly abandoned to the arms of gentle oblivion.

Walk the bridge from end to end, starting from the Old City side: the chaotic open space here is called **Eminönü**,

Istanbul and the Bosphorus by night.

the lower end of the great bazaar's labyrinth and the nerve center of the city's public transport system. The opposite side is **Karaköy**, the shipping-and-banking district of Istanbul, which sits in the shadow of the squat and heavy **Tower of Galata**.

Watch the endless stream of humanity flowing past you. This is the hub not only of Istanbul but of all of Turkey, and what you see here is the closest you will ever get to a snapshot of the country as a whole.

Note the profusion of men as opposed to women (81 percent), most of them young, nearly all wearing moustaches (87 percent). A good number are visitors from deep Anatolia, gawking at the sea seen perhaps for the first time in their lives; others have been in the city for a while, struggling along the painful path of transition from rural to urban with varying degrees of success: almost nine out of ten of Istanbul's 8 million inhabitants migrated to the city after 1960, or were born to parents who migrated after 1960.

Note the women: some wearing head-to-toe *chadors* (covering) and traveling in clusters of three or four, others in the no-nonsense grey coats of conservative folk, yet others in Chanel suits or jeans-and-sneakers, none more "typical" nor predominant than the other.

Also note the gypsies, with their florid dress and piercing eyes, and the bearded Muslim patriarchs exhibiting their proud contempt towards the sins

The interior of the Hagia Sophia.

of this world.

The spirit of the bazaar inevitably seeps in wherever crowds of Turks come together: so the fast-talking pedlar touting "the latest wonder of Japanese technology", the water-seller in glittery uniform, the snake-oil man keeping a nervous eye for the police.

Foreigners, too, are present in force, as befits a city at the crossroads of continents: East Europeans and ex-Soviets carrying large shopping bags filled with the wonders of a consumer economy and tourists from the more fortunate lands milling around with guidebooks in their hands.

Meanwhile scores of amateur fishermen cast their line from the bridge's railings, oblivious to all the hubbub around them, pulling in silvery strings of *istavrit* fish in the middle of the busiest intersection of the city.

Look beyond the bridge to the broader panorama around you. Right below you is the sea, where you can see the reflections of the City Lines manoeuvering around each other like nimble white whales, a dozen of them at a time, tooting and belching billows of black cloud, loading and unloading passengers for the 20-minute commute from continent to continent.

Further out, where the Bosphorus forms a broad basin between the Palace Point and the apartment-crowded hills of Asia, lumbered ocean liners wade slowly through the city *en route* to Russia or the Mediterranean.

The Old City

Consider now the hooked tip of the Old City, to your left, where the first of the seven hills of the city of Constantine forms a wooded headland thrusting into the Bosphorus. It is a spectacularly strategic point, astride the main overland route between Europe and Asia and dominating the important sea lane from the Black Sea to the Mediterranean. The summit of the hill is occupied with the hundred towers, cupolas, domes and baldachins of the **Topkapi Palace**, the residence of the sultans and the seat of their harem through the centuries of Ottoman splendour. It was also on this hill in 658 BC, (2,111 yearrs before any sultan had set foot in the city), that the city of **Byzantium** was founded by a shipful of Greek colonists travelling from Megara. For 1,000 years after its founding, ancient Byzantium stayed confined to this area alone. She was a fairly important city-state of the Greek-Roman world although not as important as she could or should have been. Its remains lie scattered through the Palace parks; the more interesting pieces are exhibited within in the Ar-chaeological **Museum**, also located within the grounds of the Palace.

The mammoth dome of **Hagia Sophia** stands next, sitting on giant buttresses painted the color of dried roses, surrounded by a number of minarets added as if in a afterthought. This is the symbol and masterpiece of the second 1,000 years of the city's history – a time when Byzantium at last lent its name to a great empire, yet lost its own name to the man who made it great. In AD 324, Constantine the Great chose Byzantium as the new seat of a newly Christian and newly reorganized Roman Empire. Rebuilt from the ground, the new city – the largest that the ancient world had yet seen – was henceforth known as **Constantinople**. Its dominion extended over the whole of the known civilized world, and later only over its eastern half. It also claimed the spiritual leadership of Christendom, and it was in support of this that Justinian (AD528-565), the mightiest of Byzantine emperors, wanted to furnish his capital with the largest church ever built by man. So the Hagia Sophia was built – its size and magnificence not to be surpassed until 1,000 years later, when Rome, the old and only rival of the imperial city, responded

A cityscape of minarets and domes as viewed from the
Suleymaniye Mosque in Istanbul.

through Michelangelo's dome of St Peter. However, by that time, the Hagia
Sophia was no longer a church, having
been converted into a mosque in the
hands of its Turkish conquerors.

The Turks conquered Istanbul in
1453. Their empire took over many of

the institutions and policies of the Byzantine state which they tried to perfect.
Hagia Sophia was the chief monument
of Byzantine might: with its conversion
it became the model of imperial mosque
architecture, which Ottoman architects
tried to better in size, splendour and

grace. The results of their efforts crown the hills of the Old City in a monumental procession of mosques.

Nearest to the bridge, surrounded by its perpetual cloud of pigeons, you see the grey bulbous mass of the **New Mosque**, the newest of the mosques from the classical Ottoman period (which is still over 350 years old)! Over the hill and slightly behind, the mosques of **Nuruosmaniye** and **Beyazit** rear their head.

To the right, the **Süleymaniye** covers the third hill of Istanbul in its magnificent cascade of domes and minarets: it reflects the glory of Sultan Süleyman the Magnificent (1520-66) under whose reign Istanbul reached a level of wealth and brilliance it had never matched since the days of Justinian.

The mosque of Süleyman's favorite *grand vizier*, **Rüstem Paşa**, lies in the shadow of his patron's temple as if figuratively kowtowing. The great mosques of Süleyman's ancestors punctuate the skyline further to the right: the **Fatih**, built for Mehmet II (1451-81), the conqueror of Istanbul, and **Yavuz Selim** which commemorates **Selim the Grim** (1512-20), the victor of Syria, Egypt and half of Arabia.

Watch this fabulous panorama reflected on the surface of the harbour, at sunrise when the early rays of the sun paint the murky waters of the harbour in the color that once inspired its name – the **Golden Horn** *(Haliç* in Turkish). Try to imagine that fatal day in 1453 when the inhabitants of the city woke

up to find the armada of Mehmet II transported into their harbour, sails unfurled and cannons firing, having been pulled overnight by rope and pulley across the hills and valleys of Galata – a blow to Byzantine ingenuity which had blocked the entrance of the Golden Horn with a chain drawn across the area where the bridge now stands.

Or go back to the disastrous year of 1204, when the navy of the Fourth Crusade, led by the blind and nonagenarian Dandolo the Doge of Venice, spent a winter of envy here dreaming of the untold riches of Byzantium, before setting upon the imperial city in a savage paroxysm of arson and pillage. Where their galleons once dropped anchor, feisty little motorboats now zip around in seemingly random motion, carrying men and goods across the shores of the harbour.

The Other Half

Now turn to the other half of the city. Until less than a century ago this was the alien part of the city, Beyoğlu, the "other side" (Pera in Greek). Today, Beyoğlu has grown into the more important part of modern Istanbul, the home of its banks and corporations and its smarter sort of shops. The steep hill immediately facing you gives the bridge its name: **Galata**.

Here a horde of Celtic tribes from Western Europe whom the Greeks called Galatoi camped one winter some 2,300

A cruise ship plying the clear blue waters of the Bosphorus.

years ago, having pillaged all of Greece and Thrace and threatening to do the same to Byzantium.

The Byzantines negotiated, bribed and won, no doubt with the same slow and wily patience which survives in the instincts of the men of the bazaar: they then generously named the district in memory of the western barbarians who had come to subjugate them.

The Western Connection

The Western connection lasted. Merchants of the Italian city-republics which had brought Byzantium to its knees settled in Galata in the Middle Ages, and a walled, self-governing Genoese colony was established here during the final squalid century of the Byzantine empire.

The Genoese erected the **Tower of Galata** in 1348 for the purposes of keeping an eye on the imperial capital across the harbor; its observation terrace still affords the finest bird's-eye view of the center of the city.

A European "ghetto" continued to exist in Galata through the Ottoman centuries. Its heyday was the *belle époque* of the late 19th century which came at a time when the Eastern empire had once again entered a period of mortal decline, and the "sick man on the Bosphorus" seemed doomed to fall under the supremacy of the European powers.

From the 1850s onwards, a rich, cosmopolitan and lively culture of unabashed colonialism grew in "Pera" (the Greek name for Beyoğlu), with its expatriate banking families, all-powerful embassies, cafés, opera companies and grand hotels lined along the *Grand'rue de Pera (main street of Pera)* – today's **Istiklal Caddesi**. It had its own municipal organization, the first in Turkey. The language most commonly used was French and the only natives it admitted to its ranks were the Christian subjects of the sultan – the Greeks and Armenians.

Until 1908, the Turks kept away from Pera. When they at last began moving across the harbour, the move meant a break with the past and a turn towards a western, modern, middle-class way of life. The living hub of the city was transferred in the first years of the republic to new districts like **Taksim**, **Nişantaşi** and **şişli** which grew northwards of Istiklal Caddesi. To this day they remain the core of upper-middle-class Istanbul, and the newest monuments of Istanbul's Western connection – the high-rise towers of the Hilton, Sheraton, Swissôtel and others – dominate the city's skyline behind the Tower of Galata.

Next, squint and try to look past the wharves of Karaköy where cruise ships lie at berth. You will see the long white frontage of **Dolmabahçe**, the European-style palace where the last Ottoman sultans took refuge from the grim and terrible memories of Topkapi. Beyond it, framed by the graceful outline of the first of the two suspension bridges, the suburbs of the **Bosphorus** begin. In the dying days of the empire, these suburbs were synonymous with the sad and inward-looking elegance of an imperial ruling class which built its stately mansions along the shores of the waterway; today they contain the homes of Istanbul's wealthy, mixed with those of the non-wealthy and poor in an intimate confusion that is perhaps a hallmark of the cities of the East.

Across the Sea

Look, finally, across the sea: what you see is Asia, lying less than two miles away from the tip of Europe. Nearly two-fifths of the inhabitants of Istanbul live in *Anadolu yakasi* (the Asian side), many of them commuting daily to work in the other continent *Rumeli* (the Roman side). Paradoxically perhaps, Asia is a cleaner, and better organized part of the city – and for that reason also the less interesting. Facing you almost directly is the old suburb of **Üsküdar**, a district of a much more traditional character.

Note the quaint white **Kizkulesi** "Maiden's Tower" which appears to belong to the waterfront of Üsküdar but in reality stands offshore on an islet of its own. According to legend the king's beautiful daughter was sequestered here after a prophecy that she would die of a snakebite. A reckless suitor sent her the inevitable basket of grapes, and a viper concealed in it administered the mortal bite. The terrifying moral of the story being that: you cannot escape your destiny.

Consider, however, also the story of another young woman who did. Somewhat further south on the Asian side, partly obscured by Topkapi Palace in the foreground, you will see the huge bulk of the **Selimiye Barracks**. It was in this complex that an Englishwoman of gentle Victorian upbringing risked her health and reputation to bring care to soldiers wounded in the Crimean War of 1855-58. Her name was Florence Nightingale, and she is remembered as the founding-mother of the nursing profession.

Monument Square

Several of the most impressive monuments of Istanbul lie within sight of each other in the area loosely known as **Sultanahmet**, a steep 20 minute walk up from the Old City side of the Galata Bridge. This is the hub of touristic Istan-

Istanbul by dusk.

bul, the region where great streams of sightseers flow together daily and where an army of bus drivers, fast-food halls, shoeshine boys, card sharps and instant lovers stand ready to offer their services. Join them for the next stage of your tour of the imperial city.

Start with **Hagia Sophia** or *Ayasofya*, as it is called in Turkish; The chief church of the Eastern Roman Empire, became the chief mosque of the Ottomans and then (since 1935) a museum. The Hagai Sophia has been the top architectural sight of the city for over 1,460 years.

The soothing gardens surrounding the Aya Sophia
make for a pleasant wander.

Thus the impressions of a 10th century sightseer, an envoy of Prince Vladimir of Novgorod: "We are bound to believe here one is more than elsewhere in the presence of God, for the religions of all other countries are eclipsed by a grandeur which we ourselves shall never forget. It was his report that persuaded the Russian prince, a pagan shopping around for a suitable religion for his primitive people, to opt for the Eastern Orthodox version of Christianity.

The original church of Holy Wisdom (for that is what Hagia Sophia

patriarchal church as well as the imperial palace were destroyed, and Emperor Justinian, barely escaped with his life; it ended with the massacre of 30,000 rebels in the **Hippodrome** – the monumental horse-racing arena, an area which is now occupied by the broad open space of Sultanahmet Square.

Justinian and his wife, Theodora, a former cabaret star turned empress, then ordered the reconstruction of the church so that it would surpass every temple ever erected to the glory of God. A mathematician (Anthemios of Tralles) and an architect (Isidore of Miletus) joined forces to design the largest dome ever built. Their vast and daringly flat cupola was placed on four freestanding piers (as had never been done before) with the help of the ingenious use of half-domes and arches. When their monument was consecrated on 26 December AD 537, Justinian is said to have cried: "I have at last vanquished you, O Solomon!"

Allow a margin of disappointment at the external aspect of the Great Church: it is squat and devoid of proportion, with enormous buttresses (added in the 14th century to prop up the dome) that prevent a clear view of the structure as a whole. The interior, on the other hand, cannot fail to inspire awe: a lofty space of tremendous size, lit only by a crown of windows at the base of the cupola, and framed by gigantic columns of red porphyry which sets the nave apart from the mysterious, semi-dark galleries surrounding it.

means) was built on this spot in the 4th century, though it twice perished in the course of the riots and tumults that were the common fare of Byzantine public life. The great riot of AD 532 grew out of the rivalry of the Blue and Green factions at the Hippodrome, undoubted ancestors of today's football clubs. It turned into a revolution in which the

The interior of the Byzantine church used to be entirely covered with mosaics and designs of precious marble. These were whitewashed during the centuries in which the Hagia Sophia served as a Muslim place of worship, and have only been partially recovered.

Among the best of the surviving mosaics is the *Madonna with Child*, found in the semi-dome of the apse, which dates back to the year AD 867. The splendid mosaic of the *Deesis*, in the southern gallery, the belongs to 14th century, and illustrates the remarkable artistic revival which took place in Constantinople during the dying years of the Byzantine Empire.

The entrance of a Byzantine structure far less known yet nearly as memorable lies across the street on the other side of Hagia Sophia. The **Yerebatan Sarayi** ("Sunken Palace") was one of the many cisterns with which the Byzantine capital secured its water supply throughout the centuries. Admirably renovated in 1987, its 336 enormous columns of granite and marble stand waist-high in an underground lake, silent and dark, far below the bustle of one of the busiest city crossings. There are several such subterranean wonders elsewhere in the city, few of them accessible to visitors, and a new one discovered every few years during the course of construction work.

Next proceed to the great mosque which lies across a small park as a more or less explicit riposte to Hagia Sophia. The **Blue Mosque** – named for the dominant color of its interior – forms a magnificent spectacle with the harmonious proportions of its domes and semi-domes, its extraordinarily slender minarets and its whitish grey marble which makes it look as light and graceful as the Hagia Sophia is heavy and ponderous.

In terms of size it is the largest mosque in Istanbul, though in architectural terms it is usually considered inferior to the older mosque of Süleyman. Its Turkish name, *Sultanahmet*, commemorates the founder, Ahmet I (1603-17), a weak and sensuous man whose reign marked the beginning of the disastrous decline of the Ottoman Empire. The architect was one anonymous Mehmet, a student of the great Sinan. Much of the

The nationalist courtyard of the Blue Mosque.

stone used for the construction came from the old Hippodrome, whose derelict ruins were finally pulled down for this purpose.

The interior of the mosque obtains its eponymous color from the splendid Iznik tiles which cover the entire surface of the walls to a height of several meters. Remove your shoes as you enter, keeping in mind that this is a working house of worship. Note the characteristics of mosque architecture as opposed to that of a church: First, a mosque is not a "house of God" but a simple *cami* ("place of gathering"), a Muslim can perform his devotions at any place with equal ease and is called to the mosque only to share in the collective prayers of the community.

Secondly, unlike the church which sets apart a sanctuary from the congregation, the entire space of the mosque belongs to the community. The gaze is directed, not towards an altar, but upwards to the dome, under which vast enclosure, solitary worshippers prostrate themselves in meditation, clusters of believers listen to edifying lectures, and, in another corner, a *hafiz* recites the **Quran** in a heart-rending Arabic declamation.

Only a small *mihrap* (niche) indicates the *kible* (the direction of Mecca where worshippers turn to pray). The *minber* (pulpit) in principle is a simple dais, which is used by a prayer leader to deliver the Friday sermon.

Figural decoration being strictly

The intricate splendour of the interior of the Blue Mosque.

prohibited in the code of Islam, the ornamentation of the mosque is limited to arabesque designs in tile and fresco, and to the florid lines of Arabic calligraphy, which in Islamic art developed into one of the most sophisticated expressions of artistic talent. Within the mosque, calligraphic masterpieces of enormous dash or delicacy reproduce verses from the **Quran**, or simply state the names of Allah, Muhammad and the first caliphs.

Even finer specimens are to be found across Sultanahmet Square, in the **Palace of Ibrahim Paşa**, which was converted a few years ago into a museum for Turkish and Muslim art. Ibrahim Paşa was *grand vizier* (Chief Minister) of the empire in the 1540s and 1550s, until

he fell foul of Roxelane, the Russian-born wife of Süleyman the Magnificent and got beheaded. The manuscripts, miniatures, tile and metal works on display in his erstwhile palace are among the best examples of their kind to be found in Turkey.

House of the Sultans

The residence of Ibrahim's master and employer is a five-minute walk away behind the Hagia Sophia. Reserve a good half day for touring the **Topkapi Palace**, the inner sanctum of the Ottoman sultans, for this tangle of courts, pavilions, museums, kiosks and functional buildings is more like a self-contained town-within-a-town than a palace in the European sense of the term.

The palace was first laid out in the reign of Mehmet the Conqueror (c. 1460), and it served as the principal residence of the sultans from the early 16th century through to the mid-19th century. Many of its buildings have their origin in the 15th century, although most took their present shape in the time of Murat III (1574-95). Important additions were made under Murat IV (1622-40), Mehmet IV (1648-87) and as late as during the reign of Abdülmecit (1839-56), so the ensemble represents an almost complete overview of Ottoman civil architecture through the ages.

Three great gates: **Bab-i-Hümayun** (the Imperial Gate), **Bab-üs Selam** (the Gate of Peace) and **Bab-üs Saade** (the Gate of Bliss) respectively provide access, to the three courts of the palace, each belonging to a narrower circle of the imperial establishment.

The outer court was once the camp and training ground of the *janissaries* (the feared praetorian guard of the sultans). The members of this elite force were levied from the children of Christian subjects and educated into a life of fierce devotion to the House of Osman. Technically they were slaves, yet their tumultous disapproval cost the throne and life of no less than six of their masters.

The most talented of them were chosen from an early age to be trained in the school of palace servants, located in the third court from where they rose

An aged devotee at the door of
the Süleymaniye Mosque.

to the highest offices of the empire. Standing within their court – now a park and parking lot – is the Byzantine church of **Hagia Irene**, a contemporary of Hagia Sophia which is used for concerts and exhibitions. A path behind it leads to the **Archeological Museum**, home of one of the world's most important collections of Greco-Roman and Near Eastern antiquities.

As you queue for your ticket to the palace proper at the great gateway of the second court, recall that this was where a visitor would dismount in the past, for only the sultan had the prerogative to ride beyond this point. The two *ibret taşlari* (warning stones) nearby, often carried the severed heads of those who offended the sultan and were dis-

A shady walk along the sides of the Topkapi Palace.

played thus as a matter of public instruction. Exactly 52 *grand viziers* (Chief Ministers) of the empire, ended their career in this way!

The vast porticoed cloister of the second court was once the domain of the **Palace Kitchens** (now housing a superb collection of East Asian porcelains) and the **Privy Stables** (which houses a collection of imperial carriages). Also here, (sharing elbow room with cooks and stableboys) was the great **hall of the Divan**, where the Imperial Council deliberated on the governing of the empire while the sultan watched them perform (unseen and menacing), from behind a grilled window. Next to it is the former servants' entrance to the **Harem**, where a queue forms for a half-hour guided tour of the private quarters of the sultan: this is by far the most absorbing section of the palace and for this reason best left to the end of your tour.

The gates of the third court open on a splendid **Throne Pavilion**, a free-standing *köşk* ("kiosk," is how the word entered western languages, meaning about the same as the Indian *bungalow*) where the sultan once received petitioners and envoys under a sprawling baldachin: its form echoes the royal tents where Turkish chieftains used to hold court in pre-imperial days. Another *köşk* built of marble and completely revetted in exquisite tiles, holds the Library of the pleasure-loving Ahmet III (1718-30).

Visit the two collections of stupen-

Private Lives of the Sultans

The reigns of several of the earliest Ottoman rulers were marred by bitter civil wars fought amongst the sons of the deceased sultan. Mehmet The Conqueror (1451-81) therefore felt justified to enact the draconian law which permitted a sultan to slay all his brothers upon acceding to the throne. Beyazıt II (1481-1512) failed to do so, and regretted his mercy which resulted in 20 years of civil war and diplomatic blackmail. Süleyman the Great (1520-66) was forced in old age to order the killing of his two most capable sons when the princes began to jockey for power in the terrible expectation of the day that would bring them either empire or death. At the most extreme, Mehmet III (1595-1603) was called upon to dispose of his 19 brothers on the day of his elevation.

Ahmet I (1603-17), a mild and sentimental man, introduced the more humane alternative of keeping the imperial princes under lock and key. From his time to the reign of Mahmut II (1808-39), all male members of the dynasty other than the ruling sultan spent their lives as glorified prisoners of the Golden Cage. Their education and their entertainment consisted of the company of concubines and black eunuchs. A number of them ended up mad, including at least four who succeeded to the throne. Osman III (1754-57) spent 50 years without ever stepping out of the harem, and lost the power of speech when he was then told to rule the empire. Süleyman II (1687-91) spent 39 years in a cage learning to recite the **Quran** by heart, and wept uncontrollably on public occasions during his subsequent short reign.

A life spent in the harem translated into the dominance of palace women and eunuchs over the will of the sultan. A precedent was already set by Hurrem, better known in the West as Roxelane, who dominated the old age of her husband Süleyman the Magnificent and the debauched reign of her son Selim the Drunk (1566-78). The trend peaked in the scandalous career of Kösem Mahpeyker, who first tasted power in the reign of her master Ahmet I and who later conspired after his death in the successive overthrow and the murder of two sons of his by other women and then exercised unchecked tyranny through the sultanate of her own sons, Murat IV and the Mad Ibrahim. She was ultimately brought down by a coup engineered by Turhan Hatice, the mother of Mehmet IV (1648-87), and strangled in the harem with a silk curtain cord.

The sultans had the prerogative to legally marry four wives (with one or two exceptions). However, after the 14th century none of them chose to submit to the formal sanctions of marriage. Instead, it was more convenient to procreate through concubines, who were considered disposable, and who lacked a family of good standing that might one day claim collateral rights over the imperial offspring. Murat III (1578-95) had an extraordinary harem in excess of 100 concubines.

Nearly all of the concubines were slaves, bought in the market or received as booty or gifts from some *paşa* (piratemaster). Beauty was their first qualification, but those who had the added charms of intelligence could rise to the status of *haseki* (favourite), be allowed to give birth, and advance to the point of making and unmaking the highest officers of state. None were of Turkish blood and nearly none of Muslim origin. The Conqueror's mother was Serbian, or perhaps Greek; Hurrem was Russian; Nurbanu, the mother of Mehmet III, is said to have been Jewish and Kösem Mahpeyker was the daughter of a Greek village priest.

Perhaps the most remarkable story is that of Nakşıdil – her name means "Embroidery of the Heart" – who was born Aimée de Rivery, the daughter of a Creole landowner from Martinique who was kidnapped by Barbary pirates whilst on a journey to Europe and sold to the Ottoman palace. In 1808, she single-handedly saved her young son from a mutinous mob of *janissaries* (the praetorium guard of the sultan) and later exercised a seminal influence on his reign as the reformist sultan Mahmut II.

dous value which are housed at opposite corners of the third court. First, the **Treasury** of the House of Osman, looted in the final years of the empire and early days of the republic, but still a dazzling assemblage of gold and precious stone.

A comfortable interior in Topkapi Palace.

full of Persian thrones of the most extraordinary ostentation and chunks of emerald the size of bricks: its highlight is the famous Spoonmaker's Diamond, a gem of 84 carats, which formed the centerpiece for Peter Ustinov's film classic *Topkapi*. Second, the **Hall of the Holy Relics**, which houses (in one of the loftiest rooms of the palace) the personal effects and bodily parts of the prophet and his companions. The chief treasures here are the Holy Mantle of Muhammad and the Sacred Banner of Islam, which were obtained by Selim I when he conquered Arabia in 1517, and conferred on the Ottoman sultans the title of Caliph and the exclusive right to declare *jihad* (Holy War) upon the infidel. These used to be shown to the sultan

and the highest dignitaries of the state once a year on a particular holy day: since 1962 they have been open to public viewing, but they are kept in a glass enclosure beyond the reach of sacrilegious eyes.

Next, proceed, via a narrow passage to the innermost platform of the palace, a large and multi-levelled marble terrace that commands a breathtaking view of the Bosphorus. Only the sultan and his closest (male) companions had the right of ingress here. Very aptly, its chief attractions are the two jewel-like pleasure houses of Murat IV (1622-40), a ruler whose preference for male company earned him the distinction of being the only Ottoman sultan to have never sired a child. The names of

A medieval Topkapi Palace as viewed from the outside.

the pavilions – **Revan Köşkü** and **Bağdad Köşkü** – commemorate his victorious campaigns against what are now the capitals of modern Armenia and Iraq. A third pavilion of equal beauty, the **Sünnet Köşkü**, was built for the circumcision of the sons of his brother, the mad Sultan Ibrahim (1640-48), who spent the early part of his life as a prisoner of the harem, where he developed a morbid fascination for bodily functions, involving furs, pearls, and fish. The small gilt-bronze baldachin that juts over the balustrade of the terrace is where he used to have his solitary suppers, watching the panorama of Istanbul, and scattering fistfuls of pearls to the beasts roaming in the park below.

Finally, return to the second court,

for a tour of his prison and pleasure dome. The **Harem of Topkapi** consists of a maze of courtyards, passages, gardens and some 300 rooms, all decorated with incredible abandon, yet narrow, dark, ominous and strangely oppressive. This is where the women of the sultan lived in varying numbers ranging from a dozen to more than a hundred.

The only males ever permitted to set foot among them, apart from the sultan and his children, were the staff of black eunuchs whose own stable-like quarters form one of the more memorable parts of the harem. Few of the imperial concubines who came into the harem ever left again, and the princes who were born here usually emerged only to ascend the

A Tour of the Mosques

The courtyard of the Sultan Ahmet Mosque in Istanbul.

he greatest act of piety that a good Muslim can perform is to endow a mosque out of his or her private wealth, and the Ottoman sultans strived o outperform each other in setting a public xample for this. Their wives and mothers, who ften amassed fortunes of immense size, did kewise, followed by the *viziers (ministers)* and aşas and the occasional layman. Today, 600 mosques from the Ottoman period exist in the Old City of Istanbul, and another 50 or so stand n other parts of the city. The greatest of them orm part of a *külliye* (pious complex) which in addition can include, one or more *medrese* religious schools), a *darüşşifa* (hospital), a naret (kitchen for the poor), *hamam* (public aths) and the *türbe* (tombs) of the founder and is or her family. Many also contain a *bedesten* shopping arcade) or a simple row of shops whose rental goes towards the upkeep of the stablishment.

The earliest imperial mosque of Turkish Is-

tanbul was naturally that of the Conqueror (Fatih), which was erected in 1470 over the ruins of the Byzantine Church of the Holy Apostles. This remains one of the most fascinating sights of Istanbul on account of its attractive courtyard and its colorful clientele. But, the mosque that one sees today is a late reconstruction which bears little resemblance to the original and carries no great architectural merit. The only mosque that actually survives in Istanbul from the reign of Mehmet II is that of Mahmut Paşa. A humble building standing in the bazaar district it keeps the pre-classical format of a simple rectangular structure with two independent domes.

The single-domed, centralized pattern of classical Ottoman architecture was firmly established by the era of Beyazıt II, whose simple yet attractive mosque (1506) adorns one of the central points of the Old City. By contrast, the mosque of Yavuz Selim (finished in 1522), went on a separate path with its very shallow dome which resembles that of the Hagia Sophia. Although it is one of the prettiest mosques of the city, with a superb view of the Golden Horn, yet it remains almost undiscovered by tourists.

The apogee of Ottoman architecture, which stretched over the second half of the 16th century, was overshadowed by the genius of one man – Sinan. Sinan was a *janissary* who was levied as a boy from a Christian family in Cappadocia and trained as an architect at the imperial school of Topkapi. From 1538 to his death in 1588 he held the title of Imperial Chief Architect, and as such put his signature to more than 50 mosques, countless baths, *medreses*, *türbes (tombs)*, covered markets, bridges and military munitions around the Ottoman dominions. His works include several of the greatest architectural masterpieces of any age or culture.

In Istanbul, his first important work was the **Mosque of şehzade** ("Crown Prince"), which commemorated the memory of the eldest son of Süleyman the Magnificent who was killed in a hunting accident in 1543 at the age of 22. The mosque is unique among Sinan's works in that the main dome is supported by four (rather than two) semi-domes; the *türbe* of the prince is one of the handsomest buildings of its type in existence. The mosque of the sultan himself, incontestably the most important Ottoman

building in Istanbul, was begun shortly after th and finished in 1557. The severe and simp grandeur which Sinan achieved in this mosqu – the **Süleymaniye** – was never again equale in the capital, although a later work of his, th **Selimiye**, in Edirne, is often considered the tru apex of his career. Two other mosques of Sina in Istanbul deserve notice. That of Rüstem Paş (1561), located in Eminönü near the Spic Bazaar, is famous for its very fine tiles whic cover parts of the exterior of the building as we as the interior. The *paşa* who commissioned th mosque was a *grand vizier* of Süleyman and th husband of his favorite daughter **Mihrimah** Her own mosque (1565), remarkable for it extraordinary sense of space and light, tower over the city walls at the highest point of the Ol City in the district of Edirnekapi.

The classical style perfected by Sinan wa carried on in the closing days of Ottoma greatness with the **Sultanahmet** (1616) an **Yeni Cami** (New Mosque). The latter was be gun in 1597 under the auspices of Safiye Sultar the mother of Mehmet III, then abandoned ti it fell in ruins, restarted again in the 1640s an finally completed in 1663 through the benevc lence of Turhan Hatice, the mother of Mehme IV. After this difficult achievement, no mosqu of comparable size or ambition was ever at tempted again in the Ottoman capital.

throne or to face the executioner's noose!

One of the most impressive suites in the harem belongs to the Valide Sultan, the empress-mother, who led the hierarchy of the harem and thus often wielded greater political power than her sovereign son.

The most extraordinary products of Turkish decorative art are lavished on the sultan's apartments, of which the **Hünkar Sofasi** (Imperial Reception Room) is the grandest, although the adjacent **Room of Murat III** retains the

better tiles.

One particularly rich room is iden tified by the guides as the **Golden Cage** although that ominous title probabl belongs more rightly to a series of smal and dark cells upstairs which are no included in the public tour: in thes rooms the brothers of the reigning sul tan spent their life as prisoners of fate awaiting the day when a palace revolu tion would either raise them to rul empire or bring them to death. Topkap Palace

A new manner of mosque architecture arrived in Istanbul toward the middle of the 18th century. It derived its inspiration from the European *baroque* style, with which it shared a predilection for bold, dramatic gesture and frivolous ornamentation. The **Nuruosmaniye** (1755), located near the Great Bazaar, is the earliest and finest example of this school: it was initially designed in a purely European style, but was forced to compromise when the *mullahdom* objected. The mosque of **Laleli** (1763) is another attractive product of the short-lived Ottoman experiment with the *baroque* style.

A third architectural period started in the 1820s, coinciding with the era of great reforms which tried to remold the Ottoman sultanate into a "European" image. Each of the significant mosques from this period was the work of members of the Balyan clan – an Armenian family of Imperial Architects who also built the imperial palaces of Dolmabahçe and Beylerbeyi. Their designs departed from the spirit of earlier Turkish mosques, but used stylized "Ottoman" motifs to a charming effect. The most important mosque of the Balyan era is the **Nusretiye** (1826), located in the Tophane district outside the Old City, though visually the most pleasant one is undoubtedly the mosque of **Ortaköy** (1854), which adorns the Bosphorus near the European end of the first bridge.

The Bazaar

From the monumental ostentation of the empires, walk next to the colorful chaos of the one institution that was the true basis of Istanbul's greatness and remains the nerve center of its urban life. The city at the crossroads of continents was and is, above all, a city of commerce.

The vast bazaar where that commerce still has its focus covers the broad

An indoor bazaar in Istanbul.

basin between the first and second hills of the Old City, an area defined at its edges by the mosques of Beyazbt, Süleymaniye, Rüstem Paca and

Yeni Cami. The products it handles follow the times and include plastic toy and fake Lacoste as well as ancient r gs and arcane spices, but its spirit, its rganization and even its looks have arely altered from the days of th Ottoman caravans or Byzantine guilds. The centerpiece of the bazaar is the **Gra d Covered Market** – *Kapaliçarşi* in Turkish – a walled and domed arcade of 60 streets, 20 inner courts and over 4,000 shops. Its innermost core probably dates from Byzantine times, although the present structure largely belongs to the 16th century. From its historic low-point

GRAND BAZAAR

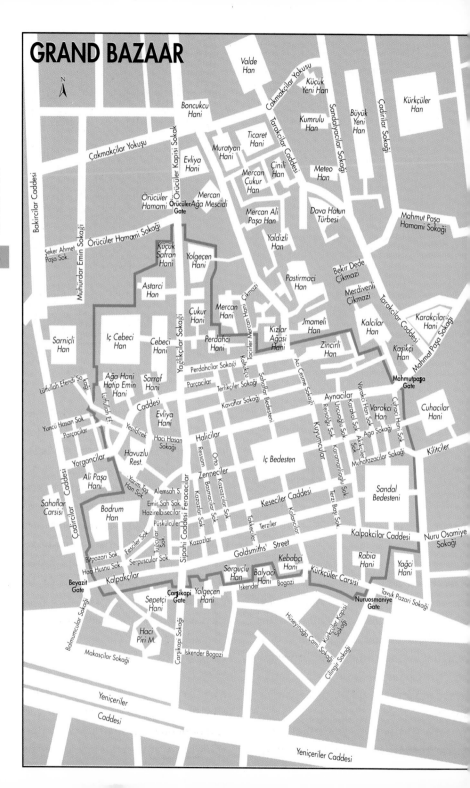

N

Valde Han

Çakmakçılar Yokuşu

Küçük Yeni Han

Kürkçüler Han

Boncukcu Hani

Kumrulu Hani

Büyük Yeni Han

Çadırlar Sokağı

Sandalyacılar Sokağı

Bakırcılar Caddesi

Çakmakçılar Yokuşu

Evliya Hani

Muratyan Hani

Ticaret Hani

Tarakçılar Caddesi

Mercan Çukur Hani

Çinili Han

Meteo Han

Orücüler Kapısı Sokak

Orücüler Hamami

Mercan

Orücüler Ağa Mescidi Gate

Mercan Ali Paşa Han

Dava Hatun Türbesi

Mahmut Paşa Hamami Sokağı

Seker Ahmet Paşa Sok.

Örücüler Hamami Sokağı

Mühürdar Emin Sokağı

Yaldızlı Han

Küçük Safran Hani

Yolgeçen Hani

Astarci Han

Pastirmaci Han

Bekir Dede Çıkmazı

Merdivenli Çıkmazı

Tarakçılar Caddesi

Çukur Hani

Mercan Hani

Tacirler Mercan Han Çıkmazı

Kizlar Ağası Hani

Jmameli Han

Kalcilar Han

Karakçılar Hani

Sarniçli Han

İç Cebeci Han

Cebeci Hani

Yağlıkçılar Sokağı

Perdahçı Hani

Zincirli Han

Kaşikci Han

Mahmat Paşa Sokağı

Perdahcilar Sokağı

Kalpakçı Sokağı

Sahaflar Bedesteni

Aci Çeşme Sokağı

Mahmutpaşa Gate

Lütfullah Efendi So.

Ağa Hani Hatip Emin Hani

Sarraf Hani

Parçacilar

Terlikçiler Sokağı

Aynacilar

Varakci Han Sok.

Karakol Sok.

Cuhaci Han Sok.

Cuhacilar Hani

Caddesi

Yuncu Hasan Sok.

Evliya Hani

Kavaflar Sokağı

Sahaflar Bedesteni

Reisoğlu Sok.

Uncuoğlu Sok.

Varakci Han

Aliköy Sok.

Aga Sokağı

Kilitciler

Parçacilar

Yeşildirek

Lütfullah Ef.

Hacı Hasan Sokağı

Halicilar

Ressam Sok.

Kuyumcular

Karamanlioğlu Sok.

Muhafazacilar Sokağı

Havuzlu Rest.

Yorgancilar

Orta Kazazcilar Sok.

İç Bedesten

Ali Paşa Hani

Yarim Taş Han Sok.

Alemsah S.

Zenneciler

Kesazlar Sok.

Kazazcilar Sok.

Sandal Bedesteni

Çadırlar Caddesi

Sahaflar Çarsisi

Bodrum Han

Emir Sah Sok.

Hazirelbiseciler

Püskülcüler

Sipahi Caddesi

Bosmacilar Sok.

Teracecilar

Kesaciler Caddesi

Terzi Başi Sok.

Kolancilar

Nuru Osamiye Sokağı

Bitpazari Sok.

Fesciler Sok.

Tuğcular Sok.

Kazozlar

Terziler

Takkeciler

Kalpakçilar Caddesi

Rabia Hani

Yağci Hani

Beyazit Gate

Hoa Husnu Sok.

Serpuscular Sok.

Goldsmiths' Street

Kebabçi Hani

Kürkçüler Carsisi

Kalpakçilar

Sepetçi Hani

Çarşikapi Gate

Yolgeçen Hani

Sorgüçlu Han

Balyacı Hani

İskender Bogazi

Nuruosmaniye Gate

Tavuk Pazari Sokağı

Haci Piri M.

Çarşikapi Sokağı

İskender Bogazi

Hüseyinağa Cami Sokağı

Kürkçüler Kapısı Sokağı

Çilingir Sokağı

Balmumcular Sokağı

Makascilar Sokağı

Yeniçeriler Caddesi

Yeniçeriler Caddesi

Fresh produce sold straight from the farm in an outdoor market.

n the 1950s and 1960s, it has returned to life with both great verve and profit, thanks largely to the tourist boom. The dominant trades are therefore those that have tourist appeal – jewelry, carpets, leather goods, antiques, souvenirs – although one only needs to turn into the back streets to realize that Kapalıçarşi is also the hub of Istanbul's trade in denimware, furniture repair, the florid print fabrics of peasant dress and in *yorgan* (old-fashioned quilts of cotton).

Resign yourself to the fact that a person of even slightly foreign appearance affects the innate instincts of the bazaar's merchants as the smell of blood attracts a school of sharks. You will be accosted, talked to, pulled by the arm and invited for tea. Keep your humor,

and drink that cup of tea. You will learn that all shops are privately owned, (though they obey a common body which carries on the habits of a medieval guild); that rents have become astronomical and that nearly all shopkeepers start out as apprentices at the age of ten or twelve – as no one can hope to survive in the bazaar if he or she has not mastered the arcane arts of customer-snatching, bargaining, supplier-pleasing and credit and tax-evasion from childhood.

And note, in passing, that that suave smile of the carpet seller who takes a sudden interest in your town's football team is perhaps the product of thirty years of rigorous training.

Kapalıçarşi is only part, albeit the

most immediately striking, of the bazaar: an extraordinary labyrinth of narrow market lanes and historic courts spread out behind it and down the hillside towards the Golden Horn. Spend half a day threading your way through this intoxicating human beehive, even if a lifetime is not enough to know it well.

You may have come into the market by the **Nuruosmaniye** gate, which leads to the street of Istanbul's best (and most expensive) carpet shops. Directly at the opposite end is the **Sahaflar** gate, which faces the entrance to the delightful courtyard of the new and used **Book Market**. Go through this to emerge into the shadow of the historic palm tree outside the Beyazit Mosque, where a chaotic flea market has come into existence in the wake of the invasion of East European traders.

Retrace your steps to the Sahaflar gate, and turn left along the permanently thronged street of coppersmiths and sellers of metal implements. Go far enough down this alley and you will get to the enclosed marketplace which was recently set up for traders from the countries of the former Eastern bloc. Or bear right into the intractable maze along the north side of the Kapaliçarşi: this is the area of *hans* (historic courtyards which are devoted to the makers of a particular type of commodity). Try **Çukur Han**, where cotton is dyed in huge vats just as it was done hundreds of years ago, or **Alipaşa Hani** which specializes in carpet repairs, or

A religious mosaic of Christ in Aya Sofia, Istanbul.

Kürkçüler Han which dates from the 15th century and belongs to makers of fur, or to the **Zincirli Han** which has one of the prettiest courtyards and produces custom jewelery.

Eventually you may end up in **Tahtakale**, which is the center of Turkey's unofficial foreign currency market where hundreds of millions of dollars change hands on little slips of paper carried around by crier boys.

Make certain that you walk down **Mahmutpaşa Street**, using your knees, shoulders and elbows against the inexorable stream of humanity which flows along this central market selling cheap clothing. At its lower end you will reach a small replica of the Grand Bazaar which is called **Misir Çarşisi** (the Corn

After Eight ...

A belly dancer wriggling to applause in Istanbul.

By hallowed tradition, dining out in Istanbul means going out to one of the fish taverns which line both shores of the upper Bosphorus. The oldest are rickety wooden structures built on stilts at the edge of the water itself. Their fare is more or less identical, consisting of a dozen types of *meze* (hors d'oeuvres) and the season's fish. Connoisseurs well know which place is likely to serve the freshest *lüfer* or add that secret twist to the recipe for *pilaki:* ordinary mortals choose on the basis of the setting and the view. Several of the most venerable taverns are located in **Yeniköy**, on the European shore: try *İskele* or *Deniz Park* for a good atmosphere. **Tarabya** offers a lively lineup of rather upmarket restaurants, featuring cacophonous music and the capacity to serve large tourist buses. Further up in **Sariyer** one finds *Urcan,* which has a well-earned reputation for serving the freshest and most varied seafood and is located next to one of Istanbul's most colorful fish markets. If you want a fabulous panorama of the city to form the backdrop of an outdoor dinner in a pleasant village square, then the place to go is **Çengelköy** on the Asian side. Also on that side is *Körfez,* one of the few true gourmet havens of the city occupying a lovely platform on the water's edge.

Two districts nearer to the city center are well-established places for eating, drinking and making merry in the company of large crowds of people who are out to do just the same. **Kumkapi**, down near the sea below Sultanahmet, features 30 restaurants in the space of three short streets which are always thronged with tourists. The area around **Balikpazari** in Beyoğlu is equally lively with a more Turkish than foreign clientele. The **Çiçek Pasaji**, a cavernous 19th century arcade filled with beer and raki parlors and a permanently tipsy crowd is located here.

The **Darüzziyafe** (which literally means "House of Banquets"), is an excellent eating experience located in the historic cloisters of the Süleymaniye, which serves the strictly authentic fare of old Ottoman cuisine. Other excellent restaurants are located, in the major hotels: the Ramada, in Laleli, is the place for Chinese cuisine and the restaurant in the **Swissôtel** serves the best French cuisine in town.

The fashion in bars and pubs changes fast, so it is pointless to name any. Just keep in mind that the places to go are on the side streets of **Taksim** and **Nişantaşi**, or in the snazzy neighborhood of **Etiler** even further north. The rooftop bar of the Sheraton retains its stature after countless years as the favorite watering hole of the foreign resident community.

Belly dancing? A thousand neon lights beckon with the charms of their featured *oryantal dansöz,* but the best in terms of taste, quality and atmosphere is the **Kervansaray Nightclub** in the Hilton hotel. Several upmarket clubs are situated along **Tarlabaşi Street**, parallel to Istiklal Caddesi on the west, while in the smoke-filled dens along the back streets off Istiklal, you also get the chance to meet the *artistes* on more intimate terms once their show is over.

More popular these days are the discotheques, three of which deserve to be named among the world's topmost decibel-bangers: **Juliana's**, in Swissôtel, was the favorite in 1992; **Taxim's** which was converted from an old warehouse and the **Andromeda** outshines all others in the lavishness of its sound and lighting effects. Here you will meet the smart and the good-looking of Istanbul's under-35 generation.

Market) which was once the domain of cereal, grocery and spice merchants. It still keeps the delightful smell of a well-stocked cellar, and its spice shops, although now reduced to only five or six, retain the fascination of a **Thousand and One Nights** with their rows of drawers and jars marked with items such as "sultan's potion", "shadow of a minaret", "snake powder" and "myrrh".

Discovering the Old City

A walking tour across the length of the Old City takes you through a landscape that is astonishingly undiscovered by tourists except for the odd landmark upon which tour buses descend. It is a chaotic territory of crooked alleys, smelly passageways and precipitous ups and downs which make the shortest route between two points anything but a straight line! Yet, nearly every street contains some striking relic of history, or some astonishing modern sight which should more properly belong to another century.

Start at the Süleymaniye, not only because it is the most sublime work of religious architecture in the city but also because it belongs to one of Istanbul's most deeply historic neighborhoods. Walk on to the **Mosque of şehzade**, whose gardens contain several of the most beautiful specimens of Turkish tomb architecture. Then cross the huge traffic-infested **Square of şehzadebaşi**, where the **Aqueduct of Valens**, dating

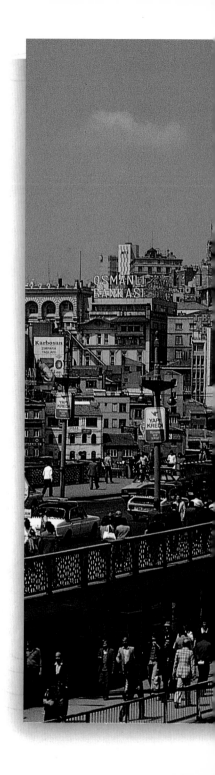

The bustling metropolis of downtown Istanbul.

from the year 410, stands like a giant theatrical backdrop.

On the other side of this square is **Fatih**, the heart of conservative, orthodox, Muslim Istanbul. At the center of the district stands the great raised platform of the mosque bearing the same name, which is where canny photographers go to stalk their stock images of "traditional Islam". Friday noon is the best time for shutterbugs.

A short distance further away is the mosque of **Yavuz Selim**, which occupies one of the highest and most panoramic points of the city. Trust your luck, and follow one of the near-vertical streets that drop towards the Golden Horn: you will end up in **Fener**, a district where a small Byzantine-Greek mercantile aristocracy continued to wield great influence under Ottoman rule.

The area is now a slum populated by immigrants from Eastern Turkey, and the contrast between old splendour and new poverty is completely apparent. A modest complex at the bottom of the hill houses the **Oecumenical Patriarchate of Constantinople** the spiritual center of a large segment of the Greek Orthodox Church and thus the theoretical (if not practical) eastern counterpart of the Vatican in Rome.

Next, explore the picturesque district of **Balat**, which was once a major Jewish neighborhood, then climb back uphill to a monument which must form part of any serious sightseeing tour of Istanbul. The **Museum of Kariye**, formerly the church of the Saviour-in-Chora, is one of the world's most important monuments of late-Byzantine art. The church itself, which forms a pretty ensemble in the midst of a recently renovated historic area, dates from the year 1081. However, its real interest, lies in its superb series of mosaics and wall paintings, which belong to 1315-21. More than 100 compositions survive, displaying a bold and vivid expressionism which reflects the influence of the early Italian Renaissance.

Kariye is a mere stone's throw away from the **City Walls** and is one of the most imposing and complex sights of Istanbul. At a length of 19 km, girding the entire peninsula of the Old City, the walls were once the longest line of urban defense in the European Continent. The landward stretch, built in AD 447 to preserve the city from an attack of Attila the Hun, is the mightiest as well as the best preserved. To fully appreciate their grandeur, drive along the outer side of the walls from the Golden Horn to the sea.

To get a better feel of their historic character, try to follow the intractable jumble along their inner edge, where you will discover strange neighborhoods that seem to exist in isolation from the city at large. One such area is **Sulukule**, inhabited by the gypsies who throw their doors open every night to provide grotesque entertainment to the men of the city.

Further towards the sea you will stumble into **Yedikule**, a great fortress of Ottoman origin which forms a forgotten and overgrown oasis in the midst of the big city. End your walk with a tour of the ancient cemeteries – Muslim, Greek, Armenian, Jewish – which lie outside the walls near the **Silivri Gate**, or visit the surreal world of the leather tanneries concentrated at **Kazliçeşme**. Then experience culture shock by taking a taxi to the **Galleria** – a shopping and entertainment complex in the modern suburb of Ataköy. It is vast and lively, the shopping is first-rate, and, above all, it helps you to realize that Istanbul is a far more complicated place than you would imagine.

The Other Side

Beyoğlu on the north side of the Golden Horn is richer in the sights of new Istanbul, but not poor in those of the old. A tottering ancient neighborhood no less historic than any other in the Old City, but of a different flavor, covers its southern spur, the **Hill of Galata**; which was once an Italian ghetto, and later the home of Sephardic Jews. Climb it by the steep alley of Yüksekkaldırım.

Climbing up to Beyoğlu you may take the Tünel, leading to Istiklal Caddesi. The Tünel is the shortest subway in the world. Many western consulates are to be found in this Beyoğlu area. The area is renowned for nightclubs but beware of rather aggressive doormen who may try to set you to buy them drinks.

The top of the hill is the beginning of **Istiklal Caddesi**, the backbone of 19th century Istanbul. An almost unbroken succession of the rich and ostentatious architecture of the turn of the century lines this avenue, which is punctuated with the former embassies of the European Great Powers and a string of pompous churches hidden behind demure façades.

A pedestrian zone since 1989, it has quickly returned to life as Istanbul's epicenter of theater, cinema, café-life, and – increasingly – of fashion and shopping. A remarkably colorful fish and produce market (**Balikpazari**) and one of the finest of Turkish baths (**Galatasaray Hamami**) lie hidden in side-streets off its midpoint.

You are in a different Istanbul once you get to the other end of Istiklal Caddesi: the city of airline companies, Japanese restaurants, jazz clubs, the Hilton and the Sheraton. The large square which concludes Istiklal Caddesi is **Taksim**; from here, it is a pleasant walk of about a mile to **Nişantaşi**, the main shopping artery of Istanbul.

Boutiques and fashion chains have grown in recent years and will (so pundits say) make themselves heard in the European markets of the 1990s. Watch people as you did earlier on Galata Bridge: you will see as many women here as men, almost none wearing head covering and of a given sample of men no more than 27 percent will be wielding a moustache. A different country? No, just the other face of the varied, pluralistic and rich land that is Turkey.

The region within a 200-mile radius of Istanbul is short of places that can excite a sightseer's imagination: one would think that the great city virtually sucked away all local color and local pride from the communities in its immediate vicinity. The exceptions being two cities of great provincial charm, both of which served as the capitals of the Ottoman state before the conquest of Istanbul, and which are therefore filled with monuments of a younger and purer era of Turkish history before 1453.

Of steps and steppes in Pergamon.

Edirne: The Balkan Capital

The monumental skyline of Edirne will impress anyone arriving in Turkey from the west by car or by train: a jumble of mosques rising like a great mound over the Meriç plain. The city owes its original name – *Hadrianopolis* or *Adrianople* – to the Roman Empire. But, the significant segment of its history

The smiling faces and shorn locks of Turkish children in Bursa.

consists of the years between 1361 and 1453 when the sultans of the young Ottoman state took it as their main residence.

Three great mosques representing three epochs in the development of Ottoman architecture, stand within sight of each other in the town center. The oldest is **Eski Cami** (Old Mosque), which dates from the reign of Mehmet I (1412-21) and follows the so-called *ulucami* plan of early Ottoman mosques – a large rectangular hall covered with a series of parallel domes: the vast dimensions enhanced by an unusually bold and sinewy calligraphy, making its interior one of the most imposing of Turkish mosques. **Üç şerefeli Cami**, named for the *şerefe* (triple balconies) of its minarets, was built by Murat II (1421-51) and represents a transitional stage from archaic *ulucami* architecture to the centrally-planned classical mosques of the 16th century.

The **Selimiye**, considered the final culmination of the classical and thus the pinnacle of Ottoman architecture, stands on high ground a few hundred meters away. Sinan, the great architect, built this mosque for Selim II (1566-78), completing it when he was 85 years old. His lofty dome minimizes the use of side-domes and is fringed by four extraordinarily slender minarets; its size and elegance were never again equaled by Ottoman architects. Other attractions in Edirne include two historic **Covered Bazaars** of considerable size (and a third which is located within the complex of the Selimiye), a splendid 16th century **Hamam** still in working order, and the **Caravanserai of Rüstem Paşa** which has been converted into an excellent hotel. The defense tower known as **Kule Kapisi** was built by Hadrian, the Roman emperor, and rebuilt by the Byzantines in the 12th century. Concentrated in the center of a small city (population 100,000), they combine to give Edirne a deeply historic character which is well worth the rewards of a day's visit.

Bursa: The Green City

In 1326, Bursa was captured by the warriors of the infant Ottoman principality and served as the capital of the sultans (at times conjointly with Edirne) for more than a century. Later on, it was reputed to be the prettiest, greenest and calmest of Turkey's provincial cities. Its wealth of pious monuments, the presence of thermal springs and the lofty backdrop of **Uludağ**, (the 2,543 meters high *Bithynian Olympus* of antiquity) made Bursa the favorite retirement spot of the empire's elite whose mansions and pious endowments continued to embellish the city through the centuries.

In the past 30 years Bursa has grown into one of Turkey's leading industrial centers, thanks in part to its vigorous and enterprising inhabitants, a large portion of whom are immigrants from the Balkan countries (Bulgarian and

A woman weaving a carpet on a loom in Kaysevi.

Macedonian Turks and Bosnians). The result is a somewhat chaotic city which nevertheless retains many monuments from its past in the attractive city center.

The most interesting of these is undoubtedly the market, centered around a historic **Covered Bazaar** which is Turkey's largest after that of Istanbul. The vast labyrinth of ancient arcades, lanes and *hans* (historic courtyards devoted to makers of a paricular commodity) surrounding it better reflect the spirit of an old Ottoman market town than the one in Istanbul. The most attractive of the dozen or so old market courts is **Koza Han**, which has been at the center of Turkey's silk trade since the 15th century. Two important mosques stand near the bazaar: that of the **Orhan Gazi**,

Locals playing backgammon on the sidewalk.

built in 1336 by Orhan I, which is the oldest Ottoman mosque in existence and the **Ulucami**, the most monumental specimen of its particular type in Turkey, which dates back from the reign of Beyazit I (1389-1402). Its construction is said to have been funded by the loot removed during the battle of Nicopolis in 1396, in which the Ottomans defeated a crusader army led by King Sigismund of Hungary and Bohemia.

Other points of interest in Bursa are clustered into three groups. The old **Citadel** which rises above the city center contains the tombs of several of the early rulers of the House of Osman as well as some of the most picturesque back streets that you are likely to find in

Turkey.

The pleasant suburb of **Çekirge**, to the northwest, offers the mosque and associated complex of **Murat Hüdavendigar**, built in 1385, whose curious architecture indicates the guiding hand of an Italian architect. Near it lies the **Eski Kaplica**, the oldest and most interesting of Bursa's baths, whose origins go back to the reigns of Justinian and Theodora and also perhaps to Roman times. The largest and most beautiful of Bursa's mosques is located on a hillside southeast of the town center. The **Yeşil Cami** (Green Mosque) was commissioned by Mehmet I and finished several years after his death in 1421. His monumental tomb, completely sheathed in green Kütahya tiles, stands at the top of

Gleaming copperware will greet the shopper in Bursa.

the nearby hill.

Iznik

On the way to Bursa it is well worth making a detour to Iznik, an attractive little town set among fruit orchards on the shore of the lake which bears its name. Iznik, formerly called *Nicaea,* was the place where in AD 325 Constantine the Great convoked the First Oecumenical Council of Christianity – a gathering of bishops from around the Roman world who met to estabish the ground rules of the religion which would soon be adopted as the official creed of the empire. The result of their deliberations was the Nicaean Creed (the "Credo" of the Latin mass), which is the nearest that the Christian religion has ever got to a unified definition.

From 1204 to 1261, when Constantinople was in the hands of the crusaders, the Byzantine court took refuge in Nicaea, organizing its forces for an eventual return and onslaught on the capital. Finally, in the 16th and 17th centuries, Iznik became the center for the manufacture of the gorgeous porcelain tiles which bear its name and which are considered by many as some of the finest achievements of Turkish art.

Sights include **city walls** which are of Hellenistic and Roman origin, a **Roman theater**, the ruined Byzantine church of **Hagia Sophia** and attractive Ottoman works of the 14th century.

Aegean Coast

S ea, sun and fun: these are the keywords that draw three million European visitors each year to Turkey's Aegean-Mediterranean shores – two thousand miles of splendid coastline where the sun shines unfailingly from April to November, the beaches are as limpid and inviting as any in Spain, Italy or Greece, and the infrastructure of hotels and entertainment is the best in Turkey. But the Turkish "Riviera" offers more than this. As one of the key theaters of ancient Greek and Roman history, it abounds in the monuments of classical civilization to an extent that few other parts of the Mediterranean world can match: the ruins of more than 80 ancient cities of striking beauty and great evocative power lie scattered from Abydus and Sestus on the Gallipoli Peninsula to the Pierian Seleuceia near the Syrian border. And the towns of the region, with their sun-drenched architecture and the

Basking in the sun on Cleopatra's Beach, Sedir Islands.

The Hellenistic kings and Roman emperors built an astonishing number of cities in Anatolia, and endowed each of them with set pieces of classical urban culture – the public monuments which set a civilized *polis* (town) apart from any old rustic backwater. Modern-day travellers who succumb to the addictive joys of ruin-hopping in western and southern Turkey soon learn to recognize the standard units of ancient city architecture. Here is a catalogue of the commonest items to look for among the heaps of toppled masonry.

Divine architecture

Temples were the greatest showpieces of Greco-Roman art. The earliest Greek temples built of stone were constructed in Ionia in the Archaic period (600 BC). The greatest temples of Western Turkey are Hellenistic (300 BC) reconstructions of these, while those in the south date mostly from the imperial Roman period (AD 1-300) and are of inferior architectural significance.

The simplest temple, called a temple *in antis*, consisted of an oblong hall *(cella)* with a front porch supported by two columns. A *prostylos* added an extra row of six columns in front; a *peripteros* was ringed by a single row of columns on four sides, while a *dipteros*, like the magnificent temple of Apollo at Didyma, was surrounded by a double row. The *pseudo-dipteros*, perfected by Hermogenes in the 300 BC at the Artemis Temple of Magnesia-by-the-Meander, omitted the inner row of columns, leaving a wide, shady walkway between the outer columns and the *cella*. Round temples like that of Aphrodite at Cnidus became popular in Roman times. One or more temples were sometimes enclosed in a *temenos*, a large rectangular courtyard surrounded by colonnades.

The three orders of classical architecture set precise patterns for the shape and proportions of the columns, the capitals and the entablature, or the superstructure carried above the columns. The *Doric Order* was characterized by simple, round capitals contrasting with a high and elaborate superstructure; most common in mainland Greece, it was rarely used in the temples of Asia Minor. The *Ionic Order*, pioneered by the Ionian temples of the Archaic era, used ram's-horn capitals on finely fluted columns. The *Corinthian Order*, which emerged in the 300 BC and found its widest application in the Roman period, introduced highly ornate capitals bearing stylized acanthus leaves.

Some Roman emperors were worshipped as gods, and the privilege to erect an imperial temple was one of the highest political distinctions that a city could aspire to. Distinguished citizens, too, were occasionally raised to the status of semi-gods or heroes; a *heroon (temple dedicated to a hero)* formed the venue for the celebration of their cult.

Theatres were used not only for dramatic performances but athletic events, battle shows, famous trials, political rallies and sessions of the general assembly as well. In Roman times gladiator fights and wild animal shows became common, and large slabs of stone were often installed around the edge of the pit to protect the spectators. On special occasions, the theater was filled with water to stage *naumachia (mock naval battles)*. Pillows were rented out at the entrance, and watermelon seeds were a popular spectator snack. As a rule women were not admitted.

The theatre of Halicarnassus (Bodrum), possibly the oldest in Asia Minor, dates from late 400 BC. Theaters of the Hellenistic era were typically built on hillsides with an unerring sense of panoramic view. The *cavea* (seating area) was often more than a semicircle, and the action took place in the horseshoe-shaped central pit, or *orchestra*. The Romans showed a preference for freestanding theaters supported on vaults and galleries. A two or three-storey stage building with an elaborate *scene* (façade) was constructed to face the audience, and most performances took place on a proscenium (elevated platform) attached to it. The *cavea* and orchestra were usually semicircular in shape — a limitation imposed by the need to face the scene.

The **stadium** acquired its name from the standard length of the course (one *stade*, or approximately 200 meters) on which foot-races

A detail from the Ephesus in the background constrasted with poppies in the foreground.

were held. Other athletic events contested in the stadium were boxing, wrestling, *pankration* (an all-out fight), horse and chariot racing, and the pentathlon, which in turn comprised the stadium run, wrestling, long jump, discus throw and javelin.

The **odeon** was reserved for musical performances and council meetings. It was often shaped like a miniature theater, although there were also some instances of rectangular construction such as one can see at Priene. Most odea had wooden roofs which have disappeared with time. Like theaters, they possessed an altar where sacrifices were offered to Dionysus before every public meeting.

The *agora* (marketplace) was the hub of public life in the ancient city. Wealthier cities paved the *agora* in marble and enclosed it by sumptuous *stoas* (colonnaded walkways) where citizens could stroll in leisure, engaging in philosophical debate or catching up the latest gossip.

Inscriptions and statues set up in the *agora* immortalized gods, heroes, political leaders, philosophers, athletes and famous actors.

The **gymnasium** was perhaps the most characteristic institution of the Hellenistic world. It served simultaneously as a school, a clubhouse and a sports center, sometimes (but not always) with separate facilities for boys, youths and adult citizens. A large courtyard called the *palaestra* was set aside for athletic exercises, which as a rule were conducted in the nude — hence the name, gymnasium, meaning a "nudehouse".

Engineering marvels

Roman architecture was characterized by a more pompous style than Greek and the wider use of vaults and arches. A typically Roman innovation that combined efficiency and monumentality were large-scale waterworks. Aqueducts carried water to the city from vast distances while impressive cisterns stored it for drier times. The nymphaeum, a public fountain and water reservoir, became a standard feature of the urban environment in AD 100. So did public latrines, some of which survive after 2,000 years.

Quintessentially Roman, too, were **public baths**. These followed a standard pattern: first came the *apodyterium* that contained changing-rooms and a public hall, then the *frigidarium* where bathers plunged in a cold pool. The *tepidarium* had basins of lukewarm water. The floor of the *caldarium* was raised on supports and heated from below by hot air from an adjoining furnace (hypocaust); the *sudatorium* (sweating-room) was made hotter still by running hot air flues all around its walls. The Turkish hamam preserves a similar pattern inherited via the Byzantines, and in many cases occupies the same spot where the Romans first built a bath.

Nearly all the ancient cities were protected by walls. The earliest settlements were usually built on a natural height offering good defense. When cities began to expand in the 400-300 BC, this original core was kept as an inner citadel or *acropolis*, reserved for public and ceremonial buildings, while residences moved down to the plain. Further expansion took place under the Roman empire, when peaceful conditions allowed some cities to neglect their defences or even to spread out without walls.

The walls of the earlier Antiquity display very high quality masonry of huge, precision-fitted stone blocks. The Roman period is characterized by a more routine workmanship of well-cut, regularly dressed stones. The quality drops markedly in the Byzantine era: post-6th C walls employ mortar and are sometimes layered with bricks. Turkish fortifications are generally built of chipped stone mixed with pebbles and mortar.

The ancient **Necropolis**, or cemetery, lay immediately outside the city walls. The pre-Hellenic Anatolian cultures had distinguished themselves for their elaborate funerary monuments. The most interesting necropoles are accordingly found in the late-Hellenizing cities of southern and inner Anatolia, notably in Phrygian Hierapolis (Pamukkale), Pisidian Termessus and the cities of Rough Cilicia; the tomb-infested landscape of Lycia is among the most memorable products of ancient civilization. Similarly it was a non-Greek, the Carian Mausolus, whose famous monument in Halicarnassus (the *Mausoleum*) yielded the generic name for funerary extravaganza.

hearty and easy-going charm of their inhabitants, offer a more immediately lovable introduction to Turkey's people than the gloomier and more alien humor of the villages of deeper Anatolia.

The Northern Aegean

From the straits of Dardanelles to the neighborhood of Izmir, the northern half of the Aegean coast is a green and pleasant land where cultivated plains alternate with large forests of the olive tree and rockier patches of the Mediterranean maquis. There are a few places of interest along the coast, but none to match the unforgettable sights further south. Plan, therefore, for several interesting stops if you are driving in from the West, but go with an easy conscience if your route takes you from Istanbul and Bursa directly to the south.

Make the short detour to the ruins of **Troy**, even if what you see there – an impressive wall from the 1600 BC, a ridiculous Trojan Horse from the 1970s – is less than overwhelming. This was

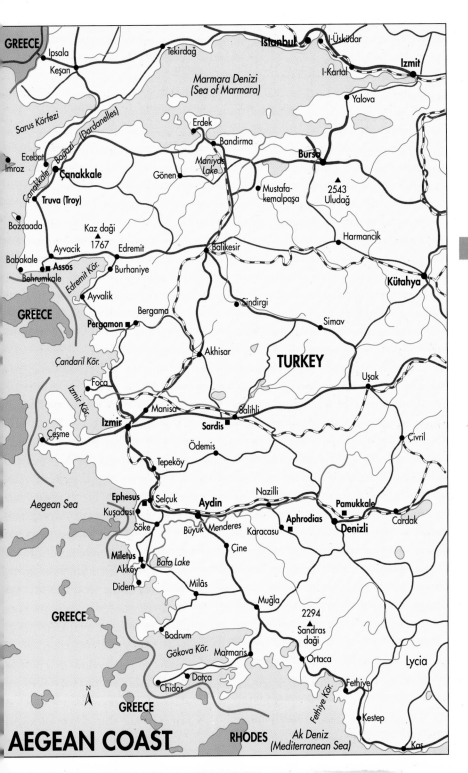

GREECE

Ipsala

Keşan

Tekirdağ

İstanbul

I-Üsküdar

I-Kartal

Izmit

Marmara Denizi
(Sea of Marmara)

Yalova

Sarus Körfezi

Erdek

Bandirma

Bursa

Ecebat

İmroz

Çanakkale

Boğazi (Dardanelles)

Gönen

Maniyas
Lake

Mustafa-
kemalpaşa

2543
Uludağ

Truva (Troy)

Bozcaada

Kaz dağı
1767

Edremit

Balikesir

Harmancik

Babakale

Behrumkale

Assos

Ayvacik

Edremit Kör.

Burhaniye

Kütahya

Ayvalik

Sindirgi

GREECE

Bergama

Pergamon

Akhisar

TURKEY

Simav

Çandaril Kör.

Foça

Uşak

Izmir

Manisa

Salihli

Çeşme

Sardis

Çivril

Ödemis

Tepeköy

Aegean Sea

Ephesus

Selçuk

Aydin

Nazilli

Pamukkale

Kuşadasi

Aphrodias

Denizli

Cardak

Söke

Büyük Menderes

Karacasu

Çine

Miletus

Akköy

Bafa Lake

Didem

Milâs

Muğla

2294
Sandras
dağı

Bodrum

GREECE

Gökova Kör.

Marmaris

Ortaca

Lycia

Chidos

Datça

Fethiye Kör.

Fethiye

GREECE

Kestep

AEGEAN COAST

RHODES

Ak Deniz
(Mediterranean Sea)

Kaş

AEGEAN COAST

the site of the first great battle of Western history: sometime around 1,200 BC, a large confederacy of the Greeks of the Heroic Age went to war here against a coalition of Anatolian cities gathered to defend Troy. Their aim was to rescue beautiful Helen, which they did after ten years of fruitless siege. Their story was told by Homer several hundred years after the event, and was treated generally as a splendid fable until a German adventurer-businessman-antiquarian by the name of Schliemann decided to dig here, in 1874, for evidence. What he discovered were the layered ruins of a town which appears to have been a rich and important city from around 3000 BC (Troy I and II) to 1200 BC (Troy VI and VIIa).

Spend a night, if opportune, in **Behramkale**, where an old and deeply picturesque village shares a steep hilltop with the ruins of ancient **Assos**. Aristotle spent several years of his life here, and his famous library was transferred to Assos after his death. The tiny fishing colony which lies below the rock of Assos has grown recently into a favorite retreat of Istanbul's educated few. Continue, alternatively, to **Ayvalik**, a larger town which was inhabited until 1922 by Greeks and which keeps many back streets of great charm. The islet of **Cunda** which is situated immediately offshore here is possibly the nearest that Turkey has to offer to the atmosphere of a "Greek" island.

Proceed, finally, to **Bergama**, which under the name of **Pergamum** was the capital of a great Hellenistic kingdom and a leading city of ancient Asia Minor. Pergamum rose to prominence after 278 BC when it successfully resisted the invasion of Celtic tribes which had been threatening Anatolia. Its kings – the Attalids – who became the power brokers of the Aegean basin after 240 BC acted as staunch allies of Rome in the wars of AD 100 and in an unprecedented act of generosity, bequeathed their kingdom to the Roman Republic in 133 BC. The Pergamene school of sculpture became a model for Roman sculptors. The Library of Pergamum was the second greatest of Antiquity after that of Alexandria: it was first to make books on bound pages, as opposed to rolling scrolls of papyrus. The thin sheets of hide used for this were called "pergamene

The amphitheatre at Knidos along the Turkish coast.

aper", or *parchment*.

The most important monument of 'ergamum, the **Victory Altar of Eumenes II**, was discovered in the 1890s and removed to Berlin where it miraculously survived the destruction of World War II. What remains *in situ* is spread over three areas.

The **Acropolis**, atop a tremendous rock, holds the ruins of a royal citadel, an impressive Theatre, a Temple of Trajan, the substructures of a Gymnasium, and somewhat lower, a fascinating section of Roman-era houses and shops which were laid free by recent excavations.

In the old town below the hill, which is of considerable interest itself for its quaint old-Turkish character, are the remains of a gigantic **Temple of Serapis** dated to the AD100. At some distance from the town, finally, one finds the widespread ruins of the medical complex of the **Asclepium**, the ancient world's leading center of medical therapy and research. Famous practicioners at the Asclepium included Galen, the Roman physician whose writings formed the basis of Western medical knowledge until the end of the Middle Ages.

Worthwhile detours on the way from Bergama to Izmir include **Çandarli**, which has a pretty and well-preserved Genoese fortress of the 14th century, or **Manisa**, which offers an excellent **Archeological Museum** and several attractive Turkish monuments.

Izmir itself, on the other hand, can

The ancient city of Ephesus.

be bypassed without a second thought: the third-largest city of Turkey (population 1.5 million) has a long history which was obliterated by the wartime destruction of 1922, and its superb seaside position has been spoiled by the awful pollution of the sea. A palm-lined har-

bour promenade known as Kordon, a relatively interesting market district called Kemeralti, a good park; the Kültürpark and a fancy new Hilton which replaces venerable Büyük Efes as the city's top hotel are things to look for if you cannot avoid going.

est times, these valleys formed important trade routes connecting the interior of Anatolia with the Aegean world. Around 1000 BC, a dozen or so towns were founded at their seaward end by Greek colonists who came to Asia as refugees from the Dorian invasions that destroyed the Bronze Age civilization of Greece.

The twelve cities of Ionia flourished after 700 BC (they were, north to south, Phocaea, Erythrea, Clazomenae, Teos, Lebedus, Colophon, Ephesus, Priene, Miletus and Myus on the mainland, and Chios and Samos on the islands. Smyrna counted as thirteenth.) Their commercial supremacy extended from Sicily to the Black Sea and Egypt. The first seeds of ancient Greek civilization sprouted here: Homer was possibly a native of Smyrna; Thales of Miletus originated mathematics and philosophy; his student Anaximander became the first author ever to publish a book that was not a sacred text or royal record; Democritus of Miletus proposed the concept of an atom; his townsman Hecataeus was the first to attempt a systematic geography and a critical history; Heraclitus of Ephesus summarized a remarkably subtle philosophy with the maxim, "one cannot step in the same river twice." The earliest great temples of Greece were built in the 560s, almost simultaneously, in Ephesus, Miletus and Samos.

Ionia declined during the superpower rivalry of Athens and Persia in the 500 BC: it returned to life after Alex-

The Cities of Ionia

The middle part of the Aegean coast is traversed by a series of parallel mountain ranges which stretch west to east, with the broad valleys of the rivers Gediz, the Lesser Menderes and the Greater Menderes lying in between. From earli-

ander's conquest (334 BC), which created the opportunity for several of its cities (Ephesus, Smyrna, Miletus among others) to rebuild themselves on grander scale. Ephesus was adopted as the capital of the province of "Asia" when the Romans became masters of western Anatolia: it grew to become one of the greatest cities of the Roman world in the early centuries after Christ.

The region fared disastrously during the Byzantine Middle Ages. Medieval Ephesus and Miletus survived, barely, until the Turkish conquest of the early 14th century, but were abandoned shortly afterward. Only Smyrna and Phocaea (modern Izmir and Foça) existed continuously to the present day.

Today, the ruins of **Ephesus** are among Turkey's most impressive sights. The ancient city used to be a seaport: a marshy plain of 6km now separates the sea from the array of marble temples, halls, colonnades, arches, gateways and marble-paved streets which cover the flanks of two low hills a short distance from the town of Selçuk.

Start your tour at the **Theatre** of Ephesus, whose upper rows command a full view of the city and the erstwhile harbor. This imposing structure, seating 24,000, dates from the rebuilding of the city early in the Hellenistic era (300 BC). On its ancient steps, where St Paul

was once shouted down by furiou crowds chanting "Great is the Artemi of the Ephesians", rock concerts and festival shows are now held each sum mer.

Note next the **Library of Celsus** whose elaborate facade – with a bit o help from Austrian archeologists – sur vives at full height. The rich ornamen tation of this Roman monument exem plifies the almost "Baroque" manne which cam into vogue i the era of th Antonine em perors (AD98 180). Procee then to **Cu retes Street** one of th most at tractiv and well-pro portioned streets to com down from classical Antiquity. On th left side of this are the graceful portico o a **Temple of Hadrian**, the extensiv **Baths of Scholasticia** with mosaics from the AD 300, and adjoining this, a build ing identified as an ancient brothel. Or the right, recent excavations have re vealed a series of patrician houses from the imperial Roman period, some of th best-preserved of their kind anywhere i the world.

Very little remains of the famou **Temple of Artemis**, one of the Seven Wonders of the ancient world. The Ephesians inherited their cult of the Vir

Lycian ruins and tombs in Fethiye.

in Goddess from that of Great Mother Cybele, who was worshipped on the same sacred spot by the pre-Hellenic inhabitants of Ephesus: it in turn inspired the cult of the Virgin Mary, which spread from Ephesus into general Christian practice in the second century. A tradition asserted that Mary had lived and died in Ephesus after the death of Jesus, and the inspired dream of a German nun traced the home of her final days to a stone hut on Mt Coressus/ Bülbül Dağı in the 19th century. The **House of Virgin Mary**, a few miles beyond the archeological site, continues to attract Catholic pilgrims from around the world.

Medieval Ephesus, which now bears the Turkish name of **Selçuk**, was formed around a **Fortress** and the enormous **Basilica of St John**, which were built on a hill further inland in the reign of Justinian and Theodora. The Basilica, ruined yet impressive, contains what is said to be the tomb of St John the Evangelist. The town, in addition, features the monumental **Mosque of Isa Bey** (1375) and several other historic buildings of the era when it served briefly as the seat of the Turkish lords of the Aydın dynasty. It has grown in recent years into a lively and rather pleasant place filled with hotels, cheap pensions, carpet shops and all the other trappings of a flourishing tourist trade.

A much more popular holiday centre is located a 15-minute drive from Ephesus. Kuşadasi is the first of the sea-

Make believe you are a soldier encased in the legendary Trojan horse.

side resorts which dot the Turkish coast between here and Alanya. From a sleepy little Aegean village 30 years ago, it has grown into a town possessing the quality that tourist brochures sometimes describe as "pizzazz": its beaches are always full and a colorful bazaar supplies 20,000 tourists a day with carpets, leatherware and imitation-Lacoste beachwear. An islet at the center of the harbor carries a little Genoese Fort of the 13th to14th century which is now used as a café and discotheque; its local name "**Bird Castle**" has inspired that of the town,"**Bird Island**". The Old Town retains some of the quaint lanes which once made Kuşadasi a pleasant place.

A virgin patch of nature lies 20 kilometers south of town. A primeval forest covers the national park of **Samsun Daği**, a giant spur of mountain (1218 meters) that juts out toward the island of Samos. Consider hiking the highly panoramic trail which leads across the mountain and down the other side to the marshlands of the lower **Büyük Menderes**. You can combine this five hour walk with visits to the ruins of two ancient Ionian cities located on the south side, **Priene** and **Miletus**, and return or continue by car or bus.

Priene is the more attractive of the two, partly because of its lovely setting on the flank of a steep mountain, and partly on account of its early Hellenistic (fourth or third century BC) architecture that is delightfully free of the pomposity of the imperial Roman style. The main

Crags and peaks in Pamukkale.

ights are a striking **Temple of Athena**, a modest **Theatre** which is one of the best-preserved and best-proportioned in Turkey, and a cozy **Council Hall** (*bouleuterion*).

The ruins of **Miletus** are without either Priene's charm or Ephesus' grandeur, except for one majestic Roman-period **Theatre** which the Byzantines converted into a defensive fortress. Do not neglect, however, to travel the further 24 kilometers to **Didyma**, where the ancient Milesians had their chief religious shrine. The **oracle of the Didymian Apollo** was the second most influential of the Greek world after that of Delphi, and his temple one of the most monumental ever attempted by ancient architects: its construction be-

gan around 280 BC, and was still imperfectly finished when the sanctuary was sacked by the Goths some 540 years later, in AD 262. Only a few of the 120 giant Ionic columns of the temple now stand to their full height of 19.2 meters – nearly twice as high as the Athenian Parthenon – but even in toppled condition they convey the beauty and precision of classical architecture as few other monuments do.

Meandering up to Cotton Castle

The Menderes is a lazy river, whose ancient name *Meander*, has become synonymous with a slow and uncertain

White statuary in Ephesus.

course. Its valley is planted thickly with fig and olive trees and fields of tobacco and cotton; their produce supports prosperous little towns with pleasant cobbled streets and big weekly markets. Take the slow but more attractive old road which follows the southern edge of the valley if your itinerary now takes you inland toward Pamukkale. Meander through such places as Karacahayit and Koçarli, modest yet delightful towns. Make sure to cross over to Sultanhisar to visit the ruins of Nysa: the ancient theatre here, overgrown with gnarled olives, is one of the most poetically evocative of all. Climb, with enough time, to **Buldan**, which is an important center of traditional hand-woven textiles, or to **Babadağ**, which is full of tottering but

beautiful specimens of traditional local architecture.

A detour of 38 kilometers bring you to one of the highlights of western Turkey. **Aphrodisias** is the most important archeological site to come to light in Turkey since World War II, with ruin that are as extensive and as splendid a those of Ephesus but much less overrun by tourism. The city is of Hellenistic origin (it is first mentioned in the 100 BC), though it flourished in the Roman era thanks to its twin assets: an important cult site of Aphrodite, the goddess of love, and a famous school of sculpture. It became an episcopal see and capital of the province of *Caria* during Byzantine times (hence the Turkish name of the village, *Geyre),* and died after an earthquake in the 14th century

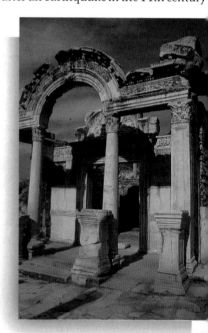

Arches and pillars dominate Hadrian's Tomb in Ephesus.

Picking cotton is back-breaking work.

Part of the charm of Aphrodisias derives from the idyllic setting of the ruins, which lie among cultivated fields full of tall poplars; sheep graze freely among the temples and colonnades. The slender columns of the 2100-year old **Temple of Aphrodite** stand against a background of gentle hills. The **Theatre**, recovered almost intact from under the soil, forms a dazzling bowl of the purest marble. The porticoes of the **School of Philosophy** evoke the picture of strolling stoics, while the delightful intimacy of the **Odeon** invites thoughts of a private recital in the delicate tunes of the Phrygian mode. A high note of the tour is the local Museum, which features a small but extraordinary collection of Roman-period statues; many of

these were discovered in what appears to have been a sculptors' workshop of the AD100.

Denizli is a fast-growing city that is of little interest except as a stepping-stone for **Pamukkale**, which appears from the city like a distant snowy patch on the flank of a mountain. The natural phenomenon which earns it the name of "Cotton Castle" (for that is what *Pamukkale* means) is the work of a hot mineral spring, whose high content of calcium hardens into limestone once the water cools down to a certain temperature. The deposit builds up into a series of shallow basins as the brook floods down the mountainside, creating the singular spectacle of a billowy cascade of white, pink and yellow rock. The dozens of natural pools which form

Ice escapades in Pamukkale, Ephesus.

Setting up the market in Bodrum.

along the slope drop by degrees from 40°C to air temperature, and are ideal for bathing.

The ancients knew about this place, and a city named **Hierapolis** grew around the hot spring in Hellenistic and Roman times. The sacred pool which was constructed below the main source is now enclosed within the grounds of a pleasant hotel, and permits the extraordinary experience of floating in hot fizzy water above the submerged columns and architectural fragments of antiquity. Other traces of the ancient city include a theatre, a triumphal arch, the ruins of several temples and early churches, as well as a most impressive **necropolis** (cemetery) that underlines the Phrygian cultural roots of Hierapolis.

Another unusual feature is the **Plutonium**, a shrine of Pluto, the god of the underworld, which is built around a hole in the ground that emits a foul and deadly gas. Strabo, the first century geographer who visited the shrine, reports that the shrine was in the charge of certain priests of Cybele who were Galli eunuchs.

A few of the best hotels of Pamukkale are near the source and the ruins; in **Palmiye**, one of the nicest of all, each room has its own private hot pool outside the door, overlooking a splendid view of the plain of Denizli. Below the cascades, a rather crazy village of pensions, hotels, restaurants and bars has sprouted from nothing within the last decade and a half. Finally, a number of good hotels have emerged recently in **Karahayit**, a village 6km beyond Pamukkale, which has its own thermal springs with a sulphurous and brackish but medically more effective, water.

From Pamukkale, a fast road brings you to Antalya in less than three hours. An alternative route leads back west via Tavas and Muğla, to the sunny towns of the southern Aegean.

Bodrum: Fun Town

People either love or hate **Bodrum**. Its very name has become synonymous with hedonism and freedom: it conjures images of narrow sunny lanes thronged with tanned limbs and rooftop bars where the juiciest scandals develop to

Boats berthed at Bodrum Marina.

wards sunrise. For a new Turkish generation breaking loose from the narrow morality of Islam, Bodrum represents a liberated zone – the symbol of "their" Turkey, lively, tolerant and moneyed. The place is empty and sad in winter: in summer people go there prepared to sleep in courtyards, on rooftops and on beaches – *if*, that is, they plan to sleep at all. All this is somewhat ironic for a town that 50 years ago was a miserable little village of fishermen and sponge-hunters, without a road, used as a place of exile for convicted criminals! There

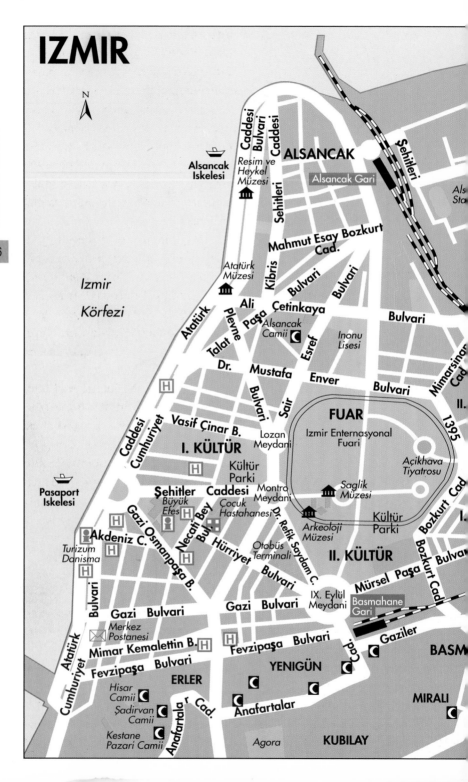

was not a hotel in town until 1968. As late as the 1970s, to go to Bodrum was to defy conventional middle-class values, something the "protest generation" – a tiny minority in Turkey – did to seek spiritual renovation in a simple and natural environment. Today, the Bodrum Peninsula has more than 100 hotels, perhaps 500 pensions, and the highest income per capita of any county in Turkey.

The panorama of the town is spectacular: an enormous medieval castle rises on a small semi-island of its own, surrounded by the graceful curves of a double harbour; Karaada island protects the harbour from the open winds, and a broad ring of maquis-covered hills closes it in.

The Castle, the largest and best-preserved monument of (Western) European origin in Turkey, is a work of the Knights of St John (also known as Hospitaller Knights, or Knights of Malta) who ran a sovereign state based in Rhodes from 1308 to 1523 and built a string of fortifications on the mainland coast facing it. Built in 1415 as Castle St Peter (Petrium, corrupted to Bodrum), it now houses a highly interesting **Museum of Underwater Archeology**, which holds finds from shipwrecks ranging in time from the Bronze Age through the Middle Ages.

The town, which in the past had a predominantly Greek population, is full of narrow lanes of great charm, whitewashed cubic houses, and tangerine orchards. Enlightened legislation has

Basking in the rays on Yalikavak Bay, near Bodrum.

protected its traditional architecture since the early 1970s, but this has not prevented the surrounding hills (and the Bodrum Peninsula, beyond the town) from being invaded by holiday-housing developments of striking ugliness.

Bodrum, once known as **Halicarnassus**, was an important naval power of antiquity. Its famous citizens included Herodotus, the Father of History; Queen Artemisia, who commanded her own fleet in the Battle of Salamis; and Mausolus, the Carian tyrant who was a major player in Aegean politics around the middle of the fourth century BC. His monumental tomb, the **Mausoleum**, was deemed one of the Seven Wonders of the World: a large pit and a few slabs of broken marble are all that

remain of it, but an attractive theatre built by Mausolus is largely intact, and fragments of ancient Halicarnassus can be seen scattered through the side streets and backyards and incorporated in the garden walls of modern Bodrum.

On the Way to Marmaris

Marmaris is the main rival of Bodrum as a place of happy abandon. The 200-km drive between the two, by contrast, provides joys of a quieter sort. Take **Milas**, an old market town which lies at the crossroads of a half-dozen points of interest. Its bazaar, covered with pergolas of vine and filled with ancient shops and muleteers in woolen caps, is one of

A Forgotten Civilization

ncient Greeks were famous for branding as barbarians" any race that spoke an alien lanuage. One of the few nations which they could ot so easily dismiss were the Lycians, who habited the region between modern Fethiye nd Antalya in early antiquity.

The Lycian image was akin to the modern wiss: a hard-working and wealthy people, neual in world affairs but fierce in defending their eedom, conservative in their attachment to ncestral traditions. Their federal system of govrnment, which seemed to solve the basic quanary of ancient politics by reconciling city-state emocracy with a working political unity, was idely admired. The ruins of all 23 cities of the ycian League have survived. Their discovery in 838 by the English orientalist Charles Fellows aused a stir in Europe, leading to a British Museum expedition which stripped Xanthus, he Lycian capital, of its finest monuments. rom that time until a few years ago the Lycian ities remained largely forgotten in the mounainous wilderness and roadless coves of the vestern Taurus.

The Lycians were probably descendants of he Luwians, a Bronze Age people of ndoeuropean origin who are often mentioned n the Hittite annals. Egyptian records of the 300s BC mention certain raiders of Lukki, and lomer's *Iliad* counts a Lycian contingent led by arpedon and Glaucus among the defenders of roy.

The Lycians, on the other hand, referred to hemselves as *Trmmli* (a Greek word meaning, ermilae) and to their country as *Trmmisa*. Their rst certain appearance in history is in 546 BC, vhen the entire population of Xanthus is reorded to have committed suicide rather than ubmit to the Persian army of Cyrus. The same ruesome episode was repeated 500 years later vhen Brutus, the murderer of Caesar, besieged anthus with his Roman legions.

The Lycian alphabet came into use in the 00s BC, about the same time as the Greek, and lisappeared towards the end of 400 BC, when Greek replaced it as the language of public ecords. Examples of the script can be seen in nany Lycian sites, notably in Xanthus and on he Kaş sarcophagus. A trilingual inscription which helped decipher the Lycian language is displayed in the museum of Fethiye.

The Lycian League was an association of free cities, each of which elected one, two or three representatives to a federal assembly. Six — Xanthus, Patara, Pinara, Tlos, Myra and Olympus — had the maximum of three votes. The assembly met each year in a different city to elect the Lyciarch and other officials, including the juries which sat in federal courts. The system continued to function even after Lycia became incorporated into the Roman Empire in AD 74, and only disappeared after the arrival of Christianity in the AD 300.

The most enduring monuments of Lycian civilization are its tombs, thousands of which dot the Lycian landscape. They testify to a preoccupation with the afterworld, perhaps even a cult of the dead, which the Lycians owed to their close cultural ties with ancient Egypt.

The tombs come in three types. *Rock tombs* are grave chambers carved into a natural cliff. The earliest of them are simple pigeonholes like the hundreds that are cut into the cliff of Pinara. Others are fashioned like the front of a timber house, perhaps copying the home architecture of the time.

Princely tombs have the form of an Ionic temple with two columns in front and a porch decorated with reliefs. *Pillar tombs*, as seen in Xanthus and Tlos, are a more archaic form, consisting of a massive rectangular block of stone which is topped with a grave chamber and a "roof". *Sarcophagi*, or sculpted caskets, date from 400 BC or later. Some of them, like the sarcophagus of Kaş and the "royal tomb" of Pinara, are splendid monuments; others stand like so many mysterious treasure boxes in the midst of wilderness — or in the sea, as in Kekova.

Like the Egyptians, the Lycians buried their dead with their valuable possessions. Each tomb was then put under the custody of a committee called the *mintis*, which took care of the safety of the tomb and collected money fines in cases of tampering or trespass. Needless to say, all tombs were broken into once the *mintises* were gone, and the chances of discovering an unopened Lycian grave after 2000 years is rather slim.

The town of Marmaris and its harbour along the Turkish coast.

the most quaintly traditional in this part of Turkey. Its big Tuesday market is attended by peasant women in resplendent traditional dress. Ancient *Mylasa (as Milaswas was once known)* was the chief town of the Carians, a pre-Hellenic Anatolian nation which flourished in the 400 BC; in the 1300's it became the seat of the Turkish *beys* of Menteşe, who controlled the mighty citadel of Peçin, nearby. Fine monuments of both periods lie, rarely noticed and rarely visited, in the back streets of old Milas.

Follow the main route northwest to **Euromus**, where a handsome Temple of Zeus stands in an olive grove by the roadside. Continue to **Lake Bafa**, where the ruins of **Carian Heraclea** blend with the weird volcanic landscape of the

Beşparmak Mountain in the isolated and beautiful village of Kapikiri. Another road which leads north of **Mila** takes you to the ancient sanctuary of **Labranda**, where the ruins of an enormous 400 BC **Temple of Zeus** lie lost in a lonely pine forest.

Just off the Milas-Muğla road, note a green rectangular patch which ha been preserved in the midst of the open work coal mines of Yatağan: it mark the site of the old village of **Eskihisar** where the monuments of ancient **Stratonicea** mix with the derelict shell of the 18th century mansions of the local feudal lords. Stratonice, who gave her name to a half dozen cities of the Hellenistic world beside this, was the wife of Seleucus I Nicator, a general and successor of Alexander the Great. He divorce from the aged general and immediate remarriage to his son Antiochu is a famous episode in the annals of historic scandal.

Marmaris beats Bodrum in the beauty of its setting, at the foot of tall and forested mountains circling a deep harbor of a striking indigo hue. It lose out in a comparison of character, charm and architecture. The historic core of Marmaris consists of a minuscule area at the foot of a small medieval fortress with an attractive seaside promenade at its edge. Beyond it, the New Town stretches out in a five-mile strip of beach facilities and highrise hotels. A brand new beach colony called **Içmeler** ha grown at its far end, around a lovely forested cove which 15 years ago con

Catching a wave while windsufring at Yalikavak Bay.

tained only two farmhouses and a few orange gardens. A similar process in now under way at **Turunç**, the next bay to the west.

A paved road leads west from Marmaris into the isolated and beautiful peninsula of **Datça**. The little town of this name is in the early stages of growing into a beach resort. Beyond it lies the meagre ruins of ancient **Cnidus**, at a wild and rocky spot more easily accessible by sea.

In antiquity, Cnidus was renowned for its statue of Aphrodite, a masterpiece

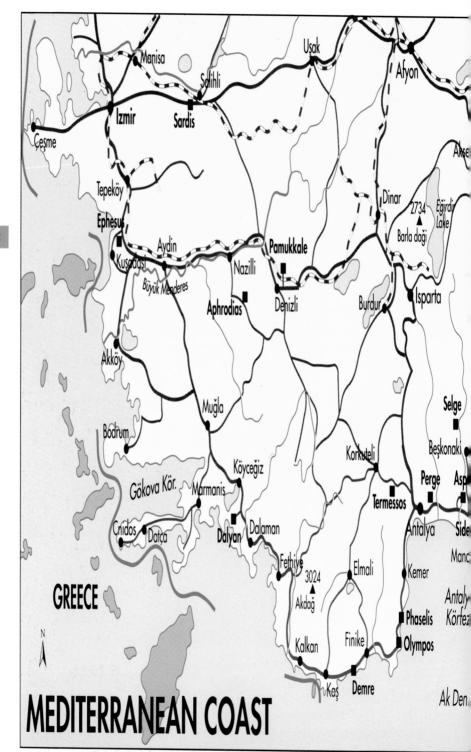

GREECE

N

MEDITERRANEAN COAST

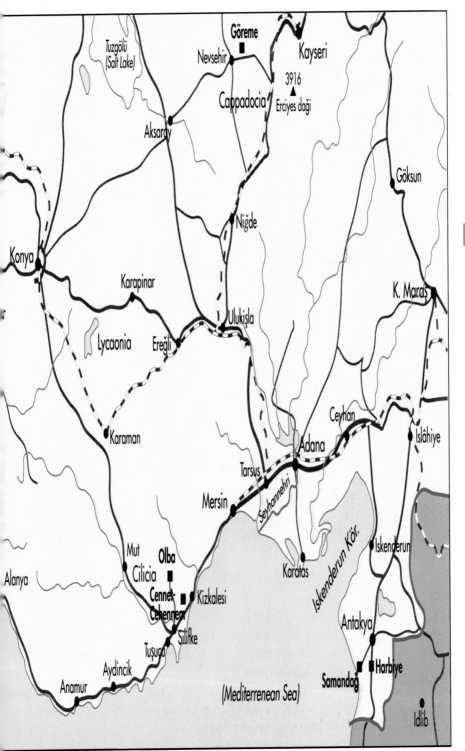

Tuzgölü
(Salt Lake)

Göreme

Nevşehir

Kayseri

Cappadocia

3916
▲
Erciyes daği

Aksaray

Göksun

Niğde

Konya

Karapinar

K. Maraş

Lycaonia

Ereğli

Ulukışla

Karaman

Ceyhan

İslâhiye

Adana

Tarsus

Seyhannehri

Mersin

İskenderun

İskenderun Kör.

Mut

Olba

Alanya

Cilicia

Karataş

**Cennet-
Cehennem**

Kizkalesi

Antakya

Silifke

Tuşuca

Samandağ

Harbiye

Aydıncık

Anamur

Idlib

(Mediterrenean Sea)

Ruins of a crusader castle in Selifke, Icelo.

of Praxiteles and one of the best-known sculptures of all times. Caesar and Cicero, among others, visited Cnidus expressly to see the statue, and one admirer was so carried away by his worship that a stain was formed on the goddess's thigh. Copies exist in the Lou-

vre and the Vatican, and the round pedestal of the temple where the original probably stood has been brought to light, but the statue itself remains elusive after 150 years of search among the rocks and the seabed of the Datça Peninsula.

lages and some of the most deeply romantic ancient ruins of the country. Its special charm lies in the combination of a gnarled topography with small, cozy towns where time seems to stand still during the long summer afternoons. The arrival of tourism is a recent phenomenon: **Fethiye** was "discovered" in the 1970s, the first paved road penetrated the wild coast of the Teke Peninsula in 1980, and Dalyan received its first batch of nature-lovers in 1984 or 1985. The number of visitors has grown in leaps and bounds, and so have hotels, pensions and souvenir shops, but the "Lycian coast" still has a long way to go for the sort of development that transformed Bodrum-Marmaris and the Gulf of Antalya into massive holiday-factories. If you are the kind of traveller who is thrilled by discovering a virgin beach or an unmarked monument, and if you can be happy with the simple comforts of a village pension, then this is your ideal place to spend a few weeks of pure escape.

Start your escape at **Dalyan**, the latest gem to join the Riviera's string of summer resorts. Unlike other beach towns, Dalyan is situated not on the sea but on the bank of a river – a slow-flowing canal actually, which connects Lake Köyceğiz to the sea across an attractive plain of cotton fields and reedy marsh. A dramatic cliff faces the village across the canal: it holds the westernmost (and in many ways most perfect) examples of that strange hallmark of the Lycian landscape, the **Royal Tombs of**

Lycia: Mountains, Beaches & Tombs

The wild and mountainous coast between Marmaris and Antalya has the best of what the Turkish Riviera has to offer: a tremendous landscape, excellent beaches, a string of attractive vil-

Turquoise waters, white beaches life on the Turkish coast.

the rulers of **Caunus**. Built in the 500 BC, the tombs loom over Dalyan like a portent from the past. They once housed, perhaps, the descendants of the eponymous founder of the city, who came to Caria – according to the legend of Ovid's *Metamorphoses* – to escape the incestuous love of his sister Byblis. The ruins of the city can be reached by rowboat and on foot in an isolated little basin beyond the tombs.

One of the most spectacular beaches of Turkey lies downriver from Dalyan. One gets there by slow river boat in 40 minutes, through the fascinating landscape of a marshy delta which constitutes one of the richest ecosystems of aquatic wildlife left in the Mediterranean world. The beach itself made headlines in the 1980s, when it was discovered to be one of the last Mediterranean hatching grounds of the giant sea turtles *caretta caretta* and *chelonia mydas*. The huge reptiles (they can be as large as 2m long) come ashore in late May to bury their eggs in the sand, and return in August when the fledglings come out at night to make the short – but very often fatal – run for the sea. In 1988, the joint efforts of local and international environmental groups defeated the plans to build a large luxury hotel on the beach, chalking up a first (and so far only) significant victory for Turkey's small Green movement.

Next along your route is **Fethiye**, a larger and more developed place than Dalyan. Fethiye itself is relatively unexciting except for a pretty pano-

Bronze yourself along the Turkish coast.

rama, a good market and a rather fascinating **Tomato Exchange**, the wholesale market for one of Europe's largest tomato-producing regions. The town is most usefully a convenient base for three wonderful excursions. First, take a boat tour of the **Gulf of Fethiye**, with its twelve small islands and scores of deserted coves to discover against a background of 2000 metre high mountains. Second, the beach of **Ölüdeniz**, 14km south of Fethiye, whose combination of white sand, translucent lagoon, forested mountain and topless bathers has become one of the most famous images of the beauties of the Turkish Riviera. A third excursion, perhaps the most unforgettable, takes you to the deserted town of **Kaya**, a short distance off the

Young children also contribute to their family.

Fethiye-Ölüdeniz road. Formerly called Livissi, Kaya (the word means "Rock") was inhabited by Greeks until their expulsion in 1922, and never resettled successfully. More than 500 abandoned houses, ruined shops, two large and countless small churches now cover the slopes of three hills, creating a ghost town of singular eeriness. Churches retain bits of their wallpaintings and their stripped iconostases. A vine grows in a fireplace, a century-old fig tree spreads its branches in a churchyard, and a half-buried inscription in Greek praises the Sultan for some benefit received.

Keep another day to explore the valley of the Eşen Stream, where the remnants of ancient Lycia are concentrated as in no other part of the region.

Cadyanda, above the town of Üzümlü is worth a visit less for its monument: than its fabulous view which takes in the whole valley as far as Patara. **Tlo** centers on a sharp outcrop of rock crowned with the fortress of an 18th century robber baron and honeycombed with Lycian rock tombs, looking dark rich and mysterious. **Pinara**, the mos extensive of Lycian sites, occupies a bowl like valley completely deserted except for the occasional shepherd. The **Letoor** possesses a sanctuary of Leto, the mother of Apollo and Artemis: at this spot, according to myth, she turned some mocking shepherds into frogs, and frogs stil infest the waterlogged ground around her temple. **Xanthus** is the best-known Lycian city, but also the most prosaic. At **Patara**, finally, the theatre, temples and

A Turk full-bearded and with steely gaze wandering close to Erzurum.

riumphal arches of what was once a great port lie half-buried in the dunes of largest sandy beach of Turkey.

Kalkan, a small village that is architecturally one of the most attractive places of the Turkish coast, is a good place to spend a night. Most of Kalkan's old houses are a legacy of the Greeks, who used to inhabit the village (then called Kalamaki) until early this century. Having stayed more or less abandoned until the mid-1980s, they have now come back to life in the form of unassuming little pensions and delightful fish tavernas.

Mediterranean Idyll

Kaş is the only resort of any size along the 300-odd kilometers of coast between Fethiye and Kemer. Its attractions include a memorable location at the foot of a 700 meters mountain, a quaint shopping lane, a jolly tavern alley, and various reminders of ancient Antiphellus (a theater, a monumental sarcophagus, rock tombs) which lie in different parts of the town.

The island directly across the harbour is **Meghisti** (or Castellorizo; *Meis* in Turkish), a Greek enclave of 200 inhabitants lying more than 100 miles from the next nearest Greek territory. Interesting excursions can be made from Kas into mountain villages, where the semi-nomadic *yörüks* perpetuate a deeply traditional way of life.

Keep the best part of your time,

A close-up of a camel in full head-dress.

however, to **Kekova** – the ultimate escape from the modern world that you can find along Turkey's Mediterranean shores. Imagine a maze of isolated bays basking in the southern sun, hundreds of islets large enough for a bunch of cactus or a fig tree, mysterious ruins sunken under the sea, a burned-out Byzantine church on a deserted beach, a medieval pirate's castle, and a stone-age village with no road connection to the rest of the world: Kekova has it all. Only a few yachtsmen ever went to Kekova until the mid-1980s, so its green-eyed, dark-complexioned natives went on living, fishing and building much as their ancestors had done in the Middle Ages. Electric current came in 1988. There is still no proper road: a car-killer

Herding the sheep in the steppes of Eastern Turkey.

path leads to the village of Üçağiz, from which one can take a rowboat to Kale, the main village of Kekova. The only other way to get there is by dolmuş boat from Kaş or Demre.

Take a room in one of the dozen pensions which have recently appeared in **Kale**, and wait for the day-trippers to leave. The fortress which gives the village its name ("Castle") was built either by Hospitaller Knights or local pirates or both; within it, and strewn throughout the village, are the much older traces of the ancient Lycian town of **Simena**: note the little ancient theatre of seven rows, perhaps the smallest in existence, which is carved into the rock.

Borrow a boat and row to the steep island which faces the village across a

narrow channel: a mile-long stretch of the island's coast is occupied by ancient structures – rock cells, stairways, houses – which in part lie under the sea surface, submerged by the gradual sinking of the Anatolian landmass over the course of millenia. An isolated beach exists near the western end of the island inside a narrow inlet called **Tersane Koyu**. A short walk here leads to the ruins of a nameless medieval town on the wild, wind-beaten south shore of Kekova. Few other places in Turkey convey so strong a feeling of solitude and timelessness.

Santa Claus's Hometown

For some, growing up means to stop

A cotton field in full bloom. South Aegean coast.

believing in Santa Claus. The truth is that Father Christmas did exist as a historical person. His name was Nicholas; he was born in Patara, became bishop of Myra and died around the year 350. His charitable acts, which did not stop growing in number and wondrousness after his death, made him one of the most popular folk saints of the Byzantine empire, the patron saint of children, poverty-stricken virgins, innocent prisoners and sailors. His cult was brought to Europe by Theophano, a Byzantine princess who married Holy Roman Emperor Otto II (973-83). In 1087 some seamen from Bari stole the saint's bones from his tomb in Myra and carried them to Italy, where the church of San Nicola di Bari was built to keep the relics. Miraculously, however, enough was left in Myra to reconstruct the saint to completeness, and St Nicholas continued to perform many more miracles in his own home. His church, built by Emperor Alexis I in 1043, remained an important site of pilgrimage until modern times.

Myra is now the modest agrarian town of **Demre**. The **Church of St Nicholas**, restored, opens its doors for an oecumenical mass celebrated on the saint's name day of December 6th. A splendid Roman-period **Theatre** can be visited at the northern edge of the town, beside a cliff carved with one of the largest groups of Lycian Rock Tombs in existence.

Another interesting Lycian site –

Rosy-cheeked and cheeky-
grinned children gathered around
a picnic tea samovar.

Andriace – exists near the **Çayağzi Beach**, a short drive south of Demre. Yet another – **Limyra** – is located a little east of Finike. None compares with the grandeur of **Arycanda**, which deserves to be named one of the lesser-known archeological wonders of Turkey. The ruins of Arycanda lie 35 kilometers from **Finike**, at the end of a dramatic gorge at an altitude of 1,000 meters.

The site is breathtakingly beautiful, with a high waterfall in background and two 3,000 meters peaks over the horizon. The monuments are extensive and very well preserved, with **Roman Baths** that retain much of their underground heating system intact and a **Theatre** whose stage building stands at its full two-storey height. The *piéce de résistance* is an **Agora**, a large court with arcades on three sides and an unimpeded view of the gorge on the fourth; a gate in the middle arcade opens to an **odeon** of delightful intimacy.

Another site call for quick visits before you leave the informal style of Lycia, at **Kemer**, for the rather different atmosphere of the Gulf of Antalya. The imposing 2,375 meters peak of **Tahtali Dağ**, the Lycian Olympus, dominates the southeastern corner of the peninsula of Teke. At its foot lies the **beach of Olympus**, a beautiful stretch of shimmering white pebble bordered by pine forest. At its southern end, engulfed in the forest and overgrown with laurel and oleander, are the unexcavated ruins of the city of Olympus, dating mostly from the late Roman and early Byzantine period. A steep climb at the north end of the beach leads to **Çırali**, where a natural flame burns perpetually as it has since antiquity.

Here, according to Lycian legend, was the home of the Chimaera, a fire-breathing dragon, a lion in front, a snake behind, and a goat in the middle. After ravaging the land for many ages it was hunted down by **Bellerophon**, on his winged horse Pegasus, and was forced to go underground.

Antalya & the Gulf

Thanks to over 50 miles of sand beach, the Gulf of Antalya is firmly established as the "hottest" holiday zone on the

The Nomads of the Taurus

The Taurus Mountains rise behind the Mediterranean coast in an unbroken row, separating a thin coastal strip from the highlands of the interior. Their roads are often no more than rocky tracks, and villages consist of primitive wooden huts lost in in a wilderness of pine forest. In the far recesses of the valleys, the ruins of ancient towns lie half-discovered and barely accessible.

From Muğla and Denizli in the west to Maraş and Gaziantep in the east, the higher zones of the Taurus are home to the tent-dwelling wanderers of the mountains, a race of people whose traditions and sense of identity set them apart from the villagers of the plains. They lived as nomadic tribes until one or two generations ago, following their herds of goats and sheep in the perpetual search for fresh pastures. Many now spend the winter in settled villages, but leave the lowlands in summer to wander with their herds in small communities of goat's hair tents. Their daughters go down to work in the cotton fields, their sons own not a few hotels and rental agencies on the coast, and Land Rovers have replaced camels as the standard mode of mountain transport; but the lifestyle that prevails in their forest villages remains very much that of another age — and so does the code of hospitality that still greets any outsider who takes the pain to discover their far habitats. They are called *yörük*, from the Turkish word *yürümek*, meaning "to wander". They claim descent from the Turkish tribes which emigrated from Central Asia and invaded these mountains, led by their independent chiefs, toward the end of the 13th century. In this connection they are also known as *Türkmen* — as distinct from *Türk*, which designates the Turkish population regardless of racial or tribal origin. Their tribes carry names like "Black Sheep", "Yellow Goat" or "Old Wanderer".

Many, though not all, belong to the aberrant Alevi sect of Islam. Some are related by name and tradition to tribal groupings which survive in the their lands of origin: thus, the Teke tribes which have given their name to the Lycian hinterland probably share the same roots as the Teke tribes which still exist at Merw in Central Asian Turkmenia; the Avşars of the highlands of Karaman-Silifke can be traced to the great Avşar confederacy whose various branches held sway in the 15th century across Afghanistan, Iran and Caucasia. Some anthropologists, on the other hand, point out to the striking similarities of manners and tradition between the Türkmens of today and the native tribes (Isaurians, Pisidians, Solymians) which used to inhabit the same mountains in Antiquity.

The Ottoman Empire, like the Byzantine before it, regarded the nomads as a menace to public order and waged a continuous battle to settle them, sometimes with much violence. It was only under the Republic that the nomads themselves came to prefer a more settled life: the absence of a fixed address meant they could not vote in elections, and the lack of educational opportunities caused an erosion of their status vis-a-vis the lowlanders. Now the *yörüks* boast a considerable number of teachers, public servants and politicians in the provinces of Muğla, Antalya and Mersin.

Summer colonies of the *yörüks*, called *yayla*, are found everywhere in the high pastures of the Taurus. A particularly colorful one shapes up each summer around Lake Kirdüve/Girdev, at the foot of the Akdağ Mountain between Fethiye and Kaş. Others exist on the Anamas mountain south of Eğirdir, and in the Bolkar range north of Mersin. Yörük villages of the Döşemealti district, immediately above Antalya, have become famous for the gorgeous *kilims* they produce.

Turkish Riviera. It owns a more developed infrastructure for mass tourism than any other part of Turkey. The airport of **Antalya** receives as many as 80 planeloads of sun-seekers a day in the high season. A string of beach hotels and holiday clubs, many operated by well-known international chains, form a self-contained world of sun and fun along the edge of the sea. It is not quite

Banana-boating a long the Turkish coast.

a Costa Brava or Rimini yet, but not too far from it either.

Four towns form the nodal points of the Gulf coast, each with its own distinct character. **Kemer**, an artificial town created by planners, has the best natural location and the most luxurious holiday complexes. Antalya preserves a picturesque walled quarter like an historic oasis in the center of a fast-growing city. In **Side**, a slapdash tourist village has grown over the ruins of ancient temples and theaters which only a couple of decades ago were home to a handful of fishermen. In **Alanya**, a stunning medieval fortress soars above a boom town of highrise hotels and the summer residences of the Turkish middle class.

The Taurus mountains, which form so intimate a part of the coastline of the Lycian peninsula, recede into the background just west of Antalya. From here to Alanya, a thickly populated plain occupies the coast. Its population centers are busy, sprawling, dusty, mostly charmless places which have grown prosperous on the income of cotton fields and citrus fruit. Apart from the resorts already mentioned, no village is located directly by the sea, and the towns of the plain – Aksu, Serik, Manavgat – have little to offer to the visitor except lively produce markets and, perhaps, a welcome break from the beach scene.

Antalya has grown into one of the richest and most progressive cities of Turkey thanks to the twin incomes of greenhouse agriculture and tourism. Its roots go back to Attalus II of Pergamum, who founded the city of *Attaleia,* in 158 BC, as a southern outlet for his kingdom. Thirteen-and-a-half centuries later, the Selçuk kings of Konya, too, found Antalya a convenient seagate for their previously landlocked realm. From Turkish conquest in 1207 until Ottoman annexation in 1423, the city enjoyed an interval of prosperity. It revived again with the rebirth of Mediterranean trade in the 19th century.

The walled Old Town of Antalya, known as **Kaleiçi** ("In-the-Castle"), had declined into a rotting slum when an intelligently managed revival project began to save it in the 1980s. It is one of the largest typically Ottoman residential quarters remaining in Turkey, with some 730 houses of authentic architec-

Picturesque housing along the banks of the Bosporus River.

ture from the late 19th century. As of this writing, about half of them stay crumbling and half-abandoned, while the rest have been renovated into the rich and beguiling mansions that they once were, and serve as hotels, restaurants, boutiques and occasionally even homes.

Monuments of Antalya's past lie scattered through the narrow streets of Kaleiçi. **Hadrian's Gate**, a triumphal arch of white marble, was built to celebrate the emperor's visit to Antalya in AD130. The **Hidirlik Tower** was perhaps the mausoleum of a Roman official. The gigantic corpse of **Kesik Minare Camii** – the Mosque of the Truncated Minaret – originated in the 5th century as a church and served a long time as a

Yachts nestled in a cosy bay on the Gulf of Gokova.

mosque until it was destroyed successively by an earthquake, a fire and lightning. Near it is the splendid stone portal of **Karatay Medresesi**, an institution of higher learning which was founded c. 1250 by a local lord who ruled as a vassal of the Mongols. **Yivli Minare** – the Fluted Minaret – Antalya's most prominent landmark, sits in a quiet courtyard above the city's rooftops: its "Persianizing" architecture belongs to the reign of Alaeddin Keykubat, the greatest of the Selçuk sultans (1219-36); the adjoining mosque dates from the Hamitoğlu dynasty, which ruled locally from the late 13th century to 1423. The main Ottoman work in town, the **Mosque of Kuyucu Murat Paşa**, commemorates a governor who acquired his epithet (*Kuyucu* or "Well-digger") from his gruesome habit of filling up wells with the bodies of slain rebels during the civil wars of the 16th century.

Not to be missed, also, is the **Archeological Museum**, which holds one of Turkey's finest collections of Roman sculpture as well as some interesting paleolithic finds from caves near Antalya. The plain which lies between Antalya and Alanya was known in Antiquity as Pamphylia, Land of All Nations. Its cities – Perge, Sillyum, Aspendus, Side and the Pamphilian Seleuceia– were of notoriously mixed background: their origin may have been Greek, but their cultural ties lay nearer to Italy and Egypt. The inhabitants of Side spoke an unknown language of their own. All grew rich on the slave trade in 100 BC, and were ranked among the wealthiest cities of the Roman Empire afterwards. The Taurus Mountains, meanwhile, were the preserve of warlike native cultures – the Pisidians in the north, Isaurians in the east, Cilicians in the southeast. Their cities, ruined and engulfed by the wilderness, are remarkable for their stunning mountain locations.

One of the most striking sites of all is **Pisidian Termessus**, which has the distinction of being the only city between Greece and India to have successfully resisted a siege of Alexander the Great. How it could do it is easy to see for Termessus stands atop a mountain, with a deep ravine at the bottom permitting access by one narrow defile alone. The ruins lie hidden among forest and tangled undergrowth, hardly touched by the archeologist's spade. The theatre is perched on the edge of a massive cliff with a drop of several hundred meters below, facing the nearly vertical thrust of Mount Solymus to one side. A necropolis extends for a half mile, with nearly a thousand tombs lying pell-mell among the woods and commanding breathtaking views of the ravine.

Pamphylian Perge, while richer in the number and quality of its monuments, is likely to prove dull after Termessus. **Aspendus**, by contrast, rarely fails to enchant. Its one edifice that really counts is a great theatre, the best-preserved Roman monument in Turkey and one of the finest in the

An intricate 12th century mosaic of the Virgin with Child.

Cotton Country

Cotton fields cover Çukurova, blanketing it in late summer with their white fluffy blobs. They make the region one of Turkey's richest, and bring it the country's largest concentration of proletarianized farm labor. The wealthiest landowners of Turkey own hunge chunks of Çukurova, exercising over them quasi-baronial authority. The textile factories clustered around Adana have in the last 20 years turned Turkey into one of the world's top exporters of inexpensive clothing.

Çukurova flourished in the Middle Ages thanks to its excellent irrigation system; under the Ottomans it became a sparsely populated malarial swamp. Cotton was introduced by Muhammad Ali, the first ruler of modern Egypt, who occupied this part of Turkey from 1832 to 1841; he also imported colonies of Egyptian and Sudanese fellaheen to work the fields.

The restored Turkish administration ran a perpetual battle over the next hundred years against Türkmen nomads of the highlands, who refused to abandon their age-old traditions of robbery and plunder, and contribute their labor to the cultivation of the plain. Muslim Circassians, driven from their Caucasian homeland by the Russians, were resettled Çukurova in the 1860s. Balkan immigrants followed in the 1870s, in 1912-13 and in the 1950s. Masses of Kurdish refugees joined them after each insurrection in the east. They created a social structure quite unlike the rest of Turkey. The owners of the land were French concerns and their local partners, some Turco-Egyptian paşas, who were more often Armenians or Christian Arabs. They had their swansong during the French occupation of 1918-21, and were driven out immediately thereafter. From the plunder of their properties

Sorting cotton prior to baling.

grew some of Turkey's richest families, including the famous Sabanciclan whose possessions include the country's top banks, the largest tire and cement factories of the Near East, and a considerable segment of Çukurova's soil.

Cotton ripens in August. Between the popping of the capsules and the first rains of September there is usually an interval of 3-4 weeks in which the crop must be picked, baled and hauled to a çirçir fabrikasi (comber plant), for

world. Built in the reign of Marcus Aurelius (AD 161-180) in the typical Roman fashion, it can seat about 20,000.

The *cavea* fully intact, supported over enormous vaults, and the stage building stands to its full height of 24m. Some seats still carry the names of contributors who had the right to reserve a seat for life.

Side, too, possesses an impressive Theatre, not to mention Hellenistic Walls, a Roman Archway, Roman Baths doubling up as an excellent archeological museum, a Nympheum, an Agora,

raw cotton is worthless once it gets wet. So the big spurt of demand for temporary labor. At the end of each summer nearly a million seasonal laborers descend on the plain, mainly from poor Kurdish villages of the east. The labor agents ("elçi" or "simsar") who recruit them wield formidable power: it is usually impossible to find work except through an agent, and whole villages are often leased out to one agent year after year. As women are preferred to men for the job of picking, entire families migrate to Çukurova with their children and household goods, living in miserable tentvilles set up near the farms. Those who try to stay and seek work in Adana after the harvest are often sent back by force, as the agent's responsibilities include getting his workers out as well as in. The secondary job market offered by the pleasure districts of Mersin and Iskenderun add another Dickensian dimension to this trade in human beings.

The plight of Çukurova is told in the novels of Yaşar Kemal, the dean of contemporary Turkish writers and himself a son of the region. His most popular work, *Ince Memed* (Mehmed My Hawk, translated into many languages) is an epic of the Türkmen rebellions of the past century. Another celebrity to rise from the squalor of the cotton fields was the filmmaker Yilmaz Güney, winner of the 1981 Grand Prix at Cannes for his film *Yol*. Güney spent a good part of his life in prison on various charges, most recently involving the murder of a judge in a bar room brawl in the town of Tumurtalik. He died in Paris after a dramatic escape from prison and from the country. His works were until recently banned in Turkey on account of their "subversive" content.

and Temples of Apollo and Athena. They all occupy a small bulb-shaped peninsula which touches on a sandy beach extending on both sides as far as the eye can see. More people go to Side these days for the beach than for ruins.

Seventy or eighty years ago, a small settlement of fishermen's huts emerged among the ruins of Side. Visitors who came for the antiquities were captivated by images of brightly painted boats moored among half-buried temples and fishing nets lying over toppled sun-bleached columns, and Side became something of a cult name among the romantics of Mediterranean archeology.

In the 1980s, it learned to make money out of its reputation: its Roman walls began to provide backing for billboards; the broken column drums found new use as bar stool and disco fixture; the lonely stretches of beach were taken over by prodigious hotel complexes; the quaint fishermen of the past became either millionnaire land developers or barmen cadging tips in five foreign languages. A unique mixture of the loftily antique and the crassly modern now gives Side its peculiar flavor: a non-stop party in an open-air museum.

Alanya has also grown fast, but in a more solid and middle-class way: rather than ramshackle bungalows, it booms with 12-storey apartment houses that seem to be in a state of permanent construction. The salient feature of Alanya is still the astounding **Citadel** which crowns a near-vertical rock 120m above the sea. Its first founders were the Cilician pirates who almost controlled the eastern Mediterranean in the 100 BC. In 67 BC they were destroyed by Pompey in the famous naval battle of *Coracesium*, which formed a prelude for the final Roman annexation of Asia Minor. Thirty years later, Mark Antony gave the citadel of Coracesium as a gift to his beloved Cleopatra: thus the beach, the stairway, the shops, the restaurant of Cleopatra which grace the town today.

In 1222 it fell to Alaeddin Keykubat, who renamed the citadel *Alaiye,* for himself, and attempted to develop it into a second capital of his kingdom after Konya. The buildings of these different epochs – Roman walls, a Byzantine church, a tower, dockyards, a hamam, a *caravanserai* of the Selçuks and an Ottoman mosque–share the citadel with a pleasant old residential district. The view from the top defies description.

Wild Cilicia

The Holiday Coast comes to an abrupt end beyond Alanya. The many-starred hotels disappear and beach crowds grow scarce in the rough stretch of the coast between Alanya and Silifke, to resume only partially between Silifke and Mersin. Yet this is a country of great scenic beauty, comparable to the Lycian peninsula in its wild physical features, with powerful mountains rising straight from the sea and miles of deserted beach lying innocent – yet – of property developers. The dusty town of **Anamur** rewards a visit with two impressive sights, located at either end of an undeveloped 15km-long beach. The ruins of **Anemurium** stand on a desolate promontory at the western edge, carrying the strange atmosphere of a recently de-

serted town; they date, in fact, from the late Roman and early Byzantine period though they seem to have been inhabited again around the 13th century. The **Castle of Mamure**, one of Turkey's most spectacular medieval monuments, rises from the sea at the eastern end. Various sources ascribe it to the Armenian kings who reigned in Cilicia from the time of the First Crusade until 1368, or to the Turkish lords of Karaman who held this stronghold from the early 14th century until the 1460s.

Silifke has an impressive castle, too, which is more certainly the work of Leo II the Armenian (c. 1190). It also has a Roman Bridge, an **Ulucami** built by the beys of Karaman and the fifth century **Basilica of Hagia Thecla** (Ayatekla), which marks the burial site of the first female Christian martyr. The town itself is dusty and charmless, but two interesting excursions make it worth devoting another day to. The first of these takes you northwest through the lovely scenery of the Göksu Canyon: 20 kilometers north of Mut, facing a great panorama of the Taurus Mountains, is the derelict **Monastery of Alahan**, one of the finest monuments of early Byzantine architecture in Turkey beside the Hagia Sophia.

A second route leads north to the primitive mountain village of **Uzuncaburç**, whose houses lie mingled with the monumental ruins of ancient **Olba-Diocaesaria**. Outstanding among these is a large **Temple of Zeus**, built around 300 BC: its priest-kings – the Teucridae –

vere the dominant political force of Cilicia through most of classical Antiquity. Historical sites succeed each other with almost tiresome regularity along the Silifke-Mersin road. The fishermen's village of **Narlikuyu** features the remains of a Roman Bath with a mosaic of the Three Graces, the fair-cheeked daughters of Zeus; "from their eyes," as Hesiod puts it, "flow love and unnerve the limbs." Near it are Heaven and Hell, two large natural chasms, one of which contains a Byzantine chapel accessible below a stairway of 452 steps. At **Kizkalesi** a medieval castle stands on an islet out in the sea while the Roman and medieval ruins of Corycus crowd the terra firma.

A picturesque gorge 3km further east contains the strange and exotic ruins of Roman Canytelis; its Turkish name, **Kanlidivane** ("Bloody Palace"), refers to a large natural pit at the center where criminals were once flung down to be devoured by wild beasts. **Viranşehir** keeps some reminders of ancient Soloi (or Soli), the atrocious Greek of whose inhabitants once gave rise to the term "solecism", meaning a grammatical gaffe. Beyond Mersin, the flat, hazy horizon of Çukurova ("Sunken Plain") stretches for 150 sweltering kilometers of identical cotton fields. Except for a few castles of medieval barons, there is nothing here to interest the casual traveler.

Mersin boasts the Ramada Towers, advertised as the "highest building between Singapore and Frankfurt". **Tar-sus** has one old well and one dusty gate to show for its famous past as the birthplace of St Paul and the scene of the legendary meeting of Antony and Cleopatra. **Adana**, Turkey's fourth-largest city, is also its ugliest. **Osmaniye** seems devoted entirely to the supply and maintenance of petroleum trucks.

Beyond this dreary interlude lies a different world. **Antakya** – the old *Antioch* on the Orontes – was once a capital of Alexander's successors, the third largest city of the Roman world, and a birthplace of Christianity. Its **museum**, with a spectacular collection of mosaics from AD 300-500, is one of the world's most important repositories of Roman art. Its citadel, set on a dizzying rock 600 meters above the city, carries memories of Bohemund and Tancred, the Norman knights who founded a Crusader principality that flourished in Antioch from 1098 to 1268.

The **Cave Church of St Peter**, rebuilt by the Crusaders in the Gothic style, may well be one of the places where the disciples of Christ first gathered to organize the universal church. Above all, however, Antakya fascinates a visitor with its cultural mosaic – a unique mix of Alevis, Orthodox Christian Melkites, Catholic Maronites, Jews, Kurds and Turks, all speaking Arabic as their common language. By atmosphere as well as history, it belongs less to the Turkish Riviera than to Turkey's "Middle Eastern" borderlands, and is thus better combined perhaps with an itinerary through eastern Turkey.

The Anatolian high plateau is vast, dusty and treeless, a lonely and primitive landscape that stretches for hundreds of miles from Kütahya in the west to Sivas in the east, from the Taurus ridge to the mountains of the Black Sea. Bald low hills take up perhaps half of its surface: for a few miraculous weeks in spring they burst into life with a dazzling display of wild flowers and grass, then they get scorched into a brownish scrub and become fodder for the huge armies of sheep. The rest is planted by a patchwork of wheat fields, cultivated by ox and hoe and seldom by tractor, subdivided into ever-tinier plots in each generation. Here and there, a spring or a stream creates an oasis of green buried in poplars and mulberry trees. Where there is water – as in Cappadocia, or the plain of Tokat – nature is almost luxuriant; where there is none, as in the salty wastes around the Great Salt

■ ■ ■ ■ ■ ■

Donkeys burdened with luggage and humans are a common sight.

CENTRAL ANATOLIA

N

Kara Deniz

Zonguldak

Safranbol

Karabük

Paphlagonia

Izmit

Bolu

Gerede

Çank

Adapazari

Köröğlutepesi
2378

Göynuk

Bilecik

Nallihan

Beypazari

Soğut

Sakaryanehri

Cayirhan

Eskişehir

Gordion

Ankara

Kütahya

Seyitgazi

Galatia

Sivrihisar

Hayamna

Kulu

Afyon

Tügzö
(Salt L

Ak

Akşehir

Dinar

Eğirdir
Lake

Konya

Isparta

Beyşehir Lake

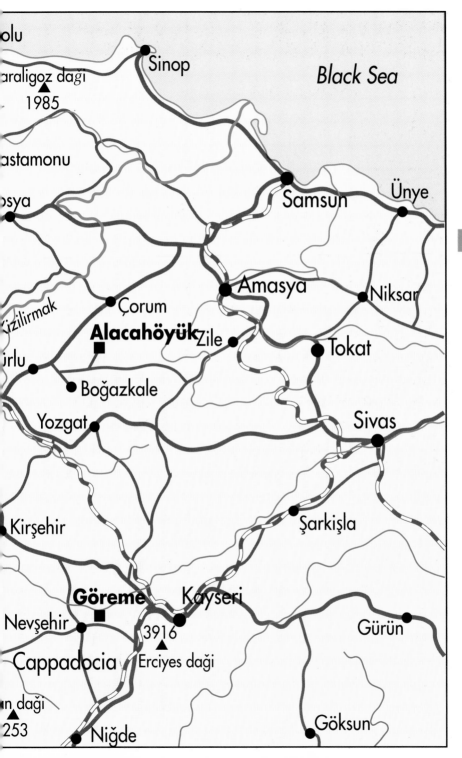

A roadside scene in Central Anatolia.

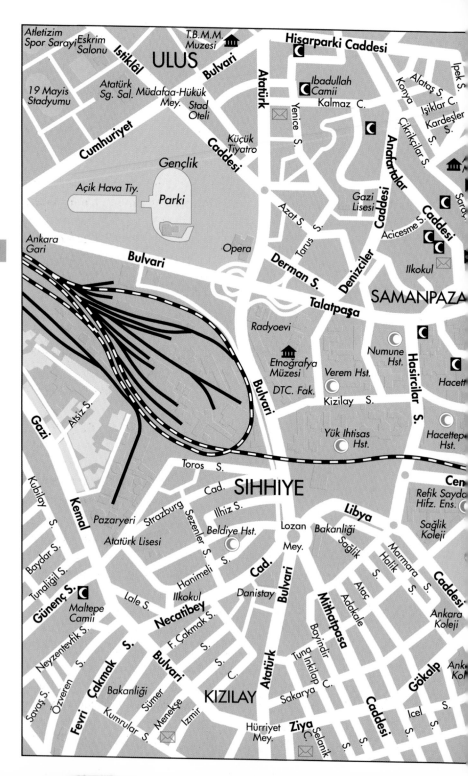

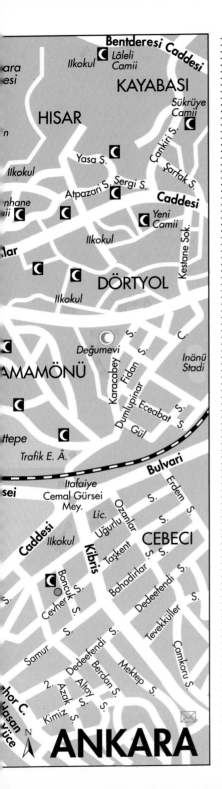

Lake, it approaches the aspect of a desert. The plateau is Turkey's heartland. It is the repository of the nation's oldest traditions and deepest instincts; the solid rock which budges least when winds of change affect the West, the East, the North and the South.

Ancestral rhythms of life predominate in its villages: their dwelling forms, agricultural techniques, handicrafts, manners, mores and superstitions took shape in the formative millenium of the early Bronze Age (3000 to 2000 BC), and only began to change, imperceptibly, with the recent arrival of roads, schools and television. Towns are small, ancient and terribly provincial: they serve first in their age-old capacity as a marketplace for villages of the vicinity, only secondarily as administrative or industrial centers.

The larger cities – **Konya**, **Kayseri**, **Sivas** above all – have always been bastions of social and religious conservatism, and are growing more so as they decline compared to the more dynamic economies of western Turkey. But their conservatism lacks the abrasive edge of modern ideologies, or the fanaticism of other parts of the Near East: it is more a way of life than a doctrine, more an instinctive defense against the modern world than a conscious attack upon it.

Historically, it is a region apart. Greek and Roman civilization took only tenuous root beyond the Meander and the Taurus mountains and the Ottoman Empire left barely a trace in the

Ankara, the Capital of New Turkey

In March 1919, a British-French-Italian allied fleet occupied Istanbul, the capital of a tottering Ottoman Empire defeated in World War I. Two months later, General Mustafa Kemal landed in Anatolia to organize the first stirrings of a movement of national resistance.

In March, the next year, the allies shut down the Ottoman parliament in Istanbul; on April 23rd, 1920, a National Assembly convened in Ankara in defiance of both the occupying Powers and the Sultan. The ragtag troops that it created from surviving bits of the Ottoman army were victorious against the Armenians and Greeks.

Istanbul was liberated in October 1922. In the historic months that followed, the Assembly voted to abolish the empire, banished all members of the dynasty, declared the Turkish Republic, and adopted Ankara as the permanent capital of the new state.

The town that thus took on the heritage of empire consisted of a bunch of dusty lanes and mud-adobe houses clustered around a medieval citadel. For the founders of the Republic it represented the stark predicament of the nation, and Ankara's transformation into a modern city became a symbol for the phoenix-like rebirth of young Turkey from the putrid carcass of the Ottoman Empire.

The early days were heroic: the Assembly met in an old schoolhouse, members commuted to work by horsecart and mule, and on desperate days any half-literate person who came off the Istanbul train would be snatched up at the station and given a ministry job. Atatürk himself cultivated a patch of the steppe into a verdant park: pictures of his model farm were reproduced on stamps and banknotes, and a patriotic march sung by schoolchildren celebrated the greening of Anatolia.

Modern Ankara evolved slowly from a wilderness mission into a full-fledged city. By the 1950s, it already had Turkey's second-largest urban population. An industrial belt grew around it after the 1960s, but the center kept the unmistakable look of a bureaucratic citadel. Today, it is a cleaner, greener, more orderly, better managed and overall more "modern" place than Istanbul. Its top places of interest

belong to that spirit: **Anıt Kabir**, the imposing post-Bauhaus mausoleum of **Atatürk** and the holiest shrine of the Republic; **Atakule**, a bold modern tower with a revolving restaurant on top; **Karum**, a post-modern atrium that was inaugurated in 1992 as Turkey's fanciest shopping center.

History, too, receives notice: Anıt Kabir incorporates Hittite and early Turkish motifs, while Karum takes its name from an Assyrian merchants' colony near Kayseri where the earliest known commercial center of Anatolia flourished some 4,000 years ago.

The Old Town

The Old Town of Ankara deteriorated into a slum until it was rediscovered a few years ago for its picturesque potential and began to experience a reversal of fortune. Several of its ancient lanes and painted 19th century houses have now been given a facelift and converted into restaurants and handicraft centers.

At its center lie the ruins of a **Temple of Augustus**, originally a Hellenistic temple built by the kings of Pergamum. Adjoining it is the medieval **Sanctuary of Hacb Bayram Veli**, an important Turkish saint of the 14th century. The City Walls were built by the 9th century Byzantine Emperor Manuel II.

Also located in the old town is the **Museum of Anatolian Civilizations**, one of the highlights of any visit to Ankara. Housed in an attractive medieval *bedesten* (covered bazaar) the museum traces the evolution of the culture of inner Anatolia from the earliest settled communities of the Neolithic era to the end of antiquity.

Displays include the reconstruction of a shrine from Çatalhöyük, one of the earliest known towns of mankind (6000 BC); fertility idols found at Hacılar (5500 BC); the astonishingly elegant metal statues of the early Bronze Age (3000-2100 BC); and extensive collections of Hittite (1800-1300 BC) and Phrygian (1300-800 BC) objects. Expertly presented and well documented, they form an excellent point to start or end a tour of central Anatolia.

Domed buildings are part of the city skyline in Central Anatolia.

Anatolian interior. The first important culture to flourish in inner Anatolia was that of the Hittites (2000-1300 BC) and their little-known Bronze Age predecessors: their descendants in the era of Greek and Roman supremacy clung jealously to their archaic traditions, and perhaps embraced Christianity as a more congenial alternative to the secular logic of antiquity.

Under the Byzantine Empire (AD 200-1000), the ancient communities of Cappadocia recovered their cultural vitality and spread their influence throughout the Christian East. The first Turkish state of Anatolia, the Selçuk Kingdom of Konya, took root in the receptive soil of the interior (AD1000-1400). And the Turkish Republic which arose from the ashes of the Ottoman Empire chose a city of Central Anatolia, Ankara, as its symbol and capital.

183

he Lake Region — the ancient country of *Pisidia* — forms a transition between the Mediterranean south and the central Anatolian plateau. By landscape it belongs more to the former than the latter: a typical karst country of sharp limestone mountains broken by fertile, basin-like small *poljes* (plains). By spirit and tradition it stands closer to the interior. On the coast, whole towns make a living from packaging and selling their natural assets; here,

The awesome Goreme Valley.

people live to a large extent outside the money-earning and money-consuming ways of modern society. In Antalya it is sometimes hard to avoid the sense of being exploited by crowds of people who have something to sell: in a place like Bucak or Uluborlu or Barla, it is not at all unlikely to run into a shop which will refuse to take a visitor's money because it is improper to send away a "guest" without a gift.

It is a highly scenic country, with a grand and unusual beauty of its own

Dwellings and houses recessed in the hills around the Lake Region.

– best appreciated perhaps on the little-traveled road between Eğirdir and Çuhut, or on the drive along the west coast of **Lake Beyşehir**. The lakes which give it its name comprise four large lakes – **Beyşehir, Eğirdir, Burdur, Acıgöl** – and countless smaller bodies of water lying at altitudes of 840 to 1110 meters above sea level.

The best time to visit is the spring, when the mountains are covered with snow and the plains put on an enchanting show of blooming apple, cherry, apricot and peach orchards. In May, rose fields blossom around Isparta, yielding the stuff for that town's distinctive rose industries (its products are rose essence, rose oil, rose water, rose jam and rose-flavored sweets).

In June, the fields of Dinar, Senirkent and Afyon are blanketed with the brilliant white and purple of the opium poppy, which is cultivated (under strict government supervision and for medical purposes) in this part of Turkey alone. All turns yellow in summer, but the crisp highland air still gives a welcome break from the muggy, enervating heat of the coast.

Consider devoting a day or two to discovering the little-known gems of the Lake Region on the way between Antalya and Istanbul or Konya. Stop in **Ağlasun** to visit the ruins of ancient Sagalassus, which lie perched on a high mountainside above the town. **Isparta** features a close-knit market district and a beautiful crater lake situated not far

A distrustful stare greets this photographer.

from the city. **Eğirdir** commands a lovely panorama of the lake of the same name, the most attractive of larger lakes in the region; an islet in the lake, now connected to the town by a causeway, holds an old residential neighbourhood of great charm.

South of Eğirdir, a bad road leads to the spectacular scenery of **Lake Kovada**, lying virtually untouched by man in a wild valley of the northern Taurus mountains. **Yalvaç** contains the ruins of ancient Pisidian Antioch, distinguished for being the first place where Gentiles as well as Jews received the Christian faith (see p 16). **Beyşehir** possesses the 13th century monuments of its eponymous Eşrefoğlu *beys*, including one of the very rare examples of a wooden mosque to

survive from that period.

Phrygia, the Lesser Cappadocia

Afyon hides an attractive historic core, with a large and traditional market, beneath its atrocious outer layer. The odd, haunted landscape of great volcanic boulders which surrounds the city announces your arrival in a land of a different character from the Lake Region: this is *Phrygia*, a volcanic plateau stretching from Denizli in the southwest to Kütahya and Eskişehir in the north.

The Phrygians who gave the region its ancient name were an Indo-European race who perhaps came to Anatolia

Cobbled roads, recesses in the cliffs and human-drawn carts — welcome to another world.

in the vanguard of the invasions which destroyed the Hittite Empire around 1200 BC. Their name derives, according to one speculation, from the same root which yields the English word "brigand"; yet these brigands taught the ancient Greeks their musical instruments and modes, their habit of capping columns with stylized ram's horns, and perhaps even their cult of the god Apollo. Their kingdom, which reached its apogee in the eighth century BC under the legendary King Midas, controlled most of Anatolia west of the river Halys

seems unchanged since the days of the Phrygians, is possibly the place which Herodotus calls *Metropolis,* the city of the Great Mother. Its primitive houses are built around scores of tombs and cave dwellings which the Phrygians carved into the volcanic rock, and which the Christians of a later age converted into churches and hermits' cells. At **Midas cehri** (Yazilikaya), a giant tombstone carved into a rock 18 by 22 meters stands at the edge of a modest village. The monument, a sixth century BC royal tomb, is decorated with a geometric maze and inscibed in the imperfectly understood Phrygian script.

An enormous walled complex, set on a hilltop, towers over the sleepy town of **Seyitgazi:** this is the sanctuary and tomb of Seyit Battal Gazi, a hero of the Turkish conquest of Anatolia who occupies a similar place in national legend as King Arthur does in the England. The complex contains Selçuk and Ottoman buildings, although it is based on Roman and Byzantine foundations.

With enough time, it pays to make the 48 kilometers detour southwest of Kütahya to the village of **Çavdarhisar.** Situated in the midst of a desolate plateau, Çavdarhisar ("Rye-castle") has grown among the ruins of Roman Aezani.

The imposing dimensions of the ancient stones contrast strangely with their rustic surroundings, where inscribed marble blocks lie mired in cowdung and the lids of Roman sarcophagi serve as communal washba-

(Kizilirmak). Their culture survived locally into the era of the Roman Empire.

More than a dozen Phrygian sites lie near the route which leads from Afyon to Eskicehir by way of Seyitgazi. At least two are as interesting as the best cave towns of Cappadocia, yet unlike them they remain virtually untouched by tourism. **Ayazini,** a village which

Seemingly extraterrestrial landscape greets the visitor to the Lake Region.

sins. A majestic **Temple of Zeus**, one of the best-preserved Roman monuments in Turkey, stands on a knoll in the middle of the village. Its vaulted underground hall appears to have been devoted to the worship of Cybele, the Phrygian Mother Goddess.

Konya: The Selçuk Capital

As little as 15 years ago, **Konya** was one of Turkey's purest outposts of medievalism. Its monuments, stemming from the city's twin distinctions as the

20th century. As late as 1965, the best restaurant in town refused to supply knives and forks on the assumption that guests should eat with their hands as their grandfathers did.

Konya, too, has now changed. The middle class has come of age with apartment blocks and Istanbul-style shops: there is even talk of building a metro. Tourism has arrived: the mausoleum of Mevlana now greets as many Europeans in improvised headscarf as it does Muslim pilgrims.

But the monuments still stamp the city with its medieval air; the bazaar is as conservative as ever, and the visitor accustomed to the easy ways of the Riviera will still suffer culture shock in a city where most men wear beards and women walk covered head-to-toe in sacks.

The city obtained the name *Iconium* in Hellenistic times, but it had been an important place much before: a walled settlement existed 3000 BC on the round hill which now forms **Alaeddin Park** in the heart of the city. The Phrygians believed it to be the first town settled by man after the Flood.

The salient period of Konya's history, however, was the time from c 1100 to 1308 when it served as the capital of the Selçuk sultans of Anatolia. The most important of Konya's monuments date from this period or from the *beys* of Karaman who ruled the region until 1467 as sworn enemies of the Ottomans. The principal sight of the city is undoubtedly the **Tomb and Sanctuary**

first Turkish capital of Anatolia and the mecca of an important Islamic order, gave it historic color. Its bazaar was the biggest and richest in inner Anatolia, as it had more or less continuously been for a few thousand years. Its people, having rebelled against Atatürk for his departure from the law of Islam, fastidiously refused to admit that they lived in the

Whirling Dervishes

"Do not search for our graves in the earth,Our graves are in the hearts of the enlightened."

Mevlana Celaleddin, surnamed Rumi, was born in 1207 in Balkh, a city now in Afghanistan. His father was one of the most prominent Muslim scholars of his time. Forced to flee his hometown by the Mongol tide of Genghiz Khan, he traveled with his son to all the great courts of the Muslim world, and at length settled in Konya at the invitation of Alaeddin Keykubad. After his death, his son took over his post as a scholar of Islamic and Greek philosophy and Quranic jurisprudence.

A sage by the name of *fiems* (Sun) of Tabriz, who appeared in Konya in the rags of a dervish — a Muslim mystic — was the author of a profound transformation in the young philosopher's soul. Mevlana withdrew from public life, dedicating himself to mystical meditation and the celebration of ecstatic love. The mysterious disappearance of *fiems* in 1247 threw him into a crisis. He tried to bury his grief in the solitude of a Greek monastery. He traveled to Damascus on a false rumour that *fiems* had reappeared there. He then composed the **Mesnevi**, a collection of several thousand odes which is not only an important work of philosophy but contains some of the finest love poetry written in the Oriental tradition. In it, in the words of its English translator, "we encounter one of the world's greatest poets. In profundity of thought, inventiveness of image, and triumphant mastery of language, (Rumi) stands out as the supreme genius of Islamic mysticism."

To his disciples, Mevlana taught a quasi-pantheistic philosophy which saw a reflection of God in all beings, and prescribed meditation, solitude and various spiritual exercises to help transcend the worldly view of things. Most original was his use of music and dance, which otherwise play little role in Muslim ritual, to help achieve a state of ecstasy. His *tekke* (dervish convent) soon became a center of art, music and philosophy. Its adherents came from the highest ranks of Selçuk society, and included the occasional non-Muslim as well. After his death in 1273, the leadership of the movement devolved to his son Sultan Veled. Devotees of Mevlana spent a period of apprenticeship under the spiritual guidance of a master, using the *tekke* as a place of celebration, discussion, meditation and penance. On *şebi arus* ("Nuptial Night"), named for the night on which Mevlana died and was assumed into the Godhead, they

of Mevlana, the founder of the order of the "Whirling Dervishes". The *Türbe* (tomb), a polygonal mausoleum sheathed in brilliant turquoise tiles, was built in 1397, more than 100 years after the saint's death. The *tekke* (santuary) took shape in the mid 13th century, although many of its buildings belong to the Ottoman period. It formed the holiest shrine of the mystic sect founded by Mevlana until the outlawing of all Muslim orders in 1925.

After lying padlocked for many years, it was reopened in the 1950s as a museum, and contains a superb collection of Islamic calligraphy and miniature painting. The "whirling" ceremonies take place each year on December 17th with the participation of devotees from around the world.

Two Ottoman mosques of radically different styles are situated near the shrine: the classic **Selimiye** was built by Selim II (1566-78), who was governor in Konya in the reign of his father Süleyman the Magnificent; the **Aziziye**, contributed by Sultan Abdülaziz (1861-76), a devotee of Mevlana, displays a unique, almost Arabic, neo-Oriental architecture.

performed the ritual of the *sema*, an ethereal dance which made the Mevlevis famous throughout Europe as the Whirling Dervishes. They sang,

> "Come, come again, and again...
> Come if you are heathen, or unbeliever, or idolater,
> Come if you have repented a hundred times and broken your vow,
> Our hearth is not the threshold of despair."

Mevlevism remained a powerful force among Ottoman elites until the final days of the empire. Its tolerance of non-Muslim ideas made it a source of progressive and enlightened opinion in the later centuries. The evolution of Ottoman music was closely bound with Mevlevism, and the greatest of its composers were practising members of the order.

The organization and practice of Mevlevism were outlawed in 1925 along with the rest of dervish orders, and the *tekkes* were seized by the state. The ban has not been lifted, although the order is known to have adherents in the highest echelons of society. Its leadership is vested with male descendants of Mevlana, who in this century included a well-known poet and prominent university scholars.

The most important mosque of Konya in both historic and architectural terms, **Alaeddin Camii**, remains closed to the public as of this writing due to restoration work.

A vast, rambling structure bearing little resemblance to the mosques of the Ottoman era, this was the principal mosque of the capital of the Selçuk sultans and the final resting place of eight of them. Its flat roof is supported by 42 columns which bear Roman and Byzantine capitals. The earliest units, including a magnificent carved-ebony pulpit, may go back to the reign of Rükneddin I Mesud (1116-56). The domed main hall was built by Kiliç Arslan II (1156-92), the sultan who first made Konya fully independent of the main Selçuk Empire of Iran, and who fought the armies of the Third Crusade at the gates of the city. Alaeddin I Keykubad (1219-36), the greatest of his successors, contributed the west wing; he is buried in an octagonal *türbe* outside the mosque.

Other highlights of Selçuk architecture in Konya include two *medreses* (schools of Islamic higher learning), whose portals are among the finest specimens of Turkish stone-carving art. **Karatay Medresesi** was completed in 1251, and now houses a splendid museum of Selçuk and Ottoman tiles.

Emir Celaleddin Karatay, its founder, was a Greek convert to Islam who became the effective master of the sultanate and led it into its disastrous confrontation with the Mongols in 1243. Emir Fahrettin Sahip Ata, his successor as *vizier* (minister) and regent, was executed by the Mongols in 1277. He endowed the **Ince Minareli Medrese**, which now serves as the setting for a museum of Selçuk stone and wood carving.

A short excursion from the city to the half-deserted village of **Sille** gives the visitor a foretaste of the cave settlements of Cappadocia. Populated mainly by Christians until 1919, Sille possesses scores of cave churches, many sadly vandalized, built into the rock of a bald gorge.

Beasts of burden and hardy animals resting in *Cappadocia, Uchisar.*

The road which leads from Konya to Cappadocia crosses the bleakest part of the Anatolian plateau, a desolate steppe where the only signs of habitation are a few hamlets of brown mud and an occasional nomad encampment. About halfway to Aksaray an enormous medieval compound appears beside the road with a magnificent portal, defense towers and buttressed walls. This is **Sultan Hani**, the largest of the scores of *caravanseraies* which the Selçuks built along the trade routes of their kingdom. It consists of a central courtyard which once gave shelter for camel caravans, and vaulted halls which provided food and lodging for merchants at public expense.

A berthed camel chews gently, oblivious to its surroundings in Uchisar.

Dryness, grit and dust seen in the plains of Cappadocia.

Landscape Changes

The landscape changes at **Aksaray**, the first town of a region that was known from prehistoric times to the Middle Ages by the name of *Cappadocia*. The hilly and fertile soil of Cappadocia lies at the foot of three extinct volcanoes, the Erciyas — the tallest at 3,916 meters — Melendiz and Hasan Daği. Their lava, turned to a soft porous rock and eroded by water and wind, accounts for the spooky landscape of Cappadocia which inspired religious reverence in the past and fascinates thousands of visitors to-day.

From the exotic destination it was some years ago, Cappadocia has grown today into an international tourist attraction with an installed capacity of over 5000 beds.

Nevşehir is the most developed town of the region with the largest concentration of modern amenities, while **Ürgüp** appeals to many visitors with its more "authentic" and small-scale charm. Excellent lodgings exist as well in Uçhisar, Avanos and other villages where only archaic warrens of stone and adobe could be found a few years back.

Wherever you choose to stay, a good place to start touring Cappadocia is **Uçhisar**, a village built in beehive fashion around the tallest of the region's "fairy chimneys". These conical pillars of rock are formed when a lump of hard

Turn your eyes upward to gaze in awe at the murals contained in
rock churches at the Goreme open air museum.

basalt acts as a protective lid for the soft volcanic *tufa* under it while the surrounding area gets gradually washed away by erosion.

From the top of Uçhisar's chimney you can see almost all of Cappadocia under your feet, from the snow-capped cones of the Erciyas and Melendiz in the south to the river Kizilirmak which appears as a shiny strip in the north.

The rock is pockmarked with man-made caves, which are turned into homes or warehouses by adding an elaborate stone facade in front. The most-photographed collection of Cappadocian fairy chimneys is found nearby in **Güvercin Vadisi**, a valley which receives its name ("Pigeon Valley") from the colonies of pigeons which villagers cultivate for their manure.

During the Byzantine Middle Ages, Cappadocia became one of the principal monastic centers of the Christian world. A leader of this movement was St Basil (AD 329-79), Bishop of Caesaria (modern Kayseri), who formulated the Rule that governs monasticism in the Eastern churches and that influenced the development of Western monasticism through the Rule of St Benedict.

Churches & Hermitages

Several hundred churches and hermitages were built in the gorges and fairy valleys of Cappadocia. In the seventh and eighth centuries, they formed a

The open-air museum at Cappadocia.

frontline of Byzantine culture and religion against Arab-Muslim invasions.
Their ascetic traditions fueled the Iconoclastic movement, which culminated in
the banning of religious images in
churches throughout the Byzantine
world (AD 726-840). Their artistic peak

was reached in the period following the
restoration of the holy icons and ended
with the Turkish occupation in the 11th
century.

Nevertheless, many churches continued in use until 1923, when the de-
portation of the Greeks of Anatolia fi-

than 10 or 20 persons.

The largest concentration of relatively well-preserved ones is in the valley of **Göreme**, where an open-air museum has been created to bring the churches under protection. The valley forms a natural amphitheater bounded by steep cliffs, where some two dozen churches, refectories, storerooms and other monastic buildings have been cut into the soft rock.

Externally, they betray no architectural details. The interiors are fully covered with frescoes, in most cases vandalized badly, but still very rich and vivid in color and composition. These originate from several epochs, from an early period (sixth to eighth centuries) of simple symbols, through the geometric designs of the iconoclastic era, to the sophisticated wall paintings of the 10th-11th century which suggest the work of imperial artists sent from Constantinople.

Further rock churches with impressive interiors are found around the village of **Çavuşin** nearby, including a so-called "Pigeon Church" which contains a portrait of Nicephorus II Phocas, a native of Cappadocia who became Byzantine Emperor (AD 963-69). The rock churches of **Soğanli**, a village further south, are interesting for being the earliest ones to employ external as well as internal architecture.

The valley of **Zelve** differs from Göreme and others in that its rock-buildings belong to a troglodyte village rather than a monastic community. The village is carved entirely into the sheer

nally ended Christian presence in Cappadocia.

Rock-carved Churches

Some 150 rock-carved churches survive today in the region, many of them minuscule chapels that can hold no more

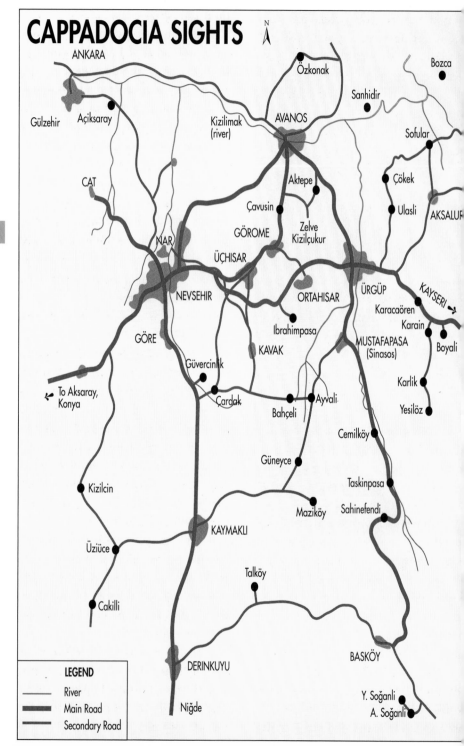

CAPPADOCIA SIGHTS

liffs of three canyons, where rope ladders are in most cases the only means of reaching houses or public places. These were inhabited by local Christians until 923 and later occupied for a while by Muslim immigrants.

The cave mosque that the latter built in the 1920s is the only rock-hewn Islamic shrine in Cappadocia.

A more extraordinary form of stone-age dwelling is characteristic of the high plateau which rises south of Cappadocia proper. This region is covered with a relatively unbroken layer of basalt that protects the underlying soft rock from exposure. Since time immemorial, villagers have built on their knowledge of the terrain to dig underground cellars beneath their houses.

In times of war, the cellars served as refuges from the enemy; during the era of Arab attacks which continued with devastating regularity for more than 100 years in the early Middle Ages, they grew into full-scale underground towns capable of accomodating thousands of people for months at a time.

Some 20 such cave-towns are known to exist in a belt between **Kayseri** and **Niğde**. Two, in **Derinkuyu** and **Kaymakli**, have been accessible to visitors for many years; a third was opened recently in **Güzelöz**, and others are reportedly being readied for imminent public debut.

The one at Derinkuyu, the largest of the three that can be toured, goes down to a depth of eight or ten stories, with an astonishing labyrinth of corridors, living quarters, public halls, storerooms – even a chapel – spreading on each level in all directions. Several ventilation shafts with hidden vent-holes secure fresh air, and wells provide an almost inexhaustible supply of water. Passages are protected at critical points by large round slabs of stone, which could be slid into place from inside to block entry by invaders.

As recently as 1839 the inhabitants are said to have gone underground to escape the invading Egyptian army of Ibrahim Pasha. Even now some reluctance exists among the local people in letting outsiders – and government officials – into the secrets of their subterranean warrens.

Other points of interest Cappadocia include the market town of **Avanos**, where artisans perpetuate handicrafts (pottery, onyx, alabaster work and carpet-weaving) as ancient as the Hittites. The village of **Mustafapaşa**, formerly Sinasos, retains some elaborate mansions and a church from its 19th century heyday which was the home of a prosperous Christian minority.

The canyon of **Ihlara** is riddled with scores of rock churches, some of which remained in use until the 1920s. **Niğde** is a town of deeply historic character which holds an excellent market on Thursdays.

The attractive **rock church of Gümüşlü** and the castle-like **Alaeddin Camii**, one of the most impressive of all Selçuk mosques, stand immediately outside the town.

Rough-hewn steps take you up for a captivating view.

Ancient Greeks called it *Pontus Euxinus,* and thought of it as the far end of the world. In a legendary age of heroes, Jason set out with his Argonauts to steal the Golden Fleece, which was said to be in the land of "cloud-bedecked Colchis", at the far edge of the Black Sea, where few ever went and fewer returned. He faced murderous moving rocks (the Symplegades, at the northern end of the Bosphorus), violent Amazons (in Themyscira, near modern Terme), killer birds (on the Isle of Aretias, off Giresun) and an array of hostile tribes. He did capture the Golden Fleece with the help of Medea, the sorceress daughter of the king of Colchis, who fell in tempestuous love with him and betrayed her own nation.

Many ages later, the Athenian general Xenophon counted some eight indigenous nations living in the 150-mile stretch from the Zigana Pass to the estuary of the Iris (modern Yeşilimak). The Mossynoeci struck him as particularly exotic: "Some boys belonging

Meet the common folk gathered around Medresa in Erzurum.

Black Sea

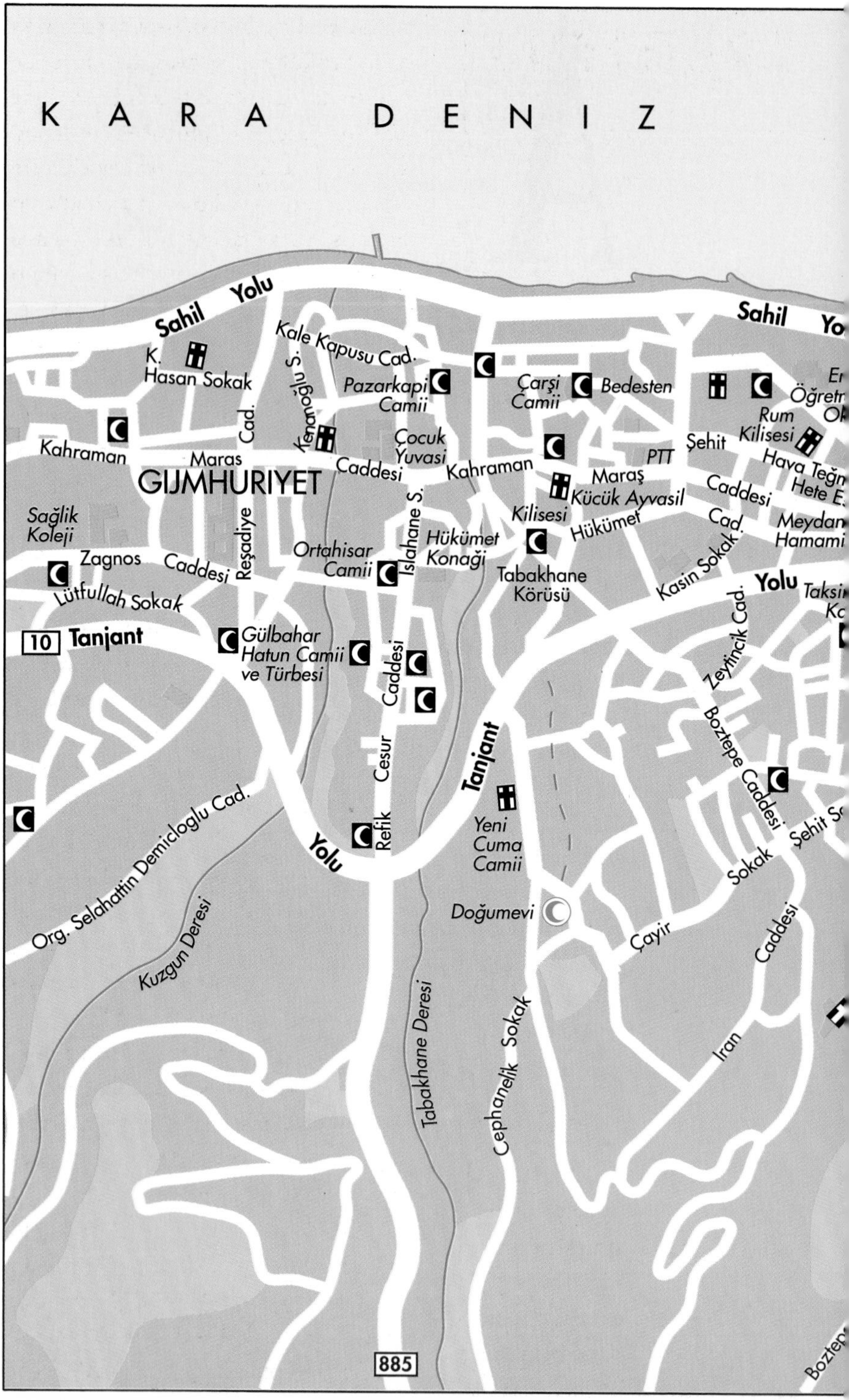

KARA DENIZ

Sahil Yolu

Sahil Yo

Kale Kapusu Cad.

K.
Hasan Sokak

Pazarkapi
Camii

Çarşi
Camii

Bedesten

Er
Öğretn
O

Rum
Kilisesi

Kahraman

Maras

GIJMHURIYET

Çocuk
Yuvasi

Caddesi

Kahraman

Şehit

PTT

Hava Teğm
Hete E.

Meydan
Hamami

Sağlik
Koleji

Reşadiye

Maraş

Küçük Ayvasil

Kilisesi

Hükümet

Caddesi

Cad.

Zagnos

Caddesi

Ortahisar
Camii

Islahane S.

Hükümet
Konaği

Kasin Sokak

Lütfullah Sokak

Tabakhane
Körüsü

Yolu

Taksir
Kc

10 Tanjant

Gülbahar
Hatun Camii
ve Türbesi

Caddesi

Zeytincik Cad.

Cesur

Tanjant

Boztepe Caddesi

Şehit Sc

Yolu

Refik

Yeni
Cuma
Camii

Sokak

Caddesi

Org. Selahattin Demicloglu Cad.

Doğumevi

Çayir

Iran

Kuzgun Deresi

Tabakhane Deresi

Cephanelik Sokak

Boztep

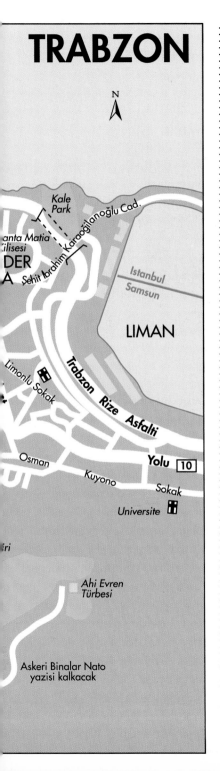

TRABZON

N↑

Kale Park

anta Matia
ilisesi
DER
A

Şehit İbrahim Karaoğilanoğlu Cad.

İstanbul
Samsun

LIMAN

Limonlu Sokak

Trabzon Rize Asfaltı

Osman

Kuyono

Yolu 10

Sokak

Universite

İri

Ahi Evren Türbesi

Askeri Binalar Nato yazisi kalkacak

to the wealthy class of people had been specially fattened by being fed on boiled chestnuts. Their flesh was soft and very pale, and they were practically as broad as they were tall. Front and back were colored brightly all over, tattooed with designs of flowers. They wanted to have sex in public with the mistresses whom the Greeks brought with them, this being actually the normal thing in their country".

A thousand years later, a Byzantine historian had this to say about the people of the Pontic mountains: "From ancient times the Tzani have lived as an independent people, without rulers, following a savage manner of life, regarding as gods the trees and birds and sundry creatures, and worshipping them, and spending their whole lives among mountains reaching the sky and covered with forests, and cultivating no land whatever".

Through much of written history, the southern shores of the Black Sea remained outside the main currents of civilization. A string of colonies were founded on the coast by the Greeks – they formed the nucleus of many of today's towns – but they never stood out for their wealth or culture, and they left few monuments that survived the passage of time. A Kingdom of Pontus emerged in the Hellenistic era with capitals in Amasia (modern Amasya) and Sinope (Sinop). Its last king, Mithridates the Great (110-63 BC), fought against Roman expansion for a half century before committing suicide in Crimea.

The hardy horse is more dependable than a modern car.

The final defeat of his army's remnants at Zela (Zile, near Tokat) was the occasion for Julius Caesar's arrogant epigram, *"veni, vidi, vici"* (I came. I saw. I conquered).

The next time Pontus appeared in the mainstream of history was 1,000 years later. A semi-independent Byzantine duchy grew in Trebizond (Trapezunt, modern Trabzon) at the end of the 11th century, when the Turkish conquest of the mainland left the Black Sea coast cut off from the imperial capital at Constantinople. When Crusaders destroyed the Byzantine Empire in 1204, a descendant of the imperial dynasty of the Comneni declared his independence in Trebizond, adopting the title of Emperor and Autocrator of Romans. He failed to recapture the Byzantine throne, but hi successors proved more fortunate in other ways. In the mid-13th century Mongol upheavals in Asia unsettled the Silk Road, the ancient trade route between the Orient and Europe, forcing i to seek a new outlet on the Black Sea Asian caravans, arriving from China via the Taklamakan Desert, Samarkand Tabriz and Erzurum, now brought their cargo of silk and spices to the port o Trebizond, where the merchantmen o Venice and Genoa loaded them for transport to the Mediterranean. The make believe empire of Trebizond began to prosper vastly. Marco Polo, who passed through the city on his way to China, admired its churches and gold-plated domes. A whole genre of popular romances grew in Europe dealing with the fabled Christian empire at the edge of the Muslim East. Don Quixote styled himself Emperor of Trebizond when he first stumbled over the boundaries of reality.

Ottoman Turks ended the dominion of the Comneni in 1461, eight years after their conquest of Istanbul. Trebizond remained a rich and important place for another century or two after this date. By the 18th century, the coast was again in the hands of semi-independent chiefs who were known by the name of *derebeyi* (valley lords). Many of the mountain tribes were first converted to Islam in the 18th century or later. Some have kept, even today, their ancestral languages or their strange dialects of Greek, Armenian or Georgian.

Isolated Valleys

The historic isolation of the Black Sea coast is a product of geography. A wall of mountains separates the Black Sea from the Anatolian interior, rising to a height of almost 4,000 meters at its eastern extremity. Except for the swampy plains of the Kizilirmak and Yeçilirmak estuaries, there is little or no coastal plain between the sea and the mountains. The predominant winds of the Black Sea are northerly and westerly: they sweep down from the Balkans and southern Russia, gather moisture over the sea, and deposit it as rain over the barrier of the Pontic Mountains. The

BLACK SEA

209

A family gathered around its hearth in the countryside close to Erzurum.

eastern "elbow" of the coast, squeezed between the Kaçkar massif and the Caucasus Mountains, has the climate of a permanently steamy greenhouse. Trabzon receives an average of 141 days of rain a year; 250 days of rain is not unusual on the northern slopes of the Kaçkar Ridge. Climate shapes the environment: a thick mantle of forest covers the mountains, taking on the aspect of a rain forest eastward of Rize; wild streams and waterfalls burst down each valley; roads get washed away every spring and have to be built anew.

In terms of tourism, it is Turkey's least-known region. At first sight this may seem fair enough: the swimming is not really the best (there are some nice beaches, but it rains a lot and the soil

A Turkish indulgence – drinking tiny cups of Turkish coffee
whilst discussing affairs.

washed down by mountain streams muddies the sea after each rain); the history, with notable exceptions, is not as impressive as other parts of Turkey. The coastal strip is thickly built with towns which are not altogether pretty. On a casual drive-through, the Black Sea does not show its best face.

To appreciate its beauty, you have to go into the mountains. Turn inland into any one of the dead-end valleys which cut deeply into the northern face of the Pontic range. Before you have time to adjust, the ever-incomplete breezeblock shanties of the coast will give way to an enchanted landscape of wild, serrated mountains buried in a riot of vegetation. The hillsides are patched with cornfields or tea planta-

tions which are often more vertical than horizontal.

There are no villages in the Anatolian sense; instead, bunches of farmhouses lie scattered all over the steep terrain, nestled like private castles over the highest and sharpest bluffs. Whether built of wood and stucco in the traditional style or as apartment buildings which look surreal in the midst of the wilderness, they are all stately and eccentric houses. Perched hundreds of feet above a valley bottom, some are only accessible by rope-and-pulley devices.

The inhabitants of this region form a people apart. Like all mountain-dwellers, they are stand out for their local pride, their clan loyalties and their in-

The women-folk cleaning carpets by the river.

tense hospitality. They cherish the idea of being the lord one's own valley, with the independence and self-respect that it engenders. Individualists and extroverts, they appreciate wit and a certain panache, and value eccentricity as a character trait. Their music is fast and boisterous, its lyrics often risqué, its rhythms unlike the melancholy strains of most Turkish music. Each valley regards the next more or less as the enemy, or too contemptible to be even the enemy, and takes pains to differentiate itself in tradition, dress, dialect, architecture, party affiliation and football club. Any outsider, however, who takes the trouble to visit these far-away valleys is automatically a guest, and will be treated to the most cordial welcome.

A few unhurried days spent among these splendid and unusual people may very well turn into the most unforgettable part of a vacation in Turkey.

West to East

The most interesting part of the Black Sea coast is the easternmost section which lies between Trabzon and the Georgian border. The western part can be passed over more quickly. **Amasra** and **Inebolu** are attractive towns suitable for a stopover on a long drive from Istanbul. **Sinop** keeps some imposing monuments from its past greatness as capital of both the Pontic kingdom (second – first century BC) and of two medi-

Going to the Yayla

Beyond a Black Sea valley and the farm belt, the landscape begins to change at an altitude of 1200 meters, where forests of giant fir replace the leaf trees, and fields of tea and hazelnut disappear. Rhododendron, yellow azalea and alpine lily become ubiquitous in a belt which lies in semi-permanent cloud and drizzle. The tree line is reached around 1,800 meters. Above this is the *yayla,* the sunny region of rolling pastures which rise at every possible angle and curvature of the plane as far as the summer snowline at 3,000 meters.

Since time immemorial, people of the Black Sea valleys have migrated each summer to the *yayla*, to escape the humid heat of the lowland and to let cows take advantage of the fresh grass. The tradition continues in force: some go for the sake of the cows, some because father did so before them, others just to enjoy the intoxication of the high mountain air. Some move up for the whole season, taking the animals and grandfather's armchair and pots and pans with them; others make the sortie for a few days at a time. Many walk, making it a trek of several days; they carry babies on their backs and struggle to keep the cattle in line. Others show up in late model Mercedes which keep getting stuck in the mud.

The *yayla* is dotted with summer settlements — clusters of ancient stone houses, sometimes at the very edge of permanent snow — which come to life overnight in a mad chaos of knee-deep mud, fiery bulls fighting to establish this year's bovine hierarchy, the pungent smells of burning pinewood and *tezek* (dried cowdung) and drunk men running wild on sheer excitement. Each *yayla* is the property of a village or a valley, with ancient imperial writs to back up the claim. Each spring, invariably, some valley goes to war against another over some obscure quarrel of *yayla*-ownership.

The yayla season begins on the first day of summer, which tradition places on the Sixth of May. The strangest folk rituals are revived on this day. Everywhere people feast and make merry in the fields. Virgins bury a ring under a rose bush, evoking mysterious un-Islamic saints. Coarse grains are thrown into the wind to feed "the birds and the wolves". At Giresun Island, large crowds gather to throw "seven pairs and one" pebbles into the sea and to circle the island thrice in rowboats. Then for three days they make music, dance the *horon,* and soak themselves in alcohol.

eval Turkish dynasties (13th-15th century). **Samsun**, a large and charmless city, can be avoided; but it is worth making the excursion inland to **Amasya**, one of the the most attractive of Anatolian cities.

Amasya is built in a narrow gorge on the banks of the Yeşilirmak, overshadowed by a cliff which exposes the grandiose rock-tombs of the kings of Pontus; the town itself is dotted with the mosques, *türbes* and *medreses* (schools of Higher Islam) of the Danişmendid Turks, Selçuks, Mongol viceroys and Ottomans, each of which treated Amasya as an important regional center. The route can then be continued to the historic town of **Tokat**, and then to the splendid valley of the river Kelkit. A reasonable road leads from Niksar across the mountains, to Ünye on the coast.

Bolaman holds the picturesque seaside Mansion of **Haznedaroğlu**, which an 18th century *derebeyi* (sea-castle) built over the foundations of a medieval Genoese fort. **Giresun** is a pleasant city with many cobblestone streets and the houses of a vanished turn-of-the-century bourgeoisie. The ancient Greek

Towers of Trebizond

Merrymaking continues in the *yayla*, where whatever remains of city culture gets stripped off by degrees. Oxcarts replace taxis, while people who normally wear suit and tie put on their traditional dress.

On appointed days, and often in between, they organize festivities. Guests from other valleys arrive on these days, along with travelling bards, professional wrestlers, trinket sellers and the best dancers of the province. For three days and three nights they drink, dance, wrestle, fight and gamble, make eternal friends and mortal enemies, bringing handguns and bagpipes out of winter storage. Bulls are decked out in festival frills. At Hidirnebi, near Trabzon, dancers form a 1,000-person *horon* ring. At Kafkasör, above Artvin, they hold bullfights. At Kadirga, on the intersection of the districts of Maçka, Torul and Tonya, the three communities get together to reenact long-forgotten hostilities. Everyone is welcome at the festivities, and every visitor becomes part of the ongoing show.

It is here in the breathtaking scenery of the mountains that the casual outsider first begins to penetrate the façade, and to catch a glimpse of the real spirit of the Black Sea.

name of the city – *Cerasus* – formed the root of the word for "cherries" in European languages when the legions of Lucullus, the Roman general sent here to fight Mithridates of Pontus, brought that exotic fruit back from the shores of the Black Sea.

At **Tirebolu**, ancient Tripolis, a little-traveled road leads inland into the beautiful valley of the Harşit. Finally in **Akçaabat**, which lies within sight of Trabzon, a detour should be made into the old hill neighborhoods which possess one of the quaintest collections of traditional Black Sea houses.

Trebizond has had the good luck of having been an important city in the past but developing slowly in the present century. As a result, it retains much of the historic flavor which no longer exists in fast-growing Samsun and perhaps never existed in more modest places like Rize. Combined with a superb natural setting and a colorful population, it amply rewards a long visit.

The historic center of Trebizond occupies a platform-like hill bordered by deep gullies whose shape accounts for the ancient Greek name of the city (*Trapezus* which means Table). The cobblestoned streets of the walled hill-quarter contain many tottering 19th century mansions and several former Byzantine churches, including the *Panagia Chrysocephalos,* the coronation church of the Comneni which has served since the Turkish conquest as the **Fatih Mosque**. At the top end of the walled quarter is the ruined **Citadel** of the Greek emperors and Turkish paşas. The attractive **Mosque** and adjoining **Türbe of Gülbahar Hatun,** built in 1512, commemorate the mother of Ottoman Sultan Selim I the Grim. She was born in Trebizond as a princess of the Greek imperial blood, was taken into the harem of Beyazit II, and returned to her birthplace when her son was appointed governor there before succeeding to the Ottoman throne. Her Turkish name means "Rose of Spring". A large and

A family hearth in a copper craftsman's house.

colorful **Market District** spreads below the Old Town around a covered *bedesten* (bazaar) of Genoese and Ottoman origin. The market has undergone a phenomenal revival since 1989 with the arrival of cross-border shoppers from ex-Soviet Georgia. Numbering almost a million in 1991, these traders arrive by the newly opened frontier gate at Sarp, sell their wares in improvised markets set up in each of the towns between there and Trebizond, and spend the hard currency they gain on foodstuff, clothes and electronics in Trebizond's bazaar.

Trebizond's most important work of art is located in the outskirts of the city, standing on a bluff by the seaside a few miles to the west. The church (now

museum) of **Hagia Sophia** dates from the reign of Manuel I of Trebizond (1238-63), a time which saw the transformation of the city from a temporary refuge of the court of Constantinople into a state on its own right. The design of the church, a cross-naved basilica with a conical dome surmounted on a tambour, shows Georgian influence, while the campanile has a distinctly Italian flavor. Most memorable are the 13th century frescoes which decorate the interior: rescued and restored in the 1960s by British scholars David Talbot Rice and David Winfield, they constitute one of the world's most important collections of late-Byzantine art.

A Byzantine monument of perhaps lesser artistic merit but far greater spec-

 A seafood restaurant in Saniyer near the mouth of the Black Sea.

tacular effect lies in the mountains about an hour's drive from the city. The highway from Trebizond to the Zigana Pass (2025 meters) and Erzurum follows the course of the historic caravan route that once formed the sole link between the Pontic coast and the cultural centers of the Near East.

At intervals along the route, in wild mountaintops overlooking the valley from afar, the Byzantines built a string of monasteries which could also play a defensive role in times of war. Some six of these, all in ruins, are accessible by more or less adventurous routes in the forest. **Sumela**, the largest and best-preserved, has grown in recent years into one of Turkey's top tourist sights.

The Monastery of the **Virgin Mary** of **Sumela** (*Meryemana* meaning "Mother Mary" in Turkish) is reached by a paved road from Maçka which follows a valley of outstanding scenery. At about 1,000 meters, the enormous white façade of the monastery comes into view perched on a vertical cliff of basalt some 300 meters above the valley floor. A steep 40-minute climb leads up to the seven-storey-high building which is built on a narrow ledge at the bottom of a cavity in the cliff. The complex includes a main church, a much older cave church, several chapels and living and guest quarters; it was gutted by fire and vandalized but retains a wealth of frescoes, some as old as the 14th century.

According to tradition, a monastery was established here during the

Women walking arm-in arm on a country road close to Erzurum.

reign of Justinian and took its name from a black icon of the Virgin which was held to have been painted by St Luke himself. The present buildings were erected in the 13th century. They formed the largest monastic establishment in Asia Minor until their evacuation by the Greek monks early this century. The traditions of Sumela are perpetuated today in a new monastery near Thessaloniki in Greece, and the holy icon of the Virgin, spirited out of Turkey, is displayed in the Benaki Museum in Athens.

The Laz Coast

East of Trabzon, the coast gets steeper, wetter and greener. The tea country starts a short distance beyond the city: past Sürmene, every slope, backyard and beachfront is blanketed with the squat, clumpy rows of tea-bush which look like endless herds of electric-green sheep. Only women work in tea fields. In summer, the enduring image of the region is hunched women wading slowly through a waist-high pile of green, cloaked in the scarlet shawls and aprons which are the hallmarks of local dress. In early morning they nip the top leaves of each bud; then they walk to the buying stations which are scattered along farm roads, carrying enormous loads of tea in conical straw baskets strapped to their backs.

The towns around Trabzon and Rize hold some of the most colorful weekly markets of Turkey: the overwhelming majority of both sellers and buyers in these markets are women, who bring down fresh produce from their mountain farms resplendent in their red dress. The days to look out for are Monday in Rize, Tuesday in Sürmene and Akçaabat, Wednesday in Çayeli, Thursday in Arsin, Arakli and Of, Friday in Rize and Saturday in Yomra.

At **Of**, a passable road branches into one of the most beautiful valleys of the Pontic mountains and climbs to the awesome pass of **Soğanli** (2,300 meters). Inhabitants speak the Pontic dialect of Greek, yet are renowned for their particularly zealous version of Islam – a fact very much in evidence in the number of gigantic new mosques dotting their mountains.

A gem of nature lies in spectacular Alpine landscape 45 kilometers up from the coast: **Lake Uzungöl**, which offers some rustic chalets for accomodation, is an ideal base for hiking tours or a nature holiday.

The five townships east of Rize/Çayeli are inhabited by an ethnic group which impersonates the quintessence of the Pontic culture. The *Laz* speak a language distantly related to the Georgian, and have predominantly blond or red hair and blue eyes. They were first mentioned in the second century, but might well be descendants of the ancient Colchians of the Argonaut legend. They inhabit the lushest corner of Turkey. They cultivate hawking as a passion and addiction, and their independent spirit, peculiar wit and business acumen are proverbial even by the standards of the Black Sea.

A stirring panorama unfolds on the short stretch of coast between Pazar and Ardeşen: the foothills recede a little from the coast to reveal the soaring range of the **Kaçkar Mountains**. On a rare cloudless day, the black horn of the Kaçkar (3,937 meters) is seen towering above the snowline, trailed to the west by the peaks of the Tatos (3,560 meters) and Verçenik (3,711 meters).

These are some of the highest spots on earth that can be seen at sea level. The highway bridge over the river Firtina, just outside Ardeşen, offers the best unobstructed view of the mountains; aptly, it is also the turnoff point for the ex-

traordinary world of the Hemşin valleys.

Hemçin, the broad triangular region of the upper valleys to the north side of the Kaçkar massif, is possibly the best that Turkey has to offer in terms of raw, magnificent, and unspoiled nature. It is by far the rainiest part of the country, with natural flora, as a result, of astonishing diversity and wealth. It is one of the most inaccessible corners of Turkey, for the Kaçkars allow no passage on the south.

Neither the Byzantines nor the Ottomans were ever fully successful in asserting their authority in the region. Its inhabitants, who are not Laz and have their own distinct dialect and dress, were perhaps only Islamized in the 19th century. They are fierce individualists, almost "nordic" in the range of their moods, people accustomed to live in endless rain and fog in solitary far-away valleys. A large diaspora has produced some of Turkey's most successful businessmen and politicians.

Çamlihemşin, the main town of the region, consists of a single street set in a narrow gulch on the bank of the thunderous Firtina; its hill quarters contain some of the most impressive specimens of the traditional all-wood architecture of the Black Sea.

Above the town, the valley branches in two. A poor road, ideally suited for hiking expeditions, follows the left (west) branch to the fantastic fortress of **Zilkale**, a moss-covered ruin set on a crag high above the cascades of the Firtina, and then on to the high *yaylas* near the glacier lakes of the Tatos massif. A paved road along the right (east) branch leads, at 1,800 meters, to the primitive thermal resort of **Ayder** which forms a base for climbing the Kaçkar or starting the 2-day trek across the ridge to the no less fascinating valleys of Artvin.

Simple accomodations exist in Çamlihemşin, Işenyuva, Çat (west valley) and Ayder. It is advisable to take a local guide for excursions into the higher reaches of the mountains.

Lost Churches of Artvin

The province of Artvin, tucked in the impenetrable mountains of the Georgian border, calls for an equally adventurous spirit as Hemşin and rewards it just as richly. Strictly speaking Artvin does not belong to the Black Sea in either landscape or history, though it has little in common with the interior plateau either. Its inhabitants are for the most part ethnic Georgians, though only some (eg. in the town of Borçka and the valleys of Meydancik) still speak the Georgian language. Its history is that of medieval Georgia.

At the start of the ninth century, a branch of the feudal dynasty of the Bagratids – cousins of the Armenian rulers of Ani – established their rule over the Georgian clans of the Chorokhi (Çoruh) valley from a base in the impregnable castle of Ardanuchi (Ardanuç). Over the next two centuries, the castles and monasteries of their isolated domain formed the source of a rebirth of Georgian national culture at a time when central Georgia itself lay under Arab rule.

The Bagratids acquired the Georgian royal title around the year 1000, and they reigned in Tbilisi as the world's longest-ruling sovereign dynasty until 1801. Their ancestral valleys, meanwhile, fell again to local clans and petty lords who came under Turkish rule in the 1540s and adopted Islam shortly thereafter.

Take the town of **Artvin**, set on near-vertical terrain several hundred feet above the river Çoruh, as your base for exploring the region, and count on spending a few more days in this wild and fascinating land than you plan at first. The trunk roads of the province follow the Çoruh and its tributaries, the şavşat and Oltu, along the bed of an arid, rocky, inhospitable canyon.

Cross any one of the old timber-and-rope suspension bridges which span the river, and drive up the obscure paths which climb the canyon wall at a crazy angle: within a few miles you will rise from the desert into an idyllic oasis of fruit orchards and some of the most attractive villages of all of Turkey, followed by the virtually Tyrolean scenery of the *yayla*, and culminating in a range of snow-capped mountains.

The utter isolation of these valleys from each other gives traveling in Artvin something of the flavor of "island-hopping" in the South Seas. Each valley has

A scenic view from Hamsuköy along the Trebizon - Erzurum Road.

a medieval fortress or two. At least a dozen of them hold an ancient Georgian church, standing out of all proportion to the rural environment with their size and splendor.

Start out with the church of **Barhal**, a huge and severe basilica from the late 10th century, now used as a mosque, set in a village in the southern foothills of the Kaçkar massif. This journey takes up a whole day, broken by a night in the pleasant town of Yusufeli. The tremendous monastery church of **Öşkvank** (c 1000), strangely reminiscent of a Romanesque cathedral, is located in a mountain village off about the midpoint of the Artvin-Erzurum road. The church of **Işhan** (1032, with a 7th century apsis) is smaller but perhaps the

more striking because of the wholly unexpected character of the village it lies in, a lush oasis at the end of a desert road.

A 12 kilometers drive south of Ardanuç leads to **Yeni Rabat** (mid-9th century), a most attractive of Artvin's churches, set like a jewel in a solitary meadow outside the village of Bulanık. The monastery church of **Tbeti** (early 10th century) is now in ruins, partly due to treasure-hunters, but visit the village of Cevizli in its splendid setting.

Other medieval churches in the area include **Dörtkilise**, **Haho**, **Dolishane**, **Opiza** and **Porta**. It is advisable to engage a local guide to reach these places, for many places are not signposted at all in this violently uneven terrain.

One of the memorable moments of any Turkish grand tour is the crossing of the mountain passes that link the Black Sea coast with the highlands of Eastern Turkey. Many travelers make that passage at the Zigana Pass on the way between Trabzon and Erzurum. Less well-known but more spectacular are the passes of Soğanli (Of-Bayburt, 2,330 meters), Ovitdaği (Rize-Erzurum, 2,600 meters), Yalnizçam (Artvin/Ardanuç-Kars, 2,650 meters) or Çam (Artvin/şavşat-Kars, 2,640 meters). The roads climb through forest and meadow, across villages resembling the Swiss uplands, and emerge, with brutal suddenness, into a landscape more easily associated with the bleak wastelands of Inner Asia.

In its eastern highlands, bordered by the Pontic mountains and the valley of the Euphrates, Turkey gives up all pretence of being the bridge be-

■ ■ ■ ■ ■ ■

Bullocks and haystacks are a common sight in East Turkey.

The East

221

Bullocks threshing grain in Vanuk, East Turkey.

tween East and West, and plunges un-ambiguously into the world of the ar-chaic Orient. The land is somewhat like the Anatolian plateau, only higher, vaster and lonelier.

Villages are not only dusty and ancient, but in many cases dug into the earth like prehistoric burrows. An un-known portion of the inhabitants do not even live in villages but wander as no-mads, following their herds of cattle or brown sheep. Two thirds of the land is too high for cultivation, and supports only a pastoral economy.

The Euphrates formed the natural boundary of the Roman/Byzantine world for more than a thousand years. The lands to its east and south were con-quered by the Arab empire in the sev-enth century and were already largely Muslim by the time the Turks arrived in the 11th. The Turks merely washed over these parts on their march to the west, and only returned in the 16th century to wrest them back from Persian hands. The earliest Turkish monuments of Tur-key were built in the southeastern towns of Diyarbakır, Urfa, Silvan, Mardin, Bitlis, Ahlat — places where, paradoxi-cally, no one is at home with Turkish today except army men and civil serv-ants holed up in concrete bunkers.

Turks & Kurds

The first trickle of foreign tourism came to Eastern Turkey in the mid-80s, when

A village waking up to greet the day in East Turkey.

several enterprising operators began carrying awestruck visitors on tours of Ani, Mt Ararat, Van, Diyarbakir and Mt Nemrut. That trickle has now all but dried up because of an armed conflict which pits Kurdish separatist groups against Turkish government forces in many parts of the region.

Kurdish is the dominant language of a well-defined zone whose boundaries run through Kars, exclude Erzurum and Erzincan, include Tunceli and Adiyaman and cut across Urfa. Other Kurds live in the neighboring parts of Iran, Iraq and Syria. Their presence in the region is documented as early as the fifth century, although their expansion over the whole area seems to have only occurred in the Middle Ages. Until the

present generation, a majority of Kurds lived in tribal groups ruled by autonomous chiefs, who were subordinated to each other and to the state in a rigid feudal hierarchy. The rapid urbanization and de-tribalization of recent years is cited by some analysts as one cause of the current crisis.

The ethnic picture of the region, incidentally, is not as simple as Kurd vs. Turk. In the historic cities of the southeast (Antakya, Urfa, Mardin, Siirt), Arabic rather than Kurdish is the traditional language of – at least – the middle class. Syriac Christians, speaking Arabic or their own Semitic language, form a sizable community in the region of Mardin. Most of the residents of Diyarbakir speak Zaza, a language said

NORTH EAST TURKEY

N

*Kara Deniz
(Black Sea)*

Batumi

Hopa

Ardeşen

Ünye

Ordu

Trabzon Rize

Camlihemiş

Fasta

Tirebolu

Kaçkar daği
3932

Yu

Giresun

Maçka (Surmela)

Niksar

Gümüsane

Coruhnehri

Mescit daği
3255

Tort

Susehri

Bayburt

Aşkale

Zara

Refaniye

Erzur

Sivas

Erzincan

TURKEY

Divriği

Ilic

Kemah

Çetinkaya

Tunceli

Bingöl

Gürün

Ağin

Muratnehri

Elâziğ

Muş

Malatya

*Firatnehri
(Euphrates)*

Ergani

Silvan

Nuruhak daği
3090

Celikan

Diyarbakir

to be related to Kurdish but mutually unintelligible. The Kurds of Tunceli and Kars, while ethnically related to other Kurds, follow the Alevi sect of Islam that sets them sharply apart from their Sunni brethren.

Finally, there are Turkish-speaking communities who consider themselves Kurdish, Kurdish-speaking clans who claim to be Turks or Arabs, and others who like to be seen as Kurds but are shunned by everyone else as Armenian converts.

Northern Highlands

Situated 1900 meters above sea level on Turkey's coldest plateau, **Erzurum** is a bleak, sullen and inhospitable city. The presence of several important monuments of the Saltuk Turks (12th century) and Mongol viceroys (13th-14th century) fails to make it an attractive place. **Kars**, built at the foot of a majestic fortress, has the altogether surprising aspect of a turn-of-the-century European town abandoned in deep Asia – a fact owing to the Russian occupation of 1877-1918, when Kars served as a garrison for the Czar's armies. The town is fascinating enough in itself, but its real interest lies in being a convenient base to visit the ruins of Ani.

The ruin-field of the medieval Armenian capital of **Ani**, situated directly on the Armenian frontier some 50 kilometers east of Kars, deserves to be counted among the most impressive

Is It Safe?

"Risk" and "safety" are notoriously relative concepts when it comes to travelling: some people rush to cancel tickets at the drop of a mullah's turban, others think nothing of tackling the Sahara or walking in the streets of New York City. The latter sort of traveller could safely skip this warning note about conditions in southeastern Tukey; the former, as of 1992, have enough reason to beware of venturing into this part of the country.

Facts first: no foreign travellers have so far suffered serious harm from going there, and apart from a couple of highly publicized cases of short-term detainment by armed groups, few have even faced much inconvenience. But the region is the scene of an armed confrontation, and the effects of the conflict are felt everywhere. Since 1986, a separatist organization called PKK (the initials stand for "Kurdistan Workers' Party") has waged guerrilla attacks in the Kurdish-speaking part of Turkey, and regular and irregular units of the Turkish security forces have fought back with increasing force. Clashes now cost around 3,000 lives each year.

Neither side has a stated policy of hostility against innocent outsiders, but mistrust, suspicion, tension and fear may sometimes affect the attitudes of individuals. Frequent roadblocks, spot checks and curfews put certain limitations on the freedom of movement. All large towns and well-known tourist sights are freely accessible, but visits to some remote places off the main highways may not always be possible or advisable. The region of Hakkari, one of Turkey's wildest and most beautiful corners, has been closed to outsiders since some years ago. Since 1988, no permission is given to climb Mt Ağri.

A travel advisory which the US State Department issued in 1991 states that "United States citizens should defer all non-essential and tourist travel to Southeastern Turkey". It recommends that "individuals who must travel to Southeastern Turkey despite this warning should be off the road well in advance of dusk and should not travel until daybreak. Travel off main highways and in remote areas should be avoided. Travelers should cooperate with travel restrictions or other security measures imposed by Turkish authorities."

These precautions apply to a zone of Emergency Rule declared by the Turkish government in the provinces of Adiyaman, Batman, Bitlis, Bingöl, Diyarbakir, Elaziğ, Hakkari, Mardin, Muş, Siirt, şirnak, Tunceli and Van. The State Department advisory also warns about possible separatist incidents in the adjoining provinces of Erzurum, Kars, Ağri, Erzincan, Malatya, Maraş and Urfa, although the level of conflict in these areas has been negligible compared to the foregoing. No significant incidents have been reported either in the eastern Black Sea coastal area (Artvin, Rize, Trabzon) or the eastern Mediterranean region (Antakya).

---

historic sights of Turkey.

The road leads across a forlorn volcanic plateau, when suddenly the massive walls and towers of Ani appear on the plain like the mirage of a ghost city. They enclose a spacious area measuring 1 kilometers by 1.5 kilometers, large enough to have once accomodated 100,000 inhabitants.

The half-ruined shells of eight medieval churches and one mosque stand scattered over the desolate plateau within. They belong to the era when Ani served as the seat of the Armenian kingdom of the Bagratids (AD 950-1040), to the brief interlude when a Turkish *bey* held court in the city (AD 1064-1089), and to the subsequent period when local Armenian chiefs ruled under Georgian suzerainty (AD 1090-1350). The city was destroyed by an earthquake in 1319, and abandoned perhaps during

The symmetrical aspect of the University of Erzurum.

Timur's invasions later in that century.

The ruins of huge and ghostly churches of the same era are sprinkled liberally along the valley of the Arpaçay and along the Kars-Digor road, across a lonely and primitive landscape dominated by the snow-capped peak of Mt Alagöz/Aragats.

The tremendous mass of **Mount Ağri** – the Biblical *Ararat* – comes into view as soon as the road enters the fertile valley of the Aras/Arax. At 5,165 meters, this extinct volcano is Turkey's highest mountain. Rising in a single, elegant thrust from a flat plain at 600 meters, it presents a more awesome sight than almost any other mountain of comparable height.

Ever since prehistoric times, it seems to have been held in reverence as a sacred place. The Old Testament names it as the site where Noah's Ark landed after the deluge, and from where all animal species spread once again over the earth. Countless climbers since the Marquis of Tournefort in 1707 have sought, and imagined to have found, fragments of the Ark in various parts of the mountain.

The most recent and sensational search party was led by the former US astronaut James Irwing. The summit, while beyond the reach of the ordinary amateur, is not particularly difficult to climb. Security concerns, however, have made it off-limits since some years.

Some of the best views of the Ağri are obtained along the Iğdir-Doğube-

Muslims in the East are rather conservative, as can be seen here in Erzurum.

yazıt road which skirts the mountain over an enormous shoulder of petrified lava. Situated on the historic Silk Route, and on the Europe-Iran transit road which still follows the same course, **Doğubeyazit** is a good place to break the journey for a night. Its main historic monument rivals the sight of the Ağrı in its grandeur.

The **Castle of Ishak Paşa**, set in a wild gully ideally suited for preying upon

the caravan route, was built by an Ottoman governor who established a dynasty here in the second half of the 18th century in virtual independence from the Sultan.

The architecture is an eclectic mix of Selçuk, late-Ottoman, Persian, Armenian and Georgian elements. The elegance of the 40-room harem and the sophistication of the stone carvings indicate an astonishing level of wealth

eastern Anatolia. The dominant sight along its coast is the snow-streaked cone of the Süphan Daği, at 4,058 meters the second-highest mountain in Turkey, mirrored in the deep-blue waters of the lake. The self-contained region which surrounds it flourished under a succession of cultures, and hides a wealth of historic sights.

The modern city of **Van** is built near the site of ancient Tushpa, the capital of a kingdom which was a contemporary and rival of Assyria. The Urartian state rose to eminence in the reign of Menua (810-786 BC) and fell to the Iranian Medes around 590 BC. At its fullest extent it controlled all of the eastern highlands from the Pontic mountains to the borderland of Iraq.

The **Citadel** of the Urartian kings crowns the great rock of Van, which commands the lake from a splendid height a few kilometers west of the modern city.

Old Van, situated at the foot of the rock, was completely destroyed during World War I when its predominantly Armenian population revolted against Turkish rule. Only the minaret of the Great Mosque, built by an emir of the Karakoyunlu dynasty in the 1390s, and a pair of attractive medieval *türbes* (tombs) stand intact among the rubble of the razed city. The new city is notable only for an active bazaar which excels in the tribal carpets and *kilims* of the region's Kurdish clans.

Two of the most interesting Urartian sites in Turkey are located, respectively,

and taste.

The ruins which cover the hillside near the castle belong to old Beyazit, which was destroyed by the Turkish air force in the course of a Kurdish rebellion in 1930.

Around Lake Van

Lake Van, by far the largest lake in Turkey, lies at an altitude of 1,646 meters ringed by the majestic mountains of

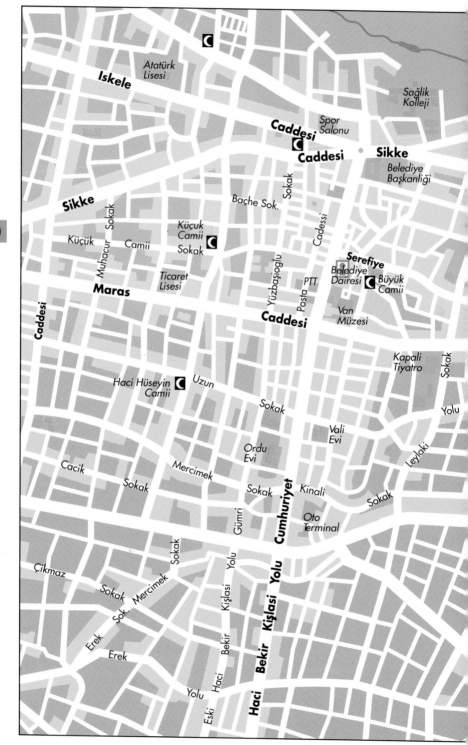

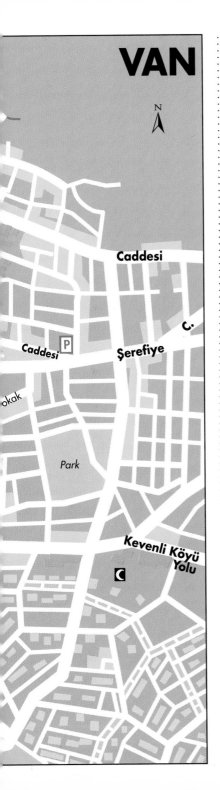

VAN

N

Caddesi

Caddesi

P

Şerefiye

C.

okak

Park

Kevenli Köyü
Yolu

C

at the royal citadels of **Toprakkale**, 3km northeast of Van, and **Çavuştepe**, near the town of şüvuştepe 23 kilometers south of the city. Not far from the latter site is the **Castle of Hoşap**, a formidable citadel built in 1643 by Sarı ("Blond") Süleyman Bey, a Kurdish warlord.

An equally fascinating monument stands on the **Isle of Ahtamar**, a short distance off the southeastern shore of the lake (ferry from Gevaş Iskelesi, 5km west of Gevaş). In the 10th and early 11th centuries, this island formed a stronghold of the Armenian kings of Vaspurakan, a rival dynasty to the Bagratids of Ani.

The **Church of the Holy Cross**, one of the greatest works of medieval Armenian architecture, was built in **Ahtamar** by King Gagik I of Vaspurakan in AD 915-21.

Today, the church stands abandoned but intact. Its most unusual feature is the great wealth of figural and ornamental sculpture which decorates its exterior. Friezes depict in a naive yet elaborate style a variety of real or imaginary creatures and Biblical scenes, including a remarkable Adam and Eve, and a series of quaint scenes from the life of Jonah.

Tatvan, the railroad terminal and ferry port at the southwestern corner of the lake, is dominated by the great mass of **Nemrut Daği** (2,935 meters), one of the two famous mountains bearing this name in eastern Turkey.

The mountain is an extinct volcano most recently recorded active in the 16th

Snow-capped peaks and cool waters greet the observer along the eastern shores.

century. Its crater, one of the world's largest with a diameter of 7km, contains an extraordinary crater lake set at 2,400m above the sea level, or 800m above the level of Lake Van. A dusty but drivable path leads over the edge of the caldera to the shore of the crater lake, where a little outdoor teashop has been set up.

Some 40km northeast of Tatvan and not far from the town of Ahlat are the ruins of medieval **Ahlat**, a key Muslim stronghold under a succession of Arab, Kurdish and Turkish dynasties. The highlight of the ruins is more than a dozen monumental tombs which constitute one of the finest collections of pre-Ottoman *türbe* (tomb) architecture in Anatolia.

The largest and most magnificen mausoleum was built in 1273 for Selçuk emir; others belong to a princes of the Karakoyunlu Turks and a ruler o the Akkoyunlu – rival dynasties o Türkmen nomads which built short-lived empires in the 14th and 15th centurie covering eastern Anatolia, Iran and Transcaucasia.

The old Muslim Cemetery which lies nearby is described by one author as "surely one of the most romantically beautiful graveyards in the world ... a veritable petrified forest of lichen-cov ered gravestones dating back to Selçuk times".

Bitlis, another town of a strikingly historic character, is set in a wild gorge controlling the land route between the

Lush verdant greenery stretches as far as the eye can see in the east.

'an basin and the plains of Upper Mesopotamia. Its citadel is of Hellenistic and
Byzantine origin; the **Ulucami**, built in
123, is one of the oldest Turkish
mosques in Anatolia.

Southeastern Borderlands

A broad arc of mountains – the eastern
spur of the Taurus – separates the eastern high plateau from the arid plain in
the south, an extension of the Syrian
desert. The plain is watered by the Tigris
(Dicle) and Euphrates (Fırat) rivers,
which carry the overflow of the Eastern
Anatolian mountains into Iraq and
Syria, ultimately joining the Persian
Gulf.

The cities of the region are among
the oldest in Turkey, originating for the
most part in the ancient civilizations of
the Near East, in the 3rd millenium BC
or earlier.

Situated at the crossroads of the
ancient Orient, their roots are mercantile and polyglot, and they have stronger
traditions of urban autonomy than the
cities of Anatolia proper. They keep a
distinctly medieval flavor in the organization of their bazaars, the architecture
of their buildings, the dress of their inhabitants, the power of their religious
institutions and the feudal structure of
their rural countryside.

A combination of factors, however,
has begun to bring rapid change to the
region. The Turkish government has

A lone building in Akhtamar Island, Lake Van.

pursued since the 1970s an ambitious hydro-power program which envisages tapping the waters of the Euphrates and Tigris with a series of huge dams and irrigation systems: this has altered employment patterns, displaced large numbers of rural people whose lands are inundated by dams, and caused them to flock to cities in search of jobs. Guerrilla warfare has been another cause of mass migration to urban centers, while a large army presence has riddled cities with huge and conspicuous military intallations.

Worst affected is **Diyarbakir**, whose population quadrupled to half a million in two decades. Its walls nevertheless stand intact for almost their entire length of over 5km, a tremendous ring

of black basalt rising in the desertlike plain.

Among the oldest and most impressive in Turkey, they were originally built by the Roman Empire, rebuilt after the capture of the city by the Selçuks in 1088, and restored with the addition of new bastions by a local Artukid emir in 1208.

The most interesting sight in the city is the **Ulucami**, the very first example of Turkish monumental architecture in Anatolia that was founded by Sultan Melikşah in 1091 and expanded on various occasions later on. The building incorporates the fully intact façade of a Roman theatre to grand and unusual effect.

Mardin retains the fabulous ap-

earance of a medieval Arab city, with
s old houses of intricately ornamented
tone forming an infinite maze of al-
ys, archways and hidden courtyards.
ost in various parts of this uncharted
abyrinth are a large number of Muslim
nonuments, built in the most part by a
uccession of dynasties between the 12th
nd 16th centuries, as well as a dozen
ncient churches belonging to as many
:hristian denominations.

Uniquely among all cities in Tur-
ey, a Christian minority formed the
lominant element of Mardin's society
until they were displaced by the up-
leavals of the last years. The Syriac
Jacobite) church split from Greek Or-
hodoxy over the doctrinal disputes of
he fifth century, and in the Middle Ages
played a key role in transferring Byzan-
ine culture to the Arabs and Muslim
earning to the West. Today's Syriac
ommunity speaks its own Semitic language (Suryani), a derivative of old Ara-
naic, although Arabic is more com-
nonly used in conducting daily busi-
 less.

The historic seat of the Jacobite
Patriarchate is the monastery of **Deyr-
Zaferan**, an ancient walled complex
ocated 5 kilometers east of Mardin. The
nonastery is still active, although the
patriarch no longer resides in Turkey.
An active monastery of still more ar-
:haic character, **Mar Gabriel**, is situated near the town of Nusaybin in the
outheast. Other Syriac communities
exist in **Midyat** and **Kiziltepe**.

The latter town is distinguished also

*Detail of Saint George on
Akhtamar Church, Lake Van.*

for the dramatic ruins of a 12th century
Ulucami, and the fortress-like residence
– Atli Kanco – of the Türk clan, one of the
most powerful Kurdish feudal families
of the region.

The bazaar of **Urfa** is one of the
most ancient and picturesque in Turkey, both for its wealth of merchandise
– fed by the contraband trade with Syria
– and the colorful character of its inhabitants: it is the only market in Turkey
where men can be seen in the flowing
robes of desert Arabs and horsemen are
still allowed to trot into the historic
Covered Bazaar.

A city named *Urha* already existed
here in the age of Babylon and Assyria;
under the name of *Edessa* it became the
seat of a post-Hellenistic kingdom whose

An old fortification set on the edge of a precipice.

king, Abgar of Edessa, is credited with receiving from Christ a miraculous shroud stamped with the holy visage. Roman rule was followed by Byzantine, Persian, Arab, Byzantine again, Syriac, Turkish and Armenian. In 1098, Edessa fell to the Crusaders under Baldwin of Flanders and became the seat of a feudal County; 46 years later it was taken by Imadeddin Zengi, the Turkish emir of Mosul who founded a short-lived empire controlling all of Syria and upper Iraq. The great Saladin, the Selçuks, Mongol Ilkhans, Egyptian Mamluks, the

A religious enclave in Urfa, Medreseh.

Karakoyunlu and Akkoyunlu Türkmens succeeded each other in the city until the Ottoman conquest of 1516.

The splendid **Ulucami** of Urfa, modeled on the Great Mosque of Aleppo, is mostly a Zengid work (AD 1180, built in part over a medieval church). Zengid emirs are also responsible for the mosque Halil Rahman Camii, 1211) and ar-

cades of the sacred complex of **Makami-Ibrahim**, an important site of pilgrimage for Muslims. This sanctuary marks the birthplace of Abraham, which Quranic belief places in a sacred cave in Urfa (the Hebrew patriarch is honored by Islam as the first prophet of monotheistic religion). Its centerpiece is the Pool of Abraham, a large rectangular reservoir fed by a natural spring and filled with thousands of sacred carp. No one is allowed to catch the fish, which are said to have been born of the flames of the fire that the evil king Nimrod lit to roast the holy patriarch.

Another site connected with Abraham is **Harran**, a town 50km southeast of Urfa: here, according to the Old Testament, the patriarch dwelled until

Another dusty day in East Turkey.

the age of 75 during the course of his wandering from Ur of the Chaldees to the promised land of Canaan.

The city known as *Carrhae* (Harran) flourished under the Roman and Arab empires: Crassus, the third member of the Triumvirate besides Caesar and Pompey, was defeated and killed in Carrhae by the Parthians, and Caracalla was assassinated here in AD217.

Under Marwan II of the Umayyads (AD 744-750) Harran briefly became the capital of the Muslim Caliphate, an empire stretching from Spain to Central Asia. Today it lies in ruins, inhabited by a few hundred wretched bedouins. Their houses are built of mud-adobe and are topped with conical domes which look like giant beehives.

The Mountain of Nimrod

No place is better suited to end a tour of Turkey on a grand and awesome note than **Nemrut Daği**, a mountain at the northern edge of the Mesopotamian Plain whose desolate summit is the setting for one of the most extravagant monuments ever erected to glorify royal vanity.

Starting point for the day-long journey to Nemrut Daği is the Kurdish town of **Kahta**, 145 kilometers north of Urfa. A partially paved route follows a tributary of the Euphrates into a wild mountain landscape.

A series of ancient ruins lie along the way, such as the wonderfully pre

An eagle's head in magnificent close-up in Nemrut Dag.

erved Roman bridge of **Cendere**, and he tumulus of **Karakuş** where a group f pillars surmounted by statues marks he burial site of the queens and prinesses of Commagene. The village of .skikahta (Old Kahta) is set at the foot f a medieval fortress and the ruins of \rsameia, the capital of the ancient .ingdom of Commagene. A magnifient relief discovered among the ruins hows Mithridates I Kallinikos, a king of Commagene, shaking hands with Hercules. The road gets worse after this oint, until at length the great Commagene **Tumulus** of Antiochus ecomes visible on a 2,200 meters peak.

Antiochus, who calls himself "Great King, God-made-manifest, the Right-ous, the Romanophile and Helleno-phile" reigned in the first century BC over a kingdom which was created by his father and which perished not long after his death.

Through his mother he was related to the Seleucids, the greatest of the Hellenistic dynasties founded by Alexander's followers, while on his father's side he claimed descent from the ancient Persian royal line. He thus represented a fusion of the imperial traditions of the East and West in his person: his tomb is a monument of cultural syncretism that brings together elements of both Greek and Persian art and religion.

The tumulus consists of a conical pile of loose shale some 50 meters high and 150 meters in diameter. The king is probably buried under this man-made hill, although all efforts to reach his tomb have so far failed.

Two terraces occupy the east and west side, respectively, of the base of the tumulus; each bears the colossal seated statues of five deities flanked by the equally gigantic figures of two lions and two eagles. Toppled long ago by earthquakes, their heads lie scattered on the ground, each as tall as a man. They represent an amalgam of eastern and western gods: one combines Apollo and Mithra, the Persian sun-god; another is identified as Zeus-Ahuramazda, father of Greek and Zoroastrian gods; Antiochus himself is shown enthroned among gods, wearing a Persian hat but sporting a beardless face in the Greek manner.

Fragments of his inscription proclaim (in Greek) that he "undertook to make this place a common throne-room of all the gods", and that he rests here in "the heroic company of my ancestors". A Persian fire altar faces the direction of the rising sun. The view from the top of Nemrut Daai is most extraordinary at sunrise and sunset, when the gods are illuminated by a strange and startling light and the landscape of vast, bald, lonely mountains takes on a grandeur suitable indeed for the gods. This, then, is a good place to reflect for a last time on a country which for many thousands of years has stood at the cross-currents of West and East, whose soil is rife with the memories of countless kings and nations and saturated with the miracles of many gods and saints.

Scene of countless photographs – Nemrut Dag.

Cuisine

The existence of abundant, varied and cheap food is one of the greatest joys of traveling in a foreign country, and in this respect Turkey scores near the top of the world league. Do not expect *haute cuisine*: sophisticated cooking is hard to come across in Turkey except at a few pricey establishments in the big cities or at luxury hotels – or if you get invited to dinner at someone's home. The typical restaurant is often an informal place where your table may not be entirely free of leftover crumbs and where a cat will always be present to share the scraps off your plate. Service will almost certainly lack finesse, if never courtesy. Yet, the food is invariably tasty and there is something new to discover at every meal.

The higher traditions of the Turkish kitchen and restaurant culture originate in Istanbul, the cosmopolitan capital of the Ottoman Empire. They have declined along with so

243

Melons for sale at a local market.

A platter full of marzipan delicacies.

much else in Turkish culture, yet they have left behind enough residue, enough hints of class and memories of tradition to please the most discriminating epicure. Similar culinary traditions are found throughout the former Ottoman realms from the Balkans to the Middle East and North Africa. But in terms of both quality and sophistication, the old adage still holds: the nearer one is to Istanbul the better.

The ingredients of Turkish cuisine are not exotic, the tastebuds are kept titillated by the freshness of the food

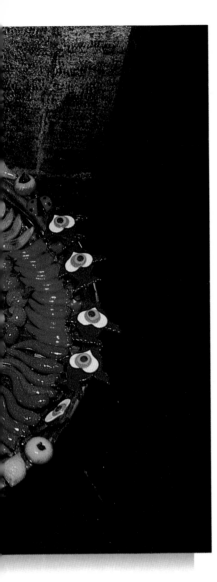

cious specialties. Game is for all practical purposes unavailable, and innards, except for such classics as *Işkembe çorbasi* (tripe soup) and *kelle* (grilled lamb's head) have quite disappeared from the culinary scene. Contrary to widespread belief, Turkish food is not spicy: peppery dishes are uncommon except in the regional cuisine of the Southeast in Adana, Urfa and Gaziantep).

A Full Meal

The most common type of restaurant, which is known as *içkili lokanta* or *meyhane,* emulates the style and lore of old Istanbul taverns. The main meal served at such establishments is simply prepared fish or meats. But, far more important is the immense selection of *meze, (hors d'oeuvre)* that are served first. One always starts with half a dozen plates of cold *meze,* continues with a potpourri of warm *mezes,* orders the main dish after the first hour or so, and end up with dessert, followed by fruit and coffee. A meal that lasts less than three hours is considered hasty!

Raki a potent anise-flavored liquor distilled from grapes, is the drink prescribed by custom, but wine and beer are also served. Some restaurants encourage the intake of alcohol downed to the accompaniment of live music: croaky plump ladies with dyed-blonde hair in classier places and gypsy strummers in seedier taverns. The atmosphere in such places can get quite jolly with advanc-

and interesting combinations rather than by unusual flavors. The basic ingredients are: fish, lamb, beef and poultry. Vegetables are used to a larger extent than in most other national cuisines; whether in pot meals with little or no meat, or cooked simply in oil and served cold. The vegetable dishes constitute a surprisingly rich category of delicious specialties.

Fresh mussels for sale along the road in Marmaris.

ing hours, but getting noisily drunk is considered very shoddy behavior in any setting and the maintainance of a certain *gravitas* in public is the quintessential Turkish instinct.

Incidentally wine, was invented in central Anatolia some 4,000 years ago from where it later spread to Greece and Italy. Nowadays, it is not widely consumed by Turks, but what does exist is remarkably good as far as table wines go. Two brands, *Kavaklidere* and *Doluca*, dominate the market for both red and white. Look out for *Kavaklidere Selection*

Fresh seafood is a popular choice for most epicures.

or Doluca if you are serious about your wine. *Nevşah, Efsane* and *Primeur* come next on the ladder of quality, while *Çankaya* (white) and *Villa Doluca* (red or white) are more common but still quite acceptable.

Meze & More

It is the wealth and quality of its *meze* that sets a good restaurant apart from the mediocre. The repertoire is almost endless. Seasoned raki-drinkers believe that the classic bean salads, *piyaz* and *pilaki* form the noblest accompaniment to a bottle of "lion's milk". A *dolma* is virtually anything (grape leaves, cabbage, mussels, mackerel) stuffed with a cinnamon-flavored mixture of rice, onions, currants and nuts. Shrimp and octopus salads are expensive and rarely good, while brain salad may not appeal to everyone. Surprisingly tasty are the various vegetable dips: *patlican salatasi,* (mashed aubergine), *humus* (mashed chick peas) and *fava* (broadbean puree). Nowadays *topik,* an old Istanbul specialty, is rarely found in restaurants neither is *çerkes tavuğu,* an altogether heavenly dish of chicken in a walnut and garlic sauce, while the consumption of *biberli ezme,* a southeastern concoction made of peppers, walnut and condiments, has now grown fashionable.

Seafood treats include the delicious *hamsi* (sour pickled anchovy), the *lakerd*

Fresh döner kebab in Bodrum.

the pan): standard *börek* filling include cheese, mincemeat and spinach *pastirma böreği*, containing a spicy vari ety of smoked beef, is delicious in th eating but leaves you stinking for th next 24 hours! *karides güveç* (shrimp casserole) is a novelty and varies ir quality from mediocre to heavenly, whil *arnavut ciğeri* (fried liver "Albaniar style") is now regarded as old fashioned *Köfte* can be eaten either as *meze* or as a main course: it consists of spiced meat balls and comes in a dozen differen varieties; finally *balik köftesi*, made o minced fishmeat, is a rarity that shoulc not be passed.

Fish Food

There may be a temptation to quit after the first dozen dishes, but the real high light of the meal is yet to come. Invari ably the salient eating experience for most visitors to Turkey, especially in coastal areas, is the fish. The delicious flavour of charcoal grilled fish is often a revelation to palates long trained on the cardboard-flavored denizens of the northern seas.

The species of fish are too numer ous to count and it is often best to leave the choice to your waiter, but a few points bear keeping in mind. First, every fish has a season: *kalkan* (turbot) is best in early summer, *lüfer* (bluefish) is fat test in mid-summer, *palamut* (baby tuna) and *uskumru* (mackerel) appear in Au gust and *hamsi* (anchovy) are abundant

(smoked bluefish) and the *çiroz* (sun– dried mackeral) which has the consist ency of wood and is merciless on your teeth.

Eggplant (aubergine) comes in vari ous shapes and is served in a variety of forms: simply fried, with tomato-garlic- vinegar sauce or, in the form of *imam bayildi*, (a splendid mix with onions, green peppers and garlic). Pickled beet root is a staple. For local specialties try Antalya's *hibeş*, (a mixture of mustard and sesame paste) and Antakya's fresh thyme salad.

In the field of warm *meze*, the all- time favourites are *midye* (batter-fried mussels) and *kalamar* (squid). Another obligatory item is *börek* (anything wrapped in pastry dough and fried in

A family eating from a communal platter.

in winter. Secondly, prices vary widely according to the season and type of fish: *barbunya* (red mullet) can be 20 times more expensive than the lowly *istavrit* although it is not necessarily tastier; so make sure you ask for the prices before you order. Thirdly, waiters sometimes do not condescend to mention small inexpensive varieties like *istavrit, hamsi* and *gümüş* (smelts): asking for them by name may save a lot of money.

Generally, fish is grilled or fried and served whole – head, tail and all. The *buğulama* (fish stew) is often unaccountably expensive and the old–fashioned fish soup made with *kirlangıç* or *iskorpit* has become harder to find outside certain venerable seamen's taverns in Istanbul.

The Kebab Family

The art of dressing and cooking meat remains surprisingly underdeveloped for a country with a rich pastoral background: meats are generally badly cut and overgrilled to the point where they taste rather like carbonized leather.

More interesting are the various *kebabs*, which are available in most restaurants but are represented with a better selection in specialized *kebab* houses. *şiş kebab* and *döner kebab* have become familiar at streetcorners around the world thanks to Turkish and Greek entrepreneurs. *Bursa kebabi* consists of slices of döner smothered in yogurt and tomato sauce; *adana kebabi* is a deadly

Streetside bread is one of the more healthy street treats.

combination of mincemeat and red peppers grilled on a skewer; *sac kebabi,* also known as *kavurma,* is a casserole of lamb bits and vegetables sauteed on high heat; *kağit kebabi* is the same thing except that it is baked and wrapped in paper; *patlican kebabi* is baked lamb served with eggplant puree, whilst *orman kebabi* is laced with thyme. The ultimate delicacy of the *kebab* family comes in the form of *tandir kebab* (also called *kuyu kebabi)* which is a whole lamb left to bake on charcoal embers in a special earthen well cemented with clay. And while on the topic of meats, how could one forget *koç yumurtasi* (the polite term for grilled ram's testicles)?

The usual accompaniment to *kebab* is rice *pilav,* which is sometimes elabo-rated into *iç pilav* with the addition of meat stock, bits of innard, pine nuts, currants and cinnamon. *Bulgur pilav* substitutes cracked wheat for rice. Customers always have the prerogative of asking for a spoonful of *fasulya* (beans) or *nohut* (chick peas) to top their plate of rice.

Humble Wonders

The unsung stars of the Turkish restaurant culture are the *lokanta* or *hazır yemek lokantasi* (pot–meal restaurants) which are typically found clustered in the bazaar district, near the bus terminal, or annexed to highway service stations. They offer a variety of home-style dishes which are displayed in the service area for patrons to inspect and choose from.

It is entirely acceptable to ask for a taste before making a choice, and most cooks will gladly combine a bit of this and a ladleful of that for your convenience. Each dish normally costs about US$2, and a full meal will rarely exceed US$5. Some establishments carry beer, although most working man's eating-shops are owned by Muslims who frown on the consumption of spirits.

For those who are in a hurry, streetside food vendors and fast food outlets offer a wide range of alternatives from *büfe* (sandwich shops) to American-style hamburger and pizza parlors. Adventurous souls may test the limits of their digestive system on *kokoreç* (grilled lamb's intestines), or *lahmacun*, (the Turkish version of pizza containing a heavy dose of half-cooked onions). Some may venture as far as *çiğ köfte*, (raw mincemeat ground to a pulp with pepper and spices) and *çöp şiş*, (lamb scraps grilled on a reed skewer), which reigns supreme in the streets of mid-Aegean towns, notably in Selçuk.

It should not come as a surprise that the most popular way to water down any of the above is with a can of good old–fashioned Coca Cola, although one could also choose from a wide selection of *meyve suyu* (bottled fruit juices) or *ayran* (a highly refreshing beverage made from watered-down and lightly salted yogurt). A characteristic of the Adana region is *şalgam suyu* (fermented beetroot juice), decidedly an acquired taste.

Sinful Sweets

Turks are unrepentant sweet-toothed. The celebrated *lokum* (Turkish Delight) is likely to prove a disappointment except in certain Istanbul establishments (notably Haci Bekir and Divan) and around the town of Afyon.

Nevertheless enough other sinfully sweet specialties exist to tempt the most tooth-conscious of human beings. *Baklava* is the standard pastry dessert: it comes in variety of shades (pistachio or walnut filling, milk or chocolate dough), and is best made by inhabitants from the southeastern towns of Gaziantep and Diyarbakir.

Other variations on the theme of crusty pastry in oozy syrup include *tel kadayif, tulumba tatlisi, lokma, bülbül yuvasi* ("nightin'gale's nest") *vezir parmaği* ("vizier's finger"), *kadin göbeği* ("lady's navel"), *revani* and *kemalpaşa tatlisi;* they are best enjoyed with a dollop of *kaymak* (thickened cream). For the ultimate dessert treat if you ever end up in the vicinity of Afyon, try the *kaymakli ekmek kadayifi.*

Helva is the generic name for a class of denser sweets. Besides the ubiquitous *tahin helvasi* which are based on sesame oil and sugar, the family includes *irmik helvasi* and *pişmaniye,* a specialty of the town of Izmit, which has the consistency of fiberglass wool. Dairy-based puddings form another large category in which *sütlaç* (a type of rice pudding), and *tavuk göğsü* (a milk dessert containing fine fibers of chicken breast), deserve mention. More recent additions to the dessert repertoire of better restaurants include *ayva* tatlisi (baked quinces served with *kaymak*), and *muz tatlisi* (bananas fried in honey and ground walnut).

Fruits are in abundance and so are the various marmalades and jams made from them. Apart from the usual varieties served at breakfast, one may try more exotic sorts like the rose petal marmalade of Isparta and the watermelon rind, date, fig and eggplant marmalades of Antalya. *Güllaç*, (a delicate traditional dessert made of rice starch, milk and the essence of roses), is normally only available during the month of *Ramazan*.

Rabbit Blood

Although "Turkish coffee" may be a more familiar concept, most Turks prefer to conclude their meal with a glass of tea! They also start the day, conduct business, express hospitality, relax and while away their spare time with a glass of tea.

A village may lack a grocery shop, but it never lacks a teahouse; no alley in the bazaar is without its teashop tucked under a gateway; nor can any office hope to maintain good employee relations without a tea-man on its payroll. Long distance buses stop every hour or two for a tea-break, and it is routine courtesy to offer a cup of tea to the customer haggling for rugs or the motorist waiting for a repair job. While 10 cups of tea a day is normal for the average Turk; 20 is definitely the mark of an intense and hyperactive man.

Tea is always carefully brewed, with water boiling in one pot and a dense infusion steeping just under the boiling point in another: not for Turks the vulgar teabag plopped in lukewarm water! At its best, tea is supposed to sport a

A traditional Turkish wine pourer trying to lighten his load.

noble hue known as "rabbit's blood" which is of a deep, dark and transparent red. To show its color, it is always served in a glass. The shape of the glass is also important, with the peculiar "tulip" form meant for ease of holding (try handling a normal glass full of hot tea). Regional characteristics also count: the Black Sea province of Rize, which produces all of Turkey's tea, is often accused of keeping the best vintages for local consumption.

In the East, where every man is a connoisseur of tea, it is considered barbaric to sweeten it with dissolved sugar, instead one holds a lump of rock sugar inside one's cheek and enjoys the clash of tastes as bitter tea meets the slowly seeping sweetness. Tea is for Turkey what wine is to the French: a national symbol, a lifestyle embodying the distilled essence of a culture.

Turkey is well and truly a Pandora's box of shopping treasures and a land of ardent entrepreneurs. The long avenues of the covered bazaars are lined with a multiplicity of family owned stores selling everything from carpets to copperware. It is indeed hard not to buy a souvenir in Turkey where there are so many classic and traditional buys and above all enthusiastic salesmen that you the tourist must only take care that the buys you make are indeed "bargains" and the goods as authentic as the salesmen claim.

A salesman displaying a swatch of fabric at a bazaar in Istanbul.

The currency in Turkey is the *lira* which has a very high inflation rate, inflating against the stable currencies at a rate of 2.5 per cent. You will therefore have to gauge the standard price of things on your arrival to make a realistic judgement on fair prices. It is extremely useful to have a number of small coins especially

Tourists and locals alike thronging the marketplace for eatables and souvenirs.

of the 25, 50 and 100 TL denominations, lower values are of little use. Payment can be made by cash, Eurocheques, travellers' cheques or visa. Traveller's cheques and cash appear to be the best methods of payment; when paying by credit card you will probably have to pay the fee that the credit card company will charge the shop-keeper; when cashing Eurocheques some discount will be made but there will be no commission charge.

The main places to shop in Turkey are the covered bazaars; these are in

compete furiously with each other and will undertake all sorts of business gimmicks to encourage purchasers, especially since in a particular avenue of an arcade most shops are selling the same goods.

Expect all kinds of flattery to encourage you to look at a stall, there is no need to be rude in response but be discerning and non-committed until you are certain you want to buy something only then should the bargaining begin. Other shops are small shops and flea markets, the latter of which can be found in the Kuledibi, Carsikapi, Üskador and Topkapi districts in Istanbul. High class shops include **Istiklal** and **Caddesi**.

Bargaining is standard practice in Turkey's street stalls and bazaars and most store owners will enjoy a bit of mischief, often fixing ridulous prices to allow for an enjoyable haggle. If you are going to take the initiative in bargaining begin at a lower price than you are prepared to pay, and remember that once a price has been agreed upon you are morally obliged to pay it. The most important thing is to be relaxed and enjoy the process yourself without losing control over your money.

Classical Carpets

The most classic purchase in Turkey, is of course a carpet. The best place to buy carpets and *kilims* (pileless carpet) are in Istanbul, but not in the covered bazaar. Popular varieties include the Islamic

fact medieval Ottoman shopping malls and are divided into arcades each of which deals with a specific trade. The most famous covered bazaar is the **Grand Bazaar** in Istanbul.

The government discourages monopolies and therefore small successful shops and stalls are disallowed to merge in order to expand, consequently stalls

A carpet merchant in Istanbul holding one of his best rugs.

prayer rug which has a representation of the place in the mosque where the position of Mecca is fixed. Kar rugs have geometrical designs. *Cicim* carpets are *kilims* with designs on them. Kayseri silk and wool rugs have floral patterns on them. When choosing a carpet there are

a number of things to look for the most important being the tightness of the weave. A tight weave will ensure good durability and you should ask how many knots there are per square centimetre. Check the warp of the weave which should be wool and not cotton. *Hereke*

An aged saleswoman waiting for the next customer.

silk rugs have approximately 36 knots per square cm and are of a good quality. Next look at the colouring, where you should ascertain animal rather than any detrimental chemical concoctions. Take a damp cloth if possible and rub on the carpet if the colour smudges then natural dyes are not being used.If the colours are brighter at the surface of the carpet than at the base of the pile the carpet is not of a good quality.

An authentic carpet such as those you see in the museums and those very expensive shops will maintain the original tone of the colour for years. To guarantee that you buy a carpet made with natural dyes, buy your carpet from DOBAG Projesi – a natural dyes Research and Development project which

has a store in Ayracik. DOBAG Projesi labels elsewhere may not be genuine as there is a huge market for fake goods.

Using these basic rules, you should leave Turkey with a carpet of a beautiful shade and hue – of your own personal aesthetic taste – and if you managed to buy a good quality carpet it should outlive you.

Leather & Suede

Leather is a traditional Turkish industry, mainly centred around Izmir and Istanbul, again especially in the Grand Bazaar. Raw hide shoes, jackets, gloves,trousers and cushions and many more small items are all available smell-

Peddlars plying some trinkets to tourists.

ing beautifully fresh.

Turkish leather is found all over the world, a pair of shoes is a particularly good buy knowing how much you would pay for the same product in the shops of northern Europe and elsewhere.

Leatherware can be made-to-measure but make sure that it is clear you are not committing yourself to the finished product as these are often rushed jobs.

Jewellery & Clothing

Turkish design is entering an era of international recognition. Rifat Ozbek has become a well known designer, his clothes having a distinctive oriental and exotic appeal. *Haute Couture* is cheaper in Turkey than the rest of Europe, as are less high quality designs, you can tailor a suit for US$100 in Turkey which when seen in comparison with northern Europe, is really very cheap.

Moreover, Turkey is known for its textiles which are of a high quality and workmanship. Bursa silk and Angora wool are favoured textiles. Bursa is also famous for its towels and bathrobes and much of Turkey for its laced cotton blouses and other items. **Vakko** and **Beymers** are two of Istanbul's top boutiques.

Turkish jewellery is increasing in fashion value and can make as fun gift. When buying – it can be found in most markets– ask for the price of gold and shop around to see how genuine this price is before deciding whether it is worth the extra expense.

There is a lot of fake jewellery around but look out for the beautiful amber and turquoise semi-precious stones especially. A certain amount will be charged for labour costs – again see what the market price is for the stone itself, but beware, a dirt-cheap price may indicate that the stone is not genuine.

Copperware

What could be more Turkish than a copper *samovar*? Used very little by the modern generation these are still classic gift-ideas and found in abundance.

Intricate copperware on display.

Other copper items such as pots, pans and cauldrons may also be found in the bazaars of Eastern Anatolia especially.

Modern copperware is of a lighter weight than traditional copperware but the important thing is if you are going to utilize these products, for cooking is that they must have a tin lining inside.

If you like an item but it does not have a tin lining you can usually have one put in by a shop nearby, ask the proprietor for details.

Ceramics

Beautiful ceramics are one of the major art forms in Turkey, which decorate many of the best known buildings, such as the Blue Mosque in Istanbul. most of these "art pieces" will have come from the kilns of Iznik, which is now reviving

A roadside scene in Bodrum along the Turkish coast.

he industry after many years in decline. Another major centre is Kîtahya where he tile factory sells a great variety of iles for souvenirs ideal to decorate the ireside. Alabaster is a famous Cappadocion product, centred on the towns of Ürgüp and Aranos. Alabaster ware consists of some beautiful vases, chess sets, ashtrays and many other small items, a mark of authenticity is that when you hold it up to the light the light should shine through it.

Handicrafts

Turkish handicrafts are intricately made. A good example would be a *tarla* (backgammon) set which may be plain or inlaid. Inlaid materials include pearls and silver. Cigarette boxes and other paraphernalia are also meticulously and delicately crafted. Again check for authenticity.

Musical instruments are slightly more original purchases the most traditional being the *Saza*, Turkish long necked lute, the *ney*, a Turkish flute and the *Daral*, a Turkish drum. For true pipe smokers, *meerschaum* pipes are one of lifes' great mellowers. The white substance turns a deep nut brown as its pores absorb the tobacco. *Meershaum* deposits are found in the Eşkişehir area of Turkey, especially in the Eşkişehir caves where they are moulded into various shapes and sizes. Since the Turks do not make much use of the pipes, they should be much cheaper than elsewhere.

Food & Film

Foodstuffs are really not generally very convenient souvenirs but there are a few good alternatives to kebabs. Turkey is the home to smyma figs, pistachio, walnuts, hazelnuts and sultana raisins. Try to squeeze a few of these delight into your suitcase or savour them during your travels.

Photographic film can be bought easily provided you are not too fussy about brands. Fuji® is the cheapest kind of film and the most easily available. Nation-wide chain stores are the best places to have your prints developed safely.

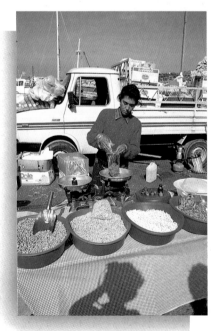

Turkish tidbits for sale.

From the spectacle of brawney young men wrestling in oil to waterskiing along a sun-kissed Mediterranean beach, Turkey has a considerable amount to offer both the casual exerciser and the sports enthusiast. All the "European" sports are available with the addition of specifically local ones such as camel wrestling, which are not merely a sport but a spectacle and cultural education in themselves. Sport in Turkey is certainly on the move, the influx of tourism and the growing prosperity of the economy introducing new and varied sports.

Even small villages are beginning to acquire their own volleyball and basketball courts so that sport may sprout and be nurtured at a grass roots level though facilities in many other sports are still rather scarce. For every sportsman and sportswoman in Turkey there is one moment in sporting history which they all

Sailboats moored at Orhaniye along the Turkish coast.

Sports & Recreation

265

Standing room only at a football match in Istanbul.

hold dear, that of the 1988 Olympic games when Niam Suleymanoglu clean and jerked to weight lifting gold. This moment has been repeated numerous times on Turkish television and has filled the hearts of many with aspirations for the future.

Soccer

The Turks certainly do not lack enthusiasm, they are a passionate people and this does not side-track in their attitude towards sport. The three most popular

The main teams are the Istanbul ones, three in paricular; Besiktas, Galatasaray and Fenerbahçe, the provincial sides of Trabzonspor, Adanaspor and Konyaspor are also popular. The top teams do have foreign players but they are limited to a maximum of two per team.

If you do chose to watch a soccer match live, beware. Hooliganism has not yet reached the proportions of certain areas in northern Europe, but the Turkish spirit is such that maniac excitement spreads in waves. It is not unknown for the vanquished side to be attacked by its own supporters after a game, on the other hand victories are delirious occasions, the streets being jammed with the cars of celebrating fans klaxoning interminably while waving their team's fans. The jam is likely to continue into the sunset.

Thankfully supporters tend to be less inebriated than their comrades in northern Europe, but charges of bribery and corruption are rife. So buy your ticket from a reputable source and hold on to it. Having said all this, to immerse yourself in the real atmosphere of a Turkish soccer match, will be undoubtedly an exciting experience, and will really open your eyes to this love of the Turkish people.

For an even more juicy and authentic Turkish spectacle, attend a wrestling match. It is a sport which has almost become a ritual and is especially popular in rural Turkey. Posters go up weeks in advance to announce the upcoming great *güreş* and the venue is some grassy

sports are basketball, wrestling and soccer, but the latter is their greatest love, in fact soccer is a national obsession. Since the 1910s their have been organized clubs and now these clubs compete in weekly meets that kick the nation into a frenzy. Every reasonable size town has a soccer stadium and every Saturday or Sunday afternoon crowds flock to them.

patch outside the town. Hordes of bar-becue-grillers and kebab sellers take up their stands on the morning of the games, women arrive in their Sunday reds and best headscarves (forming a wildly colourful enclave of their own) and men pass betting tips and trade large wads of banknotes as fighting is a serious business with both reputations and money at stake.

At Artivin's bullfights, tens of thou-sands descend from around the prov-ince armed with tents, rainshelters and gas stoves and enough *raki* to last every-body for three days. The camel fight is preceded by a late night revel laced with gypsy bands, belly dancer's, much alco-hol and much behind the scenes horse-trading. A rowdy public auction deter-mines who will be the *cazgrzr* (master of ceremonies and the *a 'a* (sponsor) for the next year's games. Overture shows fea-turing fat peroxide-blonde lady singers from the city follow bag pipe players, travelling minstrels, jugglers and little wrestling boys, to warm up the audi-ence to the climax of the day. In the end a good set of games will last for the proverbial three days and three nights whilst the less ambitious one's last a mere two or three days.

Greasy Gladiators

Yaǧi güeş (oil wrestling) is a strictly traditional game in Turkey having no national organization or official rules. The habit of lubricating wrestlers and other athletes with olive oil seems to be as old as the ancient Greeks who per-formed stark naked and immortalized champions with public statues. Today, famous *pehlivans* (wrestlers) travel from town to town in search of cash and glory. Although the champions are rarely featured in the press, they are spread by the grapevine which man-ages to elevate them from local promi-nence to a national star. Many of them later convert their wrestling success into business capital or a political career.

Since 1360 the most celebrated oilwrestling tournament has been held in Edirne's *Kzrkpzna*r fields. Turks from western and southern Turkey are avid wrestlers and thus the vicinity of Antayla is a good place to look out for a tourna-ment.

The event begins when big black cauldrons of oil are brought out to the accompaniment of pipe and drum. Wrestlers put on knee-length leather breeches and parade the field splashing themselves with buckets of olive oil. The *cazgzr* blare non-stop through a bullhorn haranguing the crowd, intro-ducing the divers and taking bets. Fi-nally a hush descends "in the name of God the compassionate, the merciful, O pehlivan! Let the holds be legal and may God guide him of the truest heart to victory. Let the rites begin."

Forty *pehlivans*, shining and glis-tening in the midday sun then throw up their hands in common prayer. To the strains of gypsy pipers they move out into the field in an elaborately choreographed gait, slapping their breeches before pairing off. The rules are simple: no biting, no gouging and no sticking of fingers into any bodily orifice. The winner is the wrestler who can force his opponents shoulder's to the ground or extract a cry of surrender.

An ordinary match will last half an hour or more whilst a good match may last for a full day, although the recent tendency is to impose a time limit on meets. The loser then leaves the field giving the winner only a few minutes in which to rest before facing another opponent, then another and another until only one of the 40 gladiators is left standing. His prize decreed by ancient tradition is a belt stuffed with gold coins.

Animal Machismo

Deve güreş (camel wrestling) is a passion, of the south and west. From the beginning of December each year, a 300-odd contingent of fighter camels riding atop trucks wrapped in warm clothes and accompanied by owners and camel boys tour the Aegean and Mediterranean region from fight to fight. They belong to a noble breed of camels called *tülü*. To them has never fallen the lowly task of hauling loads as by birth and lineage, they are destined to spend their annual mating season (December to March) trying to impress she-camels by their strength and valor!

They begin by impressing a human jury. Before each game a beauty contests (of sorts) is held in which *tülüs* are judged on their individual figures and grace of movement, as well as their finery which consists of tinkling bells, scarves, saddle carpets and the havut (an exquisitely embroidered saddle-bag thrown over the camel's hump). Dignified, with a hint of arrogance in the eye, camels going by the names Emerald, Black Lightning and Small Wolf are led before the jury by a donkey.

In order to avoid injuries in the battlefield their mouths are bound by two independent parties and checked by two others. Crazed by lust, the beasts charge towards each other with fire in their eye and foam on their otherwise gentle lips. Instantly they are so entangled that to the untrained eye it is impossible to distinguish which limb belongs to which camel. Whichever camel is brought onto its knees, or is rolled to the ground, or – shame of shame! – runs away from the arena, is the loser. Should two camels be so hopelessly entangled that no movement is possible, they are separated by a team of *urganc* whose task is to pull the beasts apart with thick strings of rope.

In the alpine pastures of the Black Sea bulls replace camels as game fighters. The most famous bullwrestling tournament takes place at the end of each June in the field of Kafkasör near Artvin. Unlike its Spanish cousins, the Artvin bull stands a fair chance: the encounter is (relatively) bloodless and its rival is another bull disputing the former's place in the annual test of bovine hierachy.

Turks haul the champs to the field a few days before the fight. As soon as they reach, the bulls charge against the embankment, their horns into the earth, raising a storm of dust and bellowing threateningly at any rivals that wander into sight – their declaration that they regard this territory as their own. Maddeningly there are some 50 other contenders who hold the same claim – and enough cows present who have an interest in the outcome. The hour of showdown strikes: the dualists emerge from their tethers from opposite ends of the field; they strut to the center, hoofing up clumps of soil, eyes shot red and nostrils flaring.

For several minutes, they stand side by side, their heads pointing in the opposite direction, sizing up the opponent, they charge towards each other and lock horns with a staggering headlong crash.

The horns part and clash again, the massive frames of belligerent muscle pushing, thrusting and stabbing each other with mad fury in a cloud of dust. Suddenly, with no warning, one of the gladiators disengages himself, stampeding at full tilt through the circle of spectators which breaks apart in wild panic, dashing straight across the far end of the field and beyond of the hillock, abandoning the territory to its rightful winner.

Apart from glory, all that the victor gets for his pains is corn fodder: the cows are kept away from him as they would undermine his fighting spirit.

Watersports

If you are looking to be a sporting participent, do not fear, there is opportunity for action as well as spectacle in Turkish sport. With its beautiful long coatline and glistening waters, Turkey is of course an ideal location for watersports enthusiasts.

For diving it is best to come equipped with your credentials and enquire in specialist shops in Marmaris and Bodrum. Because of antiquities off the Turkish coast, scuba diving is also somewhat restricted the areas where you can dive being strictly regulated. again the best places to go are Bodrum, Marmaris and Felhiye. Swimming is of course available on the beaches and in hotels.

River watersports include Kevlan Kayaks, canoeing and white water rafting. Whitewater streams can be found in the Taurus Mountdins on the Goksu river or Pontic Range. The Firtina is the favourite place for kayakers in the Black Sea region and Coruh is well known to the canoeists. For these river sports, the best time to go is April or May, as later in the year drought sets in and the rivers run very low.

Skiing

A growing inland favourite, skiing is beginning to prove its appeal. The facilities may not be as developed as Switzerland or Austria but the price is more affordable and equipment can be hired on the slopes. Uludağ near Bursa is Turkey's premier skiing resort but the mountains near Antayla especially the Begdagi Mountains are increasingly popular.

Skiing here is at high altitude such that you can combine a summer and winter holiday; ski in the morning and descend to swim and sunbathe in the afternoon sun.

There are also resorts at Erzurum, Erciyes near Kayseri, Kartalkaya near Bolu has a mixture of beginners and intermediate runs. The main criticism of skiing in Turkey (as with most places in the world) is that it is too commercialised, the hotels in Uludağ are indeed expensive. Those seeking tough runs should go to Palandökem (near Erzurum) where the olympic team trains, or Sarikamis where there is perhaps the snowiest run.

Mountaineering & Trekking

For those looking for a vacation with a challenge, Turkey has some geographical answers. For mountaineering Agri Dagi (Mount Ararat) climbed by the North slope is the best challenge (other slopes are more of an uphill walk than a rope ascent).

The Aladaglar range of the Taurus Mountains are another good bet especially at the Alaca peak. In Eastern Turkey the Kaçklar Tepe stand at 3,971 meters, but consult regional meterological offices as there is a risk of rain or fog. In Cappadocia try Hasan Daği.

The most picturesque and well marked trekking routes are at Kaçkar Daglar (running parallel to the Black Sea) Cilo, the Sat Massifs (along the Iraqi border) and the Taurus range. Consult specialist clubs for further information, it is often best to book such trips from home as facilities may not always meet your needs.

Sporting Snobs

Other sports which as you would expect can be found in Turkey are cycling and tennis. These sports are somewhat resented by ordinary Turks since in the past they the exclusive privilige of the rich. Tennis is only available in private clubs and cycling was introduced mainly by European tourists.

However these things are gradually being absorbed by the masses and you will find less resentment nowadays, if at all only in the remote areas. For this reason and others when cycling it is best to remain around the tourist areas, be prepared for bad road conditions if you chose to venture beyond.

However coastal roads can provide for the most beautiful and enjoyable rides and be worth all the hitches (take puncture repair kits with you they can only be bought in resort towns). It is not a good idea to go to Turkey for golf. This can only be found in exclusive private clubs and even there the turf is not good.

The Turks are fond of the night hours, and love to live it up until the early hours, no matter what day it is. If you do not want to miss a vital part of Turkish culture, venture out into the night and sample a whole host of activities. Do not worry too much, since most people go out at night, there will be plenty of people around – in the big cities that is – violent crime is uncommon and theft is rare, but keep an eye on your belongings just in case. Shops are generally open to 7 or 8 pm but bazaars – which are generally keen to do business – are usually open until at least 9 pm.

Folk dancers in traditional native garb entertain the masses.

The various eating establishments nurture a classic evening form of entertainment – eating out. Facilities range from *lokanta* (restaurant), *gazino* (club) and the lest elegant but hearty *salonu* (eating hall). Restaurants are usually well decorated and

Clap your hands and stand mesmerized by the swivelling hips of a belly dancer.

have a distinctly Turkish ambience, specializing in either meat or fish so you must make a decision beforehand as to what you want to eat. The most exclusive places to eat are however in the hotels where you can find some truly authentic ancient recipes, but prices tend to be rather steep. The younger crowds tend to prefer the various bar restaurants such as the Terrace and Samden in Istanbul where European fare is available.

Bars & Clubs

Turkish entertainment is to be found in various clubs around the cities, the most famous form of entertainment being belly dancing. In Istanbul the best place to head for such club is the Beyogles region, where the most well-known and trustworthy club is Maksims. At other clubs be careful of the aggressive bouncers and people who loiter around cajoling you into buying them drinks. These clubs tend to be smoke-filled and the music of a low-standard, but they cannot be beaten for their authentic Turkish atmosphere; with a sleazy tinge, and the aroma of alcohol is never far away.

Women be warned: Turkish women do not go out at night except in groups and any women found on premises where they sell alcohol will be regarded as of ill repute.

There are a number of clean casinos to be found with floor acts which often include belly-dancers and a number of foreign acts. Korean discos are the in thing for the wealthy, but most hotels also cater for those want to bop to western tunes, particularly in the resort towns of Bodrum and the capital Istanbul. The disco at Halikamas Hokel in Bodrum is one of the most famous in Turkey, well known for its laser strokers.

Bars are popular in Turkey among the men. Raki is the favourite form of alcohol which the men like to gather around and slowly savour to mellow down after a days work. Bars also form an oasis for intellectual banter and discussion, often to the accompaniment of a little folk music, such an establishment is the Mari Ev in Bodrum, and in Istanbul the café under the bridge. Foreigners tend to favour the Hadigari Bar in Bodrum which is the 'in' place for more upmarket local residents.

For those with Bohemian inclinations the Çiçek Pasaji is a quaint area of bistros and outdoor restaurants, open into the night it is a good area to congregate and savour.

The Istanbul nights, preferably with a little music – folk, pop or jazz which can be found in abundance in the cities. Turkish cinema is emerging as a popular form of entertainment, and an appreciated and form, the films of Yilmaz Güney being the most popular. Films are however heavily censored in this predominantly Muslim country, but cinemas can be found in most of the major towns.

Outside of the main towns and resort areas, nightlife as a form of entertainment is hard to find. Turkish people in the promies tend to be poorer and there are no clubs and exclusive restaurants. Bars are however just as popular, the men habitually gathering around their raki. A quiet walk on the beach is a relaxing thing to do at night, or for those who prefer a bit more action, attend a Turkish cultural activity or a *hamam* (turkish bath).

Turkish nights have an exotic flavour, inspired by the legendary belly-dancers and clubs. There may not be many chic and trendy places to go outside of your hotel, but to experience Turkey as the Turkish people know it, you will understand something of its lure and mystique.

Please be aware as you enjoy Turkey's nightlife that conspicous behaviour is generally disapproved of, in this sense Turkish people are distinctly un-Mediterranean. Though a passionate people it is believed that a certain *gravitas* (composure) should be maintained in public – foreigners who remember this will be treated with respect.

Hamams

You can of course take your shower in the hotel, but a journey in Turkey would be incomplete without a visit to the *hamam,* or Turkish bath. One or more of these exists in every town and in each neighborhood of larger towns. Many

A Turkish folk dancing troupe whirling to their own tune in Istanbul.

are of historic vintage: the Ottoman Empire, drawing on both Roman and Persian traditions, took it upon itself to build a public bath – beside a mosque, a school, a hospital, an almshouse and a fountain – in every town of the realm. Some (like Bursa's Eski Kaplica or Adana's Old Hamam) were built on existing Roman or Byzantine foundations; others were the work of imperial architects, including the great Sinan who designed scores of hamams throughout the country in addition to his famous mosques.

The better ones possess sumptuous interiors, with enormous domed halls and vaulted chambers lined in precious marble; even modest back-street baths often hide a graceful dome behind the nondescript façade of the bathkeeper's house.

Larger ones have separate sections for men and women; others offer separate hours. In touristic places it is often possible to rent out a *hamam* for private parties for an absurdly low fee.

The bathing procedure starts with putting on a loincloth in a private cubicle. So clad, clients move into the steamy-hot domed central hall to lounge around as long as they wish, splashing themselves with water or working up a sweat. Then, they may employ a *tellak,* who will scrub them with a rough cloth to peel off the dead skin, then give them a thorough soaping.

Tea and refreshments are served back at the cubicle, and the towel-men

A candle dance being performed at Club Kervansary.

or women stand ready to offer their services. Tips are obligatory but the amount is entirely up to you. All included, the experience should cost no more than about US$5. Prudishness is the order of day, so you are not even supposed to take off your loincloth while you wash yourself.

Three of the best *hamams* of Istanbul are given below. All three are popular with tourists, and so charge somewhat more than the run-of-the-mill Turkish bath.

Cağaloğlu Hamami. Prof. K. Ismail Gürkan Cad. 34, Cağaloğlu. Tel 522 24 24. Men 7am-9.30pm; women 8am-8pm.

Çemberlitaş Hamami. Vezirhan Cad. 8, Çemberlitş. Tel 522 79 74.

Galatasaray Hamami. Turnacibaşi Sok. 24, Beyoğlu. Tel 249 43 42. Men 6am-11pm; women 8am-8pm.

Turkish Music

The latest rock hits make a nearly simultaneous appearance in the bars and discotheques of western Turkey with those of London or New York. Jazz is common in establishments frequented by the intelligensia of Istanbul and Ankara. Common people, of course, prefer the various strands of Turkish music. These may at first strike foreign ears as so much indiscriminate wailing, but one soon learns to distinguish several distinct traditions.

Foot stamping and arms flailing in unison, a troupe performs for tourists.

Classical Turkish music, based on an elaborate tonal theory and a 24-note scale, was the music of the Ottoman upper classes. It peaked in the early 19th century in the work of Dede Efendi, a dervish of the whirling sort, and went through a final, nostalgic revival in the 1930s through the immensely popular songs of Münir Nurettin Selçuk, Pinar, Selahattin and others. It is now for all practical purposes a dead art, surviving in the vulgarized forms which one hears in musical restaurants and on television entertainment programmes. The norm is a small orchestra playing in unison with a singer who plumbs the finer shades of love.

The traditional **folk music** of villagers is extremely varied and often colourfully rhythmical. The Republic in its younger days promoted peasant music as the purest expression of the

common sight in the less modern parts of the country. The Southeast is distinguished for its particular genre of wild, ululating songs sung in a heart-rending falsetto. This has become popular recently, with superstar Ibrahim Tatlises.

Turkish pop was a product of the cultural revolution of the 1970s and 1980s whose driving forces were urbanization, television and mass-produced cassette tapes. Its core constituency was young, urban and mobile (and often on wheels: the early pejorative term for pop was *dolmufl müziği* – taxi-driver's music), dissatisfied with peasant music yet unconvinced by Western pop. The great Orhan Gencebay, with Ferdi Tayfur set the ball rolling with his sentimental tunes which borrowed a lot of Arabic and Indian elements. The genre he created was dubbed **Arabesk** and abominated by the literati, yet became a runaway success. **Taverna** emerged in the 1980s in reaction to Arabesk looking for inspiration in the Mediterranean rather than the Middle Eastern world, though the actual distinction is sometimes hard to perceive.

The categories were further blurred as the hit-song market became more susceptible to folk, on the one hand, (thus Tatlises, referred to above) and to Western-style tunes on the other (thus Sezen Aksu, the "Little Sparrow" of songdom). Many songs are now simultaneously released in two versions – an "Arabesk" version featuring throaty modulations and mournful strings, and a "Pop" along Yamaha rhythms.

Turkish national genius: schools introduced classes of folk dancing and government scholars scoured the countryside for nuggets of folk tunes. The sanitized repertoire that they built up over the years bears little relationship to the rambunctious, uncensored stuff one actually hears in rural areas – try a village wedding. *Davul* (kettledrum) and *zurna* (pipe) are the instruments of choice at festive occasions, while itinerant minstrels singing to the accompaniment of a *saz,* a string instrument, are still a

TRAVEL TIPS

ACCOMMODATION

Finding a hotel is never a problem except in the remotest parts of Eastern Turkey. The big tourist destinations (Istanbul, the coast from Izmir and Alanya, Cappadocia) are chock-a-block with good, new, clean hotels making a bona fide effort to follow international norms of comfort and service. And even the smallest of out-of-the-way town has a few simple inns whose personnel will go out of their way to humor the rare foreign tourist who strays their way.

Hotels fall in two categories: those certified by the Tourism Ministry are supposed to follow certain well-defined norms, and are rated one, two, three, four or five stars accordingly. Locally licensed "no-star" hotels offer more spartan facilities. These usually feature common bathrooms which range in quality from acceptable to abominable.

Private pensions, consisting mostly of a couple of rooms in a village home, form a good alternative for accomodation if you are not too fussy about appearances. They are invariably clean and friendly places making the best of the Turks' universal instinct for hospitality and equally universal aversion to professional service. Relax and take your time when you are attacked by an army of pension-keepers' boys at the bus station: it means there are enough empty rooms in the town, so you have the freedom to choose and bargain.

Prices are subject to the vagaries of season, competition and inflation. A five-star hotel in Istanbul or the beach resorts of the Riviera will typically cost US$180 to US$250 for a double room in high season, including breakfast and all taxes. A good three-star hotel in a big city or a popular beach resort will charge US$50 to US$80 for a double room with private bath/shower (in summer, breakfast and taxes included), while the same room in a three-star hotel in a town outside the main tourist routes may cost as little as US$30. Pensions in Aegean and Mediterranean towns charge US$15 to US$25 per double, with breakfast, with or without private shower. Double rooms in an inexpensive hotel in the back country cost from US$10 to US$20. The cheapest hotel room one can possibly expect is in the range of US$6-8 for two.

AIR TRAVEL

International flights to Turkey arrive in Istanbul (Atatürk Airport), Ankara (Esenboğa Airport), Izmir (Menderes Airport), Adana, Antalya and Dalaman. More than half of the incoming international passengers arrive in Istanbul, which has connections to all major European, Middle Eastern and Asian cities. Izmir, Antalya and Dalaman receive a busy traffic of charter flights in summer.

Scheduled **domestic flights** are available to the following airports: Adana; Ankara; Batman (Diyarbakir); Dalaman; Denizli;Erzurum; Gaziantep; Istanbul; Izmir; Malatya; Sivas; Trebizond;Van;

The largest operator on both domestic and international lines is Turkish Airlines (*Türk Hava Yollari*, THY), the state-owned airline company. Several private carriers have been founded in recent years, but only one, Istanbul Airlines, has so far proven its staying power.

Turkish Airlines information and reservation numbers:

Adana:	(71) 143 143, 137 247
Ankara Res:	(4) 309 0400
Info:	(4) 312 4910
Antalya:	(31) 126 272, 112 830
Dalaman:	(6119) 1291
Denizli:	(621) 486 61
Diyarbakir:	(831) 132 14
Erzurum:	(011) 119 04
Istanbul Res:	(1) 574 8200
Airport:	574 7300

Izmir	Res:	(51) 258 280
	Info:	141 200
Konya:		(33) 112 000
Malataya:		(821) 119 22
Trabzon:		(031) 134 46
Van:		(061) 112 41

Istanbul Airlines information and reservation numbers:

Istanbul	(1) 570 3400, 574 2443
Antalya	(31) 124 888
Airport:	(31) 211 920
Dalaman	(6119) 1780

AIRPLANE HIRE

The following companies rent private airplanes and provide air-taxi service to various points in the country.

Gökkuşağı.
Yeşilköy, Istanbul
Tel: (1) 541 2917

Mach Air
Mecidiyeköy, Istanbul
Tel: (1) 274 9860

Maş Air
Karaköy, Istanbul
Tel: (1) 251 7845

Sancak Air
Sefaköy, Istanbul
Tel: (1) 598 4484

Top Air
Yeşilköy, Istanbul
Tel: (1) 599 0227

BOOKS

Here is a short selection of reading matter for those who wish to take their interest in Turkey deeper. Two good bookstores where you can find these and many other books in the major European languages are:

Can Kitabevi
Bebek, Istanbul
Tel: 265 7103

Kuydaş (Ada) Kitabevi
Kibris Cad. 10
Kuşadasi.

Bookstores with a reasonably good selection of foreign-language publications exist in the lobbies of the Hilton and Sheraton hotels in Istanbul, the Sheraton in Ankara and the Hilton in Izmir. The titles
Aegean Turkey; Turkey beyond the Meander; Lycian Turkey and *Turkey's Southern Shore* written by George Bean, Ernest Benn (London) and WWNorton (New York) is archeological guide to Western and Southern Turkey, written with erudition and humor by a dean of the field and published in four volumes.

A Book of Middle Eastern Food
Claudia Roden, Penguin, 1970.
First published in 1970, and still the best introduction to Turkish cookery.

The Emergence of Modern Turkey
Geoffrey Lewis, Ernest Benn 1974.
The classic account of Turkey's modernization efforts from the early 19th century to the 1950s.

Lords of the Golden Horn
Noel Barber, Macmillan, 1973.
An entertaining account of the lives of the Ottoman sultans.

Strabo's Geography (Books XII, XIII, XIV)
Loeb Classics.
Highly detailed classical Greek source on the geography of Anatolia in Antiquity, enriched with anecdotes and snippets of history.

Strolling through Istanbul
Hilary Sumner-Boyd and John Freely, Redhouse, 1972.
By far the best guide to the old monuments and historic corners Istanbul.

Turkey: A Short History
Roderick Davidson, Huntington (UK) 2nd ed. 1988.
A good introduction to Turkish history from the early Ottomans to the 1980s.

BUS TRAVEL

The bus is the standard mode of long-distance transport. A testimony to the wonders of free-wheeling private enterprise, hundreds of companies serve every imaginable route in the country in a fast, cheap and efficient way. Each town has its **Intercity Bus Terminal** *(otogar)*, a wonderfully crazy mix somewhere between an Oriental bazaar and the Tower of Babel. An inexperienced traveller is instantly spotted and attacked tooth and nail by the touts from rival companies. On board, passengers are regaled to generous sprinklings of eau de cologne and frequent tea stops "courtesy of the company".

As a rule of thumb, assume a speed of 60 km/hour and a price of about US$1 per hour.

Most buses (except those designated "express") will stop for passengers anywhere along the road. Several big companies belong to a somewhat higher class and charge slightly higher prices. Here are some with their Istanbul telephones (phone code 1):

Akdeniz (Antalya)	582 1320
Aydin Tur (West, South)	576 4650/
	255 3247
Kamil Koç (West, South)	582 2930/
	249 2510
Nevtur (Cappadocia)	249 7961
Özkaymak (Konya, Central)	582 2920
Pamukkale (West, South)	582 2934-35/
	249 2791
Ulusoy (Black Sea)	251 6108
Varan (Ankara, Izmir)	582 1090/
	251 7476

The main bus terminal of Istanbul is in Topkapı, a district outside the western city walls (unrelated to the palace of the same name). Many companies have passenger pickup points in Taksim and Harem (Asian side) as well.

BUSINESS HOURS

Banks and most government offices open from 9 am to 12 noon and from 1.30 pm to 5 pm, Monday through Friday. Otherwise there are no hard rules. Many shops work from 9 am to 7 pm including Saturdays, usually with no midday break.

Groceries and bakeries open earlier from 7.30 or 8 am, while fancier shops rarely start the day before 10 or 11am. Some shops in the southern resorts observe a long siesta in the afternoon, typically until 5pm, then work until 9pm or midnight. Most shops are closed on Sunday, though groceries, bakeries, kiosks and souvenir shops may open for a few hours in the morning. The only time, in fact, when every business will certainly be closed is the first day of the two major Muslim holidays, fieker Bayramı and Kurban Bayramı.

CAMPING

Organized campsites are common along the Aegean-Mediterranean coast, near Istanbul, and in Cappadocia, but unusual elsewhere. The **Turban** and **BP/Mocamp** camping chains feature excellent standards of cleanliness, service and security, with facilities that include hot water, showers, power hook-up, common kitchen, shop,

swimming-pool, restaurant and bar. Other sites range from well-managed and well-equipped to the backyard of some country restaurant trying to supplement its tourist income.

Outside populated areas, it is possible to camp out in the wild. In places where foreign tourists are uncommon, it is a good idea to inform the *jandarma* (rural police) before you camp out: you do not *have* to do so, but it is the friendly thing to do, and it saves irritating complications at midnight. On country roads, a gas station with a restaurant is often the best place to set up camp.

CAR RENTAL

Car rental companies with a nationwide network include the following, with phone numbers of their Istanbul head offices (phone code)

Avis	Tel: 241 7896/241 2917
Budget	Tel: 243 0343/245 1276
Europcar	Tel: 254 7788
Hertz	Tel: 241 5323

At least one (in most cases, several) of these firms have branches in the following localities. Local rental companies can be found in many towns of the western and southern coast, but they are less common in the interior of the country.

Adana (city and airport); Alanya; Ankara (city and airport); Antalya (city and airport); Ayvalik; Bodrum; Bursa; Çeşme; Dalaman (airport); Diyarbakir; Erzurum (city and airport); Fethiye; Gaziantep (city and airport); Istanbul (multiple branches in city and airport); Izmir (city and airport); Kemer; Konya; Kuşadasi; Marmaris; Mersin; Nevşehir; Samsun; Side; Trebizond and Van.

Caravan rentals
Anadolu Karavan, Istanbul
Tel: 260 1480
Limousine service
Inter Limousine, Istanbul
Tel: 246 0393

CAR TRAVEL

Valid registration, national driver's licence and international insurance ("green card") are documents required of visitors who arrive by car. A foreign-plated vehicle can enter Turkey for a total of six months in each calendar year before it becomes subject to import duties.

The road network is almost wholly paved in the western half of the country; in the east, secondary roads are more likely to be of stabilized gravel or earth but are still quite passable. **Traffic rules** and signs conform to international standards, but their observance does not, so great care is needed to avoid unpleasant surprises. Night driving should not be attempted except by drivers with steely nerves and devotees of high-adrenaline video games.

It is mandatory to report all **accidents** to the police, and a police report is essential for insurance purposes. The **Turkish Touring and Automobile Club (TTOK)** will assist with necessary repairs, and forward the bill to your insurance company. However, as repairs in Turkey are relatively inexpensive, it may save time and money to bypass insurance procedures in case of minor accidents.

Repair shops are found in great abundance, often concentrated in a so-called *sanayi sitesi* (industrial park) in the outskirts of towns. Most *tamirci* mechanics) are able, fast, honest and very inexpensive by Western standards. *Yedek parça* (spare parts) are easiest to find for Ford, Fiat and Renault models; for most other makes, a trip to the big city may be necessary. In case of repairs it is essential to insist on "original" spare parts, as locally manufactured copies can be of poor quality.

Highway **breakdown service** exists in theory but in practice the quickest and cheapest way of getting on when your car gets stuck in the middle of nowhere is to hitch a ride to the next town and find a repairman who will help. Even at night and on Sunday it is often possible to fetch someone at his home. Go to a coffeehouse and look helpless: people will first suggest you stay and take it easy, then volunteer to repair your car on an amateur basis and finally remember that Ahmet the Repairman lives down the street.

The head office of **Turkish Touring and Automobile Club** (TTOK) is located at Halaskargazi Cad. 364, Istanbul. Tel: (1) 231 46 31. Fax: (1) 248 9661.

CLIMATE

The weather in **Istanbul** is drizzly and miserable most of the time between October and April, warm or tolerably hot for the rest of the year.

The **Riviera** enjoys bright sunshine from late March through late November, although some chilly/rainy days can occur in early spring and late autumn; the Mediterranean is warm enough for swimming from mid-April to mid-December.

The Interior gets extremely cold from October to April and unpleasantly hot in July and August.

Large parts of the East are made inaccessible by snow in winter, and in higher areas it may snow as early as September and as late as May.

The best time to travel is April-May for the southern coast, May-June for Istanbul and the interior, and June-July for the east.

CLOTHING

What you wear depends on the season and the region that you are in. In summer you need lots of shirts in Istanbul (it is dusty and humid), light cotton summerwear and a bathing suit in the Riviera.

You can wear anything you like in the resort towns, but in cities and non-tourist areas you might prefer "modest" clothing (no shorts or miniskirts, no extra-bold T-shirts) for the sake of courtesy and comfort. You will not get lynched if you do not, but boys will stare at you as if you were an alien from outer space and grown-ups will turn away in embarrassment.

Allowance should be made for rainy days except in mid-summer. The interior of the country can get extremely cold outside the high summer: bring sweaters for late spring and early autumn, a heavier coat for other times. Formal dress is unlikely to be necessary unless you intend to engage in business in Istanbul or Ankara: in places like Bodrum or Antalya only waiters and ministry inspectors ever wear suit and tie.

CUSTOM REGULATIONS

Incoming visitors can import duty free any item that they may reasonably claim for personal use, as well as 400 cigarettes or 50 cigars, five bottles of perfume and five liters of spirits. There are no limitations on what can be taken out of the country except for two red-alarm items: narcotics and antiques. Turkish law carries severe penalties against the illegal export of antiquities and visitors are strongly warned against buying and exporting any item that might be of genuine historic value.

Cars brought into the country must be taken out again within six months. Visitors arriving by car are issued a temporary import permit and have this fact stamped in their passport; under normal circumstances, they can not leave unless they surrender this permit at exit customs.

Pets must have a rabies vaccination certificate issued at least 48 hours and at most one year before departure, accompanied by a Turkish translation certified by a Turkish consulate.

DISABLED TRAVELERS
Special facilities for disabled persons are rare or non-existent in most parts of the country. Only a small number of luxury-class hotels are equipped with ramps, special bathrooms and similar amenities for handicapped guests.

ELECTRICITY
Standard power supply throughout Turkey is 220V AC (50MHz).

FERRYBOAT
Turkish Maritime Lines operate a car and passenger ferry between Venice and Izmir. The boat departs from Venice on Saturdays at 7 pm every two weeks from April to mid-June, and every week from mid-June through October. The passage takes three days. For information call TML in Venice (041) 709211. Istanbul (1) 244 02 07, 249 92 22. Izmir (51) 21 00 77, 21 00 94.

British Ferries run a weekly ferry on the Venice-Ancona-Brindisi- Piraeus-Kuşadasi-Istanbul line, sailing from Venice every Friday between April and October. Their boats are considerably more comfortable than those of TML.

Major domestic ferry routes:

Istanbul-Izmir (Departure: Istanbul Mon, Wed 2 pm; Arrivals: 9 am next day. Return: Tue, Thu 2 pm).

Istanbul-Sinop-Samsun-Giresun-Trabzon (Departure: Istanbul Mon; Departure: Trabzon Thu).

GOVERNMENT
The official name of the country is *Türkiye Cumhuriyeti* (Republic of Turkey), abbreviated TC. A unicameral **Parliament** of 450 members (*Türkiye Büyük Millet Meclisi*, abbreviated TBMM) is elected by proportional representation every five years. Elections were last held in 1991. The **President of the Republic** is elected for a seven-year term by parliament and performs a largely ceremonial office. The **Prime Minister** is the head of the executive branch of government.

As of 1992 seven parties are represented in parliament; ranked by size from the largest down, they are the True Path Party (DYP, center-right), Motherland Party (ANAP, center-right), Socialdemocratic People's Party (SHP, center-left), Prosperity Party (RP, Islamic), Democratic

Left Party (DSP, center-left), National Labor Party (MÇP, Nationalist) and People's Labor Party (HEP, Kurdish Left). The President was **Turgut Özal** (1989-1993). Prime Minister **Süleyman Demirel** leads a coalition government of DYP and SHP.

The country is divided into 73 *il* (provinces) subdivided into *ilçe* (districts). *Vali* (province governors) and *kaymakam* (district prefects) are civil servants appointed by Ankara. Towns with more than 2000 inhabitants elect a *belediye baflkani* (mayor). Smaller communities elect a *muhtar* (village headman).

HOLIDAYS
National holidays are celebrated on the following dates:

January 1	New Year.
April 23	First National Assembly in 1920.
May 19	Start of the War of Independence in 1919.
August 30	Defeat of the Greek Army in 1922.
October 29	Proclamation of the Republic in 1923.

Government offices, banks and schools close on national holidays, but a majority of private shops stay open.

The two **Islamic holidays** are observed more widely. These return 11 or 12 days earlier each year in accordance with the 354-day lunar calendar. When they occur in mid-week, they are usually combined with the weekends before and after to create a 9-day mega-holiday, during which the country comes to a complete standstill.

LANGUAGE
Turkish is the official language of the state and the native tongue of a large majority of the population of Turkey. It is written in the Roman alphabet, which since 1928, has replaced the Arabic script previously in use.

The pronunciation of Turkish is relatively easy, as each letter has a single value which remains almost always the same regardless of context. All syllables are evenly articulated, with a slight stress usually falling on the last syllable.

Pronunciation Guide

c	always j as in *jam*
ç	ch as in *church*
g	always hard g as in *gap*
ğ	lengthens the preceding vowel:
"doğan"	sounds like *dawn*

h	always articulated clearly:
"Ishak"	is pronounced *iss-huck*
i	without dot, is like the silent e in *open* or *her*
j	like the French *j,* or the second g in *garage*
ö	like the German *ö* or French *eu*
fl	sh as in *she*
ü	like the German *ü* or French *u*

Turkish is a member of the Altaic family of languages, which includes Mongolian and Tungusic (Manchu). A closely related dialect of Turkish is spoken in Azerbaijan, while more distant variants of the language are used by the inhabitants of Turkmenia, Kazakhstan, Kirgizia, Uzbekistan and by various national groups in the Russian Federation. Turkish-speaking minorities exist in the Balkan countries and in Iraq and Iran.

An estimated 10 to 15 million Turkish nationals speak, in addition to Turkish, various native languages of their own. Ranked by approximate number of speakers, these languages include Kurdish, Arabic, Laz, Circassian, Pontic Greek, Georgian, Armenian and Old Syriac.

LOCAL CUSTOMS

On entering a **mosque**, all have to remove their shoes and women will be asked to cover their head and limbs. How rigorously the cover rule is enforced depends on the degree of local orthodoxy (Konya is most systematic) and level of tourism (people tend to get testier as tourist crowds invade their places of worship). Mosques are open to all regardless of religion or nationality, but some discretion should be exercised during times of public prayer.

Outside hotels and top-notch restaurants, finding a clean **toilet** is a matter of luck. Public toilets are marked *Bay* (men) and *Bayan* (ladies), and are (as a rule) guarded by a caretaker who expects a tip of a few hundred lira. Toilet paper is usually unavailable, as most locals prefer to use water instead. In case of need, keep in mind that just about every mosque has a public toilet.

Topless bathing has become the norm in the beach resorts of the Riviera, but will create a scandal anywhere else in the country. Nude bathing is not tolerated, and male nudity is especially considered highly offensive even in the Turkish bath or the locker room.

Loud and conspicuous behavior is generally disapproved in all situations; maintaining a certain *gravitas* in public earns good marks all round. Remember that Turks are distinctly un-Mediterranean in this respect.

The sanctity and privacy of the family is scrupulously respected. One avoids showing undue affection to members of the opposite sex in someone else's family. One does not lightly comment on the wife, mother, sister or daughter of a Turkish man. Many restaurants and public places reserve a section for *aile (families)* where unaccompanied men are not welcome.

Men of the lower classes often hold hands in public and engage in other acts of physical intimacy with male friends. This is said to have no connection with homosexual behavior, and any suggestion otherwise is likely to cause much surprise and offence.

MEASUREMENTS

Turkey uses the metric system. Commonly used units of measurement are the *kilo* (kg), *santim* (cm), *metre* (m), *kilometre* (km) and *litre* (lt).

MEDICAL ASSISTANCE

There are no special health hazards to worry about. Some visitors may suffer a bout of diarrhoea before they adjust to the change in diet. Water is almost always safely drinkable, though those who wish to take no risks may keep to bottled water.

Cities and most larger towns have one or more **hospital** (*hastane*) and many doctors in private practice (*doktor)* have generally excellent qualifications. Smaller places provide government health clinics (*sağlik ocaği).* State hospitals are usually staffed with well-meaning personnel, but suffer from undermanning, underequipment and bureaucratic chaos, so it is often better to go to a private clinic where one exists. Their fees, while higher than state hospitals, are negligible by western standards. The average private doctor charges around US$15 for a routine visit.

Pharmacies *(eczane)* provide simple first-aid, give injections and advise on the treatment of minor ailments in addition to selling drugs and suntan lotion. In principle they require a prescription to sell drugs, but will not make a fuss if you have forgotten yours at home. At least one is always on duty *(nöbetçi)* in each town, its address and telephone prominently displayed by all others.

MONEY MATTERS

The Turkish Lira (TL) comes in various coins and in bills of 1,000, 5,000, 10,000, 20,000, 50,000 and 100,000. It has been fully convertible since 1989, which means that anyone can walk into a bank and buy or sell any reasonable amount of TL at will. There are no limitations on the amount of foreign currency that can be taken in or out of the country.

Daily exchange rates are published in newspapers and displayed by banks, and practically everyone in main tourist regions will accept major western currencies at the published *efektif* aliş (cash purchase) rate. That rate as of June 1, 1992 was about 7000 TL per US$1, but inflation at the rate of about 70 percent per year can be expected to continue to gnaw into its value.

Eurocheques, travellers checks and major credit cards (Visa, Eurocard/Mastercard, American Express and Diners Club) are widely honored by banks, hotels, restaurants, travel agencies, car rental firms, carpet and souvenir shops, jewelers and others, although many shops will make a surcharge of 5 to 10 percent on card transactions. Cash advances are available to credit card owners through participating banks. The quickest way to transfer cash to Turkey from abroad is to have it wired to a local bank branch via SWIFT, an inter-bank fund transfer system.

NEWS, RADIO, TELEVISION

The leading Turkish newspapers are **Hürriyet** and **Sabah**, which combine the roles of serious reporting and the popular tabloid press. Five television channels are owned by TRT, the state broadcasting company. Several private channels were created after the legalization of private broadcasting in 1992.

Major international newspapers and magazines are available, one day late, in Istanbul, Ankara, Izmir, Bursa, Adana and the resort towns of the Riviera. The *Turkish Daily News* carries selections of Turkish and international news in English. The third channel of the radio gives news headlines in various languages at 9 am, 12 noon, 5 pm, 7 pm and 9 pm. The second channel of the television broadcasts an English-language news bulletin at 10 pm. In addition, many better-category hotels have satellite dish antennas which receive CNN, BBC and other international broadcasts.

POSTAL SERVICES

Post offices *(postane)* are marked with a yellow PTT sign. The main office in each town stays open until midnight on weekdays and Saturdays and until 9 pm on Sundays. Stamps are only sold at post offices. Airmail reaches western Europe in four to five days, North America in about a week.

RAIL TRAVEL

The railroad network was developed in the 1920s and 1930s, but received little attention or investment afterward. Trains are infrequent and slow, but astonishingly inexpensive (example: Istanbul to Kars, a distance of over 1400 km, lasts 50 hours by train and costs US$13.50 in second class). They can be an interesting way of meeting the local people.

In Istanbul, trains to Thrace and Europe depart from the Sirkeci Terminal (near Eminönü), while trains to all other parts of the country depart from the Haydarpafla Terminal on the Asian side (near Kadiköy). Schedule information can be obtained from Tel: (1) 527 0051 (Sirkeci) and (1) 348 8020 (Haydarpafla). Ankara, Izmir and lesser cities have one main *istasyon* (train station) each.

RELIGIOUS SERVICES

Functional Christian churches exist in the following localities:
Roman Catholic and Uniate: Adana, Antakya, Ankara, Diyarbakir, Iskenderun, Istanbul (19 churches), Izmir, Konya, Mardin, Mersin, Samsun and Trabzon.
Protestant (Anglican/Episcopalian): Ankara, Istanbul and Izmir.
Protestant (Evangelical/Lutheran): Istanbul.
Armenian: Adana, Antakya/Vakifköy, Diyarbakir, Elazığ, Istanbul (34 churches) and Kayseri.
Greek Orthodox: Antakya, Bozcaada, Imroz and Istanbul.
Syrian (Jacobite): Diyarbakir, Istanbul and Mardin.
Jewish Synagogues are located in Antakya, Istanbul and Izmir.

SHOPPING

Hand-woven carpets and *kilims* (flat-weave carpets) are by far the most interesting items to buy: their quality, which has been traditionally high, has improved over recent years thanks to increased foreign demand.

Other popular buys include leatherware (high quality and relatively cheap), gold jewellery (relatively cheap) and imitation designer clothes (cheap, and often as good as the original).

An area of traditional handicrafts which is nearly as fascinating as carpets but not half as tourist-oriented is hand-woven fabrics. These are used to make women's traditional clothing, and widely vary in terms of pattern, color and material in the different parts of the country. A good place to look for them is the bazaars of provincial centers like Afyon, Bursa, Kayseri, Konya, Trabzon, Urfa or Van.

TELECOMMUNICATIONS

Automatic long-distance dialing is widely available everywhere except the remotest villages. For international calls dial:

99 – ccountry code – city code – number.
For long distance calls within Turkey dial:
9 – city code – number.

Dial 011 if you need assistance for unknown telephone numbers anywhere in the country. Public telephones work with *jeton* (special tokens) which come in three sizes and are sold at post offices and kiosks; it is a wise habit to keep a few of them in your purse at all times. Phone cards and public telephones that accept them, are becoming more common. For local calls made in a hurry, the place to go is your friendly neighborhood *bakkal* (grocer).

Nearly all hotels with two or more stars have a fax machine and will graciously allow guests and sometimes non-guests, to use it.

TIME

All of Turkey belongs to one time zone, which is two hours ahead of Greenwich Mean Time (GMT), and seven hours ahead of Eastern Standard Time (EST). Summer daylight saving time begins and ends at the same time as in Europe, which is different from the dates observed in North America.

TIPPING

A tip is expected at restaurants even when a *servis ücreti* (service charge) is added to the bill: leave about 10 percent at a full-scale restaurant, but only the small change at a little back-street *lokanta*. Taxi drivers in general do not expect to be tipped unless they have performed some extra service: leave the small change to be on the safe side. A 5,000 bill left in your hotel room in appreciation of the housemaid's services will earn you a good mark for generosity and will perhaps produce more smiling service for the next guest belonging to your nationality.

URBAN TRANSPORT

All cities and bigger towns operate municipal **buses**. In Istanbul, Ankara and Izmir, tickets must be purchased before boarding a bus. They are sold at major bus stations and kiosks and by itinerant vendors. Published bus network maps and timetables do not exist, and the numbering and routing systems are of daunting complexity.

Equally common are private **minibuses**, which run along set routes and pick up and discharge passengers anywhere along the way. Their ability to speed through clogged traffic and their expertise in squeezing together a prodigious number of customers border on the phenomenal.

A **dolmuş** is any sort of vehicle (car, bus, boat) which will only depart when a minimum number of passengers have shown up. In cities *dolmufl* cabs run between specific end-points; in the countryside, *dolmufl* minibuses are the standard mode of transport between towns and outlying villages. In a hurry, it is always possible to cover for the missing number of passengers rather than wait forever.

Taxis are plentiful, inexpensive and admirably well-regulated in the bigger cities. Every taxi is required to own a meter by law and to use it under *all* circumstances. Foreign visitors must be particularly careful to make sure that it is turned on at the beginning of a ride, and that it is not set to the more expensive *gece* (night) rate. Day rates in Istanbul fluctuate around US$0.50 for starters in addition to US$0.30 per kilometer. Tips are not mandatory but are appreciated.

USEFUL PHONE NUMBERS

Police (in urban areas only)	055
Medical emergency	077
Telegrams by phone	041
Car breakdown service (TTOK)	(1) 277 8339

VISA REGULATIONS

Technically, a residence permit is required of all non-nationals staying in Turkey for more than a month, but this limit is automatically extended to three months in the case of the citizens of most European, North American and East Asian countries. When in doubt (or to extend your stay beyond three months), contact the Aliens Office *(Yabancilar fiubesi)* of the Directorate of Police *(Emniyet Müdürlüğü)* in the capital city of the province where you plan to stay. In Istanbul, that office is located in Cağaloğlu. Tel: (1) 528 5173.

British and Irish nationals are required to obtain a visa before entering Turkey. This is a mere formality which costs £5 and can be paid at the point of arrival.

DIRECTORY

AIRLINE COMPANIES

Turkish head offices of international airline companies are located in Istanbul (phone code 1). Indicated below are direct flight destinations from Istanbul. See above under *Air Travel* for the information and reservation numbers of **Turkish Airlines**.

Aeroflot
Taksim
Tel: 243 4725
Moscow

Air China
Harbiye
Tel: 232 7111
Peking

Air France
Taksim
Tel: 256 4356
Airport: 573 9453
Paris

Alia Jordanian Airlines
Elmadağ
Tel: 233 0744
Airport: 573 6260
Amman

Alitalia
Elmadağ
Tel: 231 3391
Airport: 573 8103
Milan, Rome

American Airlines
Harbiye
Tel: 230 2211
New York

Austrian Airlines
Taksim
Tel: 232 2200
Airport: 573 2854
Vienna

Balkan (Bulgarian) Airlines
Taksim
Tel: 245 2456
Airport: 573 2920
Sofia

British Airways (BA)
Elmadağ
Tel: 234 1300
Airport: 573 8107
London

Dan Air
Harbiye
Tel: 231 1604
London

Delta Airlines
Taksim
Tel: 231 2339
Airport: 573 7709

Egyptair
Harbiye
Tel: 231 1126
Airport: 574 6001
Cairo

El-Al Israeli Airlines
Elmadağ
Tel: 246 5303
Airport: 573 8899
Tel Aviv

Emirates
Harbiye
Tel: 232 3216
Airport: 574 4680
Frankfurt, Dubai

Finnair
Taksim
Tel: 234 5130
Helsinki

Gulf Air
Harbiye
Tel: 231 3450
Airport: 574 3799
Bahrain

Iberia
Elmadağ
Tel: 255 1968
Airport: 574 3775
Barcelona, Madrid

Iran Air
Elmadağ
Tel: 241 1916
Airport: 573 8329
Tehran

Japanese Airlines (JAL)
Elmadağ
Tel: 241 7366
Direct flights from Ankara to

Tokyo

JAT Yugoslav Airlines
Elmadağ
Tel: 248 2904
Airport: 573 2856
Belgrade

Royal Dutch Airlines (KLM)
Nişantaşi
Tel: 230 0311
Airport: 573 8635
Amsterdam

KTHY Northern Cyprus Airlines
Elmadağ
Tel: 246 5138
Airport: 573 5992
Lefkoşa (Nicosia)

Kuwait Airlines
Harbiye
Tel: 240 4081
Airport: 574 3860
Kuwait

Libyan Arab Airlines
Harbiye
Tel: 232 4976
Airport: 573 8598
Tripoli, Benghazi

Lot Polish Airlines
Elmadağ
Tel: 241 5749
Warsaw

Lufthansa
Taksim
Tel: 251 7180
Airport: 573 3750
Frankfurt, Munich, Dusseldorf,
Berlin, Stuttgart

Malev Hungarian Airlines
Elmadağ
Tel: 241 0909
Airport: 574 4985
Budapest

Malaysian Airlines (MAS)
Elmadağ
Tel: 230 7130

Harbiye
Tel: 248 2241
Airport: 573 2920
Beirut

Olympic Airways
Elmadağ
Tel: 246 5081
Airport: 573 8731
Athens

Qantas Australian Airlines
Elmadağ
Tel: 240 5032
Sydney via Singapore

Sabena
Taksim
Tel: 254 7254
Airport: 573 4623
Brussels

SAS
Elmadağ
Tel: 246 6075
Airport: 574 4498
Copenhagen

Saudia
Elmadağ
Tel: 256 4800
Airport: 574 1056
Medina, Jiddah, Riyadh

Singapore Airlines (SIA)
Harbiye
Tel: 232 3706
Airport: 574 2656
Şingapore, Amsterdam, Man-
chester

Swissair
Taksim
Tel: 231 2844
Airport: 573 2573
Zurich

Syrian Air
Taksim
Tel: 246 1781
Airport: 574 8477
Damascus

Tarom Romanian Airlines
Taksim
Tel: 243 6514
Bucharest

Tunisair
Elmadağ
Tel: 241 7096
Tunis

TWA
Elmadağ
Tel: 234 5327
Airport: 574 1256
New York via Frankfurt

BANKS (FOREIGN)
Istanbul (phone code 1)
Banco di Roma
Karaköy
Tel: 251 0917

Banque Indosuez
Levent
Tel: 279 7311

Bank Mellat
Levent
Tel: 269 5820

Chase Manhattan
Esentepe
Tel: 275 1280

Citibank
Maçka
Tel: 241 4300

First National Bank of Boston
Esentepe
Tel: 274 5222

Habib Bank
şişli
Tel: 246 0220

Manufacturers Hanover
Maçka
Tel: 231 4010

Midland Bank
Maçka
Tel: 231 5561

Ottoman Bank
Karaköy
Tel: 252 3000

Saudi American Bank
Harbiye
Tel: 233 0009

Standard Chartered
Levent
Tel: 280 2941

CREDIT CARD COMPANIES

American Express
Nişantaşi
Istanbul
Tel: 232 9556/240 6254

Diners Club
Elmadağ
Istanbul
Tel: 230 0918

Eurocard/Mastercard
Taksim
Istanbul
Tel: 250 6070/230 6567

Visa
Taksim
Istanbul
Tel: 250 6070

FOREIGN MISSIONS

Embassies are located in Ankara. Many countries maintain a consulate in Istanbul. A few countries have consulates in Izmir, Adana, Mersin and elsewhere.

Australia
Etiler
Istanbul
Tel: 257 7050

Canada
Gayrettepe
Istanbul
Tel: 272 5174

China, People's Republic
Mecidiyeköy
Istanbul

Tel: 272 5200

Egypt
Cevdetpaşa Cad
257 Bebek
Istanbul
Tel: 265 9780

France
Istiklal Cad
8 Taksim
Istanbul
Tel: 243 1852

Germany
Inönü Cad
16-18 Ayazpaşa
Istanbul
Tel: 251 5404

Greece
Turnacıbaşi Sok
32 Galatasaray
Istanbul
Tel: 245 0596

India
Cumhuriyet Cad
257/3 Harbiye
Istanbul
Tel: 248 4864

Israel
Valikonaği Cad
73/4 Nişantaşi
Istanbul
Tel: 246 4125

Italy
Tomtomkaptan Sok
19 Beyoğlu
Istanbul
Tel: 243 1024

Japan
Inönü Cad
24 Ayazpaşa
Istanbul
Tel: 251 7605

Korea (S)
Aydede Cad
24/10 Taksim
Istanbul

Tel: 249 8223

Malaysia
Şişli
Istanbul
Tel: 247 1728

Mexico
Ortaköy
Istanbul
Tel: 259 0000

Netherlands
Istiklal Cad
393 Beyoğlu
Istanbul
Tel: 251 5030

Pakistan
OTIM A Blok
Ihlamur
Istanbul
Tel: 272 1636

Russia (Commonwealth of Independent States)
Istiklal Cad 443
Tünel
Istanbul
Tel: 244 2610

Saudi Arabia
Esentepe
Istanbul
Tel: 275 4396

Spain
Teşvikiye Cad
143/6 Teşvikiye
Istanbul
Tel: 240 3444

Switzerland
Hüsrev Gerede Cad
75/3 Teşvikiye
Istanbul
Tel: 248 5070

Thailand
Cumhuriyet Cad
349/7 Harbiye
Istanbul
Tel: 231 1585

UK
Meşrutiyet Cad
34 Tepebaşi
Istanbul
Tel: 244 7540

USA
Meşrutiyet Cad
104 Tepebaşi
Istanbul
Tel: 251 3602

Vatican
Ölçek Sok 87
Harbiye
Istanbul
Tel: 234 0707

GAMBLING CASINOS

Istanbul (phone code 1)
Büyük Sürmeli Hotel
Gayrettepe
Tel: 272 3120

Casino Ataköy
Ataköy
Tel: 560 4734

Dedeman Hotel
Gayrettepe
Tel: 274 8800

Hilton Hotel
Elmadağ
Tel: 231 4646

The Marmara Hotel
Taksim
Tel: 251 4696

Princess Hotel
Suadiye
Kadiköy
Tel: 386 3118

Ramada Hotel
Laleli
Tel: 511 2768

Sheraton Hotel
Taksim
Tel: 231 2121

Tarabya Hotel
Tarabya
Tel: 262 1000

HOTELS

The following hotels are recommended for their comfort, cleanliness, service, attractive architecture or convenient location. We list some of the "top" hotels in each locality, but also include relatively modest establishments which we know by experience to be reliable and pleasant places.

Hotels are certified * to ***** according to such criteria as number of rooms, presence of restaurants, bars, shops, swimming pool, parking facilities, elevators, telephones and television in rooms, air-conditioning and facilities for handicapped guests. Hotels located in historic buildings or architectural landmarks are granted the special category **S**: this does not correspond to any particular "star count" but indicates fairly high quality. Holiday villages, which are self-contained hotel and entertainment complexes usually located by a beach, are classed as **HV1** (top quality) or **HV2**. A small number of top-class pensions (small establishments with less than 20 rooms) carry the classification **P**; private family pensions are often licenced locally, and so do not have any classification. A handful of motels, usually operated by state-owned chains, are designated **M**.

Adana (phone code 71)
Büyük Sürmeli *****
Özler Caddesi 175
Tel: 123 600
Fax: 121 945

Zaimoğlu ****
Özler Caddesi 72
Tel: 113 401

Fax: 116 811

Adiyaman Nemrut Daği
Euphrat Hotel
Nemrut Daği
Tel: (8795) 2428

Nemrut Tur **
Kahta
Tel: (8795) 1967
Fax: (8795) 1967

Alanya (phone code 323)
Including *Incekum/Avsallar* (24-20km west), *Konakli* (14km west), *Kargicak/Dimçayi* (7-10 km east) and *Mahmutlar* (12-14 km east)

Alaaddin ****
Avsallar/Alanya
Tel: (3237) 1491

Alantur ****
Dimçayi/Alanya
Tel: 144 16
Fax: 144 19

Ananas *****
Oba Mevkii
Alanya
Tel: 191 10
Fax: 109 13

Bedesten (S)
Içkale
Alanya
Tel: 212 34

Club Aquarius (HV1)
Konakli/Alanya
Tel: 112 96
Fax: 120 39

Club Hotel SVS ***
Mahmutlar/Alanya
Tel: (3175) 1173
Fax: (3175) 1027

Serapsu *****
Konakli/Alanya
Tel: (3235) 1476
Fax: (3235) 1072

Syedra Princess ****
Mahmutlar/Alanya
Tel: (3175) 1060
Fax: (3175) 1041

Akçay/Altinoluk (phone code 671)
Chalet Chopin (S)
Altinoluk
Tel: 610 44
Fax: 606 97

Turban Akçay (HV1)
Akçay
Tel: 412 02
Fax: 418 92

Amasya (phone code 3781)
Turban Amasya **
Tel: 4054
Fax: 4056

Ankara (phone code 4)
Bulvar Palas ***
Atatürk Bulv
143 Bakanlıklar
Tel: 417 5020
Fax: 417 4943

Grand Hotel Ankara *****
Kavaklidere
Tel: 425 6655
Fax: 425 5070

Hilton Ankara *****
Tahran Cad
12 Kavakidere
Tel: 468 2888
Fax: 468 0909

Sheraton Ankara *****
Gaziosmanpaşa
Tel: 468 5454
Fax: 467 1136

Antakya (phone code 891)
Büyük Antakya ****
Atatürk Cad 8
Tel: 358 60
Fax: 5869

Antalya (phone code 31)
Argos (S)
Kaleiçi

Tel: 172 012
Fax: 117 552

Club Hotel Sera *****
Lara Yolu
Tel: 231 170
Fax: 231 279

Marina (S)
Mermerli Sok, Kaleiçi
Tel: 175 490
Fax: 111 765

Perge *
Park içi
Tel: 123 600
Fax: 118 587

Sheraton Voyager Antalya *****
100 Yil Bulv
Tel: 182 182
Fax: 118 995

Sultan Pension
Kaleiçi
Tel: 173 346

Turban Adalya (S)
Kaleiçi
Tel: 118 066
Fax: 123 679

Artvin (phone code 0581)
Karahan **
Tel: 1800
Fax: 2420

Assos
Behram Hotel (S)
Tel: (081) 127 58 or (1969) 1437

Bergama (phone code 541)
Tusan Motel (M)
Tel: 1173
Fax: (633) 119 38

Bodrum (phone code 6141)
Halikarnas (S)
Cumhuriyet Cad 128
Tel: 8000
Fax: 1237

Manastir ***
Barış Sitesi

Kumbahçe
Tel: 2854
Fax: 2772

Maya **
Marina/Bodrum
Tel: 4741

Mylasa (P)
Cumhuriyet Cad
Tel: 1846

TMT Holiday Village (HV1)
Akçabük/Bodrum
Tel: 1232
Fax: 2647

Bursa(phone code 24)
Çelik Palas *****
Çekirge/Bursa
Tel: 343 400
Fax: 361 910

Kervansaray Termal *****
Çekirge/Bursa
Tel: 353 000
Fax: 353 024

Cappadocia
Including *Aksaray, Avanos, Kaymakli, Nevşehir, Ortahisar, Uçhisar, Ürgüp.*
Ağaçli Motel (M)
Ankara-Adana Asfaltı
Aksaray
Tel: (481) 149 10
Fax: (481) 149 14

Dedeman Nevşehir *****
Ürgüp Yolu
Nevşehir
Tel: (485) 199 00
Fax: (485) 121 58

Kaya (HV1)
Uçhisar
Tel: (4856) 1007
Fax: (4856) 1363

Lapis Inn ****
Kaymakli
Tel: (4855) 1411
Fax: (4855) 1111

Perissia ****
Ürgüp
Tel: (4868) 2930
Fax: (4868) 1524

Robinson Lodge ***
Uçhisar
Tel: (485) 199 45
Fax: (485) 150 92

Turban Ürgüp (M)
Tel: (4868) 2290
Fax: (4868) 2299

Çanakkale (phone code 196)
Tusan ***
Güzelyali/Çanakkale
Tel: 282 10
Fax: 280 28

Dalyan (phone code 6116)
Antik ***
Tel: 1136
Fax: 1138

Happy Caretta Pension
Tel: 1109

Diyarbakir (phone code 831)
Demir ***
Izzet Paşa Cad 8
Tel: 123 15
Fax: 243 00

Edirne (phone code 181)
Rüstempaşa Kervansaray (S)
Tel: 121 95
Fax: 2046

Eğirdir (phone code 3281)
Eğirdir ***
Tel: 1798

Fethiye (phone code 615)
Likya ***
Yat Limani
Fethiye
Tel: (615) 122 33
Fax: 131 00

Hotel Meri **
Ölüdeniz/Fethiye
Tel: (6156) 6060
Fax: 6456

Robinson Club Lycia (HV1)
Kidrak/Ölüdeniz
Tel: (6156) 6214
Fax: (6156) 6313

Istanbul (phone code 1)
Ayasofya Pensions (S)
Soğukçeşme Sok
Sultanahmet
Tel: 513 3660
Fax: 513 3669

Çirağan Palace Kempinski *****
Beşiktaş
Tel: 258 3377
Fax: 259 6686

Hilton Istanbul *****
Cumhuriyet Cad
Harbiye
Tel: 231 4650
Fax: 240 4165

Pera Palace****
Meşrutiyet Cad 98-100
Tepebaşi
Tel: 251 4560
Fax: 251 4089

The President ****
Tiyatro Cad 25
Beyazit
Tel: 516 6980
Fax: 516 6999

Ramada Istanbul*****
Ordu Cad 226
Laleli
Tel: 513 9300
Fax 512 6390

Richmond ****
Istiklal Cad 45-47
Beyoğlu
Tel: 252 5460
Fax: 252 9707

Sheraton Istanbul *****
Gezi
Taksim
Tel: 231 2121
Fax: 231 2180

Swissôtel Bosphorus *****
Taşlik
Maçka
Tel: 259 0101
Fax: 259 0105

Yeşil Ev (S)
Kabasakal Cad
Sultanahmet
Tel: 517 6785
Fax: 517 6780

Istanbul Vicinity
Hidiv Kasri (S)
Çubuklu/Istanbul
Tel: 331 2651
Fax: 322 3434

Klassis *****
Silivri/Istanbul
Tel: (1887) 4050
Fax: (1887) 4049

Splendid (S)
Büyükada/Istanbul
Tel: 381 6950

Izmir (phone code 51)
Büyük Efes *****
Gaziosmanpaşa Bulv 1
Tel: 144 300
Fax: 258 695

Hilton Izmir *****
Tel: 416 060
Fax: 412 277

Kalkan (phone code 3215)
Balikçihan Pension
Tel: 1075

Kalkan Han Pension
Tel: 1131

Patara Prince *****
Tel: 1338
Fax: 1337

Kaş (phone code 3211)
Aqua-Park Hotels ***
Tel: 1901
Fax: 1905

Club Hotel Phellos
Tel: 1953
Fax: 1890

Kemer (phone code 3214)
Including **Beldibi/**Kiziltepe (8-12 km north) and **Çamyuva/Tekirova** (8-13 km south)

Club Marco Polo (HV1)
Çamyuva/Kemer
Tel: (3184) 6336
Fax: (3184) 6346

Club Mediterranée Kemer (HV1)
Tel: 1009
Fax: 1018

Club Robinson Çamyuva (HV1)
Çamyuva/Kemer
Tel: (3184) 6383
Fax: (3184) 6392

Club Salima Beldibi (HV1)
Beldibi/Kemer
Tel: (3184) 8361
Fax: (3184) 8083

Eldorador Phaselis (HV1)
Kemer
Tel: 2993
Fax: 2299

IberoTel Art *****
Kiziltepe/Kemer
Tel: (3214) 2611
Fax: (3214) 2617

Phaselis Princess *****
Tekirova/Kemer
Tel: (3185) 4070
Fax: (3214) 2079

Ramada Renaissance Resort *****
Beldibi/Kemer
Tel: (3214) 3255
Fax: (3214) 3256

Roman Plaza ***
Deniz Cad
Kemer
Tel: 3900
Fax: 3111

Konya (phone code 33)
Özkaymak Park Hotel ***
Otogar Karşisi
Konya
Tel: 133 770
Fax: 155 974

Kuşadası (phone code 636)
Club Mediterranée Kuşadasi (HV1)
Tel: 111 35
Fax: 111 25

Ephesus Princess *****
Pamucak/Kuşadasi
Tel: (5451) 4700
Fax: (5451) 4703

Kismet ****
Tel: 120 05

Imbat *****
Kadinlar Denizi
Kuşadasi
Tel: 120 00
Fax 149 60

Marmaris (phone code 612)
Altinyunus/Golden Dolphin *****
Tel: 136 17
Fax: 112 14

Iberotel Marmaris (HV1)
Içmeler/Marmaris
Tel: 163 77
Fax: 163 86

Lydia ***
Tel: 129 40
Fax: 114 78

Mavi ***
Atatürk Cad 72
Tel: 136 18
Fax: 142 95

Turunç ****
Turunç/Marmaris
Tel: (6126) 7024
Fax: (6126) 7032

Mersin (phone code 741)
Hilton Mersin *****

Menderes Bulv
Tel: 650 00
Fax: 650 50

Pamukkale (phone code 6218)
Koru Motel(M)
Tel: 1430

Kur-Tur (M)
Karahayit/Pamukkale
Tel: (6228) 4117
Fax: (621) 308 18

Palmiye Motel (M)
Tel: 1014
Fax: 1018

Pamukkale Motel ***
Tel: 1024
Fax: 1026

Polat ***
Karahayit/Pamukkale
Tel: (6228) 4110
Fax: (6228) 4092

Samsun (phone code 36)
Turban Samsun ****
Tel: 110 750
Fax: 110 740

Selçuk/Ephesus (phone code 5451)
Tusan Motel (M)
Tel: 1060

Side (phone code 321)
Cesar Hotel /Casino *****
Kumköy/Side
Tel: 324 80
Fax: 318 52

Le Meridien ****
Titreyengöl/Side
Tel: (3211) 4830
Fax: (3211) 1967

Novotel Turquoise *****
Sorgun/Side
Tel: (3211) 4722
Fax: (3211) 4721

Robinson Club Pamfilya (HV1)
Acısu/Side

Tel: 147 00
Fax: 147 08

Turtel Konak (S)
Tel: 122 25
Fax: 122 26

Yat Pension (Stone House)
Tel: 314 65

Silifke (phone code 7596)
Altinorfoz Merit International
****
Susanoğlu/Silifke
Tel: 1211
Fax: 1215

Trabzon (phone code 031)
Özgür **
Atatürk Meydani
Tel: 113 19

Urfa (phone code 871)
Harran ***
Atatürk Bulv
Tel: 347 43
Fax: 349 18

Turban Urfa *
Köprübaşi Cad 74
Tel: 135 20

Van (phone code 061)
Urartu ***
Hastane Cad 60
Tel: 206 50
Fax: 216 10

NIGHTSPOTS

Istanbul (phone code 1)
Andromeda
şan Müzikholü Arkasi
Elmadağ
Tel: 246 0168
Disco with laser show

Bebek Bar
Cevdetpaşa Cad 15
Bebek
Tel: 263 3000
Terrace bar by the Bosphoru

Caz Bar
Korukent Levent

Tel: 266 6788
Live jazz

English Pub
President Hotel
Beyazit
Tel: 516 6980
Pub with English humor

Galata Tower Nightclub
Galata
Tel: 245 1160
Belly dancing

Garibaldi
Odakule Yani
Beyoğlu
Tel: 249 6895
Bar with Russian music

Juliana's
Swissôtel Maçka
Tel: 259 0101
Disco

Kervansaray
Elmadağ
Tel: 247 1630
Nightclub, belly dancing

Taxim
Nizamiye Cad
12-16 Taksim
Tel: 256 4431
Disco, bar, restaurant

Zindan Han
Ticaret Odasi Yani
Eminönü
Tel: 512 4270
Rooftop bar in historic prison

RESTAURANTS

Price guide (for full dinner for
one, including tax and tips):
$$$ Expensive (over US$ 30)
$$ Moderate (US$15-30)
$ Inexpensive (under
           US$15)

Ankara (phone code 4)
Cengiz Kaan ($$)
Köroğlu Sok
Gaziosmanpafla

Tel: 437 5101
Chinese

Dönen $$$
Atakule top floor
Tel: 440 7412
Revolving restaurant with pano-
rama

Mangal $$
Kuloğlu Sok 26
Çankaya
Tel: 440 0959
Regional meat dishes in historic
mansion

Marco Polo $$$
In the Hilton
Kavaklidere
Tel: 468 2888
Turkish and international cui-
sine

RV $$$
Atatürk Bulv
243 Kavaklidere
Tel: 427 0376
Elegant restaurant

Washington $$
Bayindir Sok 22
Kizilay
Tel: 431 2218
Turkish cuisine with good selec-
tion of mezes

Zenger Pasha Konaği $$
Ulus
Tel: 311 7070
Turkish cuisine

Antalya (phone code 31)
Gaziantep (Çobanoğlu) $
Traditional restaurant in the ba-
zaar

Gürvis $$
In Beldibi/Kemer
Tel: (3184) 8201
Nouvelle cuisine conceived by
Dutch chef

Marina $$
Kaleiçi

el: 159 906
urkish cuisine

Kiral Sofrasi $$
Kaleiçi
el: 112 198
Good selection of mezes

Bodrum (phone code 6141)
Han $$
Kale Cad 29
Tel: 1615
Turkish cuisine in historic court-
yard

Zeytin $
Cumhuriyet Cad
Good traditional cuisine

Istanbul (phone code 1)
Abdullah Efendi $$$
Koru Cad 11
Emirgan
Tel: 277 5721
Turkish cuisine

Beyti $$
Orman Sok
Florya
Tel: 573 9373
Kebab, meats

Çiçek Pasajı $
Istiklal Cad
Galatasaray
18 taverns

La Corne D'or $$$
In Swissôtel Taşlik
Maçka
Tel: 259 0101
French

Darüzziyafe $$
Süleymaniye
Tel: 511 8414
Turkish cuisine in historic domed
hall

Deniz Park $$
Daire Sok 9
Yeniköy
Tel: 262 0415
Bosphorus fish tavern

Gelik $$
Sahil Yolu
Mobil Karşisi
Ataköy
Tel: 560 7283
Turkish cuisine

Haci Abdullah $
Sakizağaci Cad 19
Beyoğlu
Tel: 244 8561
Turkish cuisine

Hacibaba $
Istiklal Cad 49
Taksim
Tel: 244 1886
Turkish cuisine

Hasir Beykoz $$
Abraham Paşa Korusu
Beykoz
Tel: 322 2901
Turkish cuisine

Iskele $$
Yeniköy
Bosphorus fish tavern

Iskele $$
Iskele Meydani
Çengelköy
Tel: 321 5505
Bosphorus fish tavern

Japan Club $$$
Haciağa Çikmazi 15
Balmumcu
Tel: 171 1819
Sushi bar and restaurant

Körfez $$$
Körfez Cad 78
Kanlica
Tel: 332 0108
Seafood, international cuisine

Palet $$
Yeniköy Cad 80
Tarabya
Tel: 262 4005
Seafood restaurant

Rejans $$
Emir Nevruz Sok
17 Beyoğlu
Tel: 244 2610
Russian and international cui-
sine

Reşatpaşa Konaği $$$
Bağlarbaşi Cad 34/1
Erenköy
Tel: 361 3411
Turkish cuisine

Sarnıç $$
Soğukçeşme Sok
Sultanahmet
Tel: 512 4291

Urcan $$
Ortaçeşme Cad 2
Sarıyer
Tel: 242 0367
Bosphorus fish tavern

Yeşil Konak $$
Kabasakal Cad 5
Sultanahmet
Tel: 517 6786
Turkish and international cui-
sine in a historic home

Izmir (phone code 51)
Deniz $$
Atatürk Cad 188/B
Alsancak
Tel: 220 601

Kemal'in Yeri $$
1453 Sokak 20/A
Alsancak
Tel: 223 190
Excellent selection of seafood

Pina $
1382 Sokak 32/B
Alsancak
Tel: 218 417

TRAVEL AGENCIES AND TOUR OPERATORS
Istanbul (phone code 1)
Active Turizm
Bağdat Cad 1657
Kadıköy

Tel: 349 5590

Anadol Turizm
Cumhuriyet Cad 261/4
Harbiye
Tel: 246 8084

Bosfor Turizm
Mete Cad 18
Taksim
Tel: 251 2474

Camel Tour
İnönü Cad 33/1
Taksim
Tel: 252 9713

Duru Turizm
Istiklal Cad 365
Beyoğlu
Tel: 251 5960

Ekin Turizm
Cumhuriyet Cad 295
Harbiye
Tel: 234 4300

Gürkay Turizm
Abidei Hürriyet Cad 43
şişli
Tel: 230 0217

Kültur
Cumhuriyet Cad 243/4
Harbiye
Tel: 241 5253

Setur
Cumhuriyet Cad 107
Elmadağ
Tel: 230 0336

Tantur
Sheraton Hotel Lobby
Taksim
Tel: 247 8048

Tura Turizm
Cumhuriyet Cad 129
Elmadağ
Tel: 241 6082

Türk Express
Cumhuriyet Cad 91/1

Elmadağ
Tel: 230 1515

VIP Turizm
Cumhuriyet Cad 269/2
Harbiye
Tel: 241 6514

Other towns
Diana Turizm
Kuşadasi
Tel: (636) 148 11

Ege Tour
Atatürk Cad 176
Alsancak
Tel: (51) 223 447

Era Turizm Bodrum
Tel: (6141) 2310

Pegasus Turizm
Marmaris
Tel: (612) 134 19

Pamfilya Turizm
30 Ağustos Cad 577B
Antalya
(head office; branches in all
southern resorts)
Tel: (31) 121 401

Roman Tour
Fethiye
Tel: (6151) 2735

DIRECTORY

298

.ce Photo Agency/Erik Pelham : 252/253
.ce Photo Agency/R Richardson : 27, 111
.ce Photo Agency/H Schwarz : 176/177
.ntiques of Orient : 8/9, 14, 20/21, 23
.anda Bishop : x (top), xiv (top), xiv (bottom), 43, 58, 86, 96, 117, 118/119, 127, 131, 142 (top), 161, 268/269, 277
Vendy Chan : back cover (top left), xiii (top), xv (bottom left), 4, 36, 38, 40, 41, 42, 61, 75, 76, 78 (top), 128, 135, 136/137, 143 (top), 144, 145, 148, 150, 151, 157, 164, 165 (bottom), 168, 242, 246, 248, 262, 263, 264
;lenn Baker Archives/Bob King : 18, 259
;lenn Baker Archives/Glenn A Baker : front cover, xi (top), 52, 56/57, 59, 90/91, 106/107, 110, 124, 142 (bottom), 160, 184, 185, 186/187, 197, 202/203, 208, 215, 244/245, 266/267
;reg Evans Photo Library : xi (top), xvi, 5, 10, 11, 13, 24, 25, 26, 30, 48, 50/51, 103, 104, 109, 126, 154/155, 156, 172, 181, 182, 232, 233, 236/237, 274
'hotostock/J Binstead : 72, 196, 219, 220, 222, 223, 234, 235, 237, 238, 239, 240/241
'hotostock/S Garnier : 81
'et Groves : xiii (bottom)
R Holzbachová/P Bénet : back endpaper, 39, 49, 65, 68/69, 70 (top), 70 (bottom), 71, 83 (top), 158 (top), 158 (bottom), 162, 204, 209, 210, 211, 214, 216, 227, 228/229, 249, 250
Retna Pictures/Chris Beall : 19, 122
Retna Pictures/Daniel Jungman : 15, 44, 46, 62, 82, 83 (bottom), 94, 98/99, 100/101, 105, 141, 143 (bottom), 192/193, 194, 198/199
Retna Pictures/Ray Rampton : xii (top), 261
Stockphotos/Derek P Redfearn : 159
The Image Bank/Charles Allen : x (bottom)
The Image Bank/Derek Berwin : xv (bottom)
The Image Bank/Tim Bieber Inc : 54/55, 92
The Image Bank/P & G Bowater : 165 (top)
The Image Bank/Kay Chernush : 16, 116
The Image Bank/Werner Dieterich : 125
The Image Bank/Andre Gallant : xii (bottom)
The Image Bank/Larry Dale Gordon : 256/257
The Image Bank/Gilles Guittard : 3, 276
The Image Bank/Jake Rajs : 66, 115, 167
The Image Bank/Mahaux Photography : 78 (bottom)
The Image Bank/Paul Trummer : 2, 113, 139, 140, 254, 258
Turkish Embassy : xi (bottom), 6, 33, 47, 74, 77, 79, 188/189, 247, 270/271, 272, 278/ 279

INDEX